The Equality Complex

A new series of books from Cassell's Sexual Politics List, Women on
Women *provides a forum for lesbian, bisexual and heterosexual
women to explore and debate contemporary issues
and to develop strategies for the advancement of feminist
culture and politics into the next century*

COMMISSIONING:
Roz Hopkins
Liz Gibbs
Christina Ruse

The Equality Complex

Lesbians in therapy: a guide to anti-oppressive practice

Val Young

CASSELL

Cassell
Wellington House
125 Strand
London
WC2R 0BB

215 Park Avenue South
New York
NY 10003

First published 1995

British Library Cataloguing-in-Publication Data
A catalogue record for this book is available from the British Library.

ISBN 0–304–32961–4 (hardback)
      0–304–32959–2 (paperback)

Typeset by York House Typographic Ltd, London
Printed and bound in Great Britain by Biddles Ltd, Guildford and King's Lynn

contents

Dedication

To the counsellors on the frontline:
the lesbian volunteers at switchboards,
befriending groups, and
support projects everywhere.

*a*cknowledgements

To Thea, the first adult to treat me as an equal, for 35 years of wisdom, unconditional support and philosophical musings. I wish you peace at last among the tulips – I'm so glad you don't have to eat the bulbs now. In Australia, to the women of all ages and political inclinations who have helped to make life there so meaningful to me as a lesbian. In the UK, to Sarah, most loyal and constant friend and soulmate despite our different directions, for her inspiration, practical help in every possible crisis, and truly original humour. I hope we will see each other through all the 0 years.

Special thanks to the lesbians at London Friend who helped with the early stages of research. Love and appreciation to Michele, for always putting children's needs first.

Valuable assistance was also given by several members of the Association for Lesbian, Gay and Bisexual Psychologies (UK), and Pink Therapy, and in particular Jan Bridget of LYSIS.

Most important of all, particular thanks are due to all the lesbians, and women who thought they might be lesbians, whom I have worked with in therapy and in women's groups, for their strength, resourcefulness, creativity, warmth, survival abilities, natural loving natures and spirit – not forgetting 'comic relief'.

The final word goes to all the lesbians in therapy, who offered so much valuable insight, time and networking to this book, for their openness in contributing their experiences.

Honour is due to the determinedly woman-identified woman whose modesty, need for personal privacy and gratitude for sanctuary prevented her from challenging the British psychoanalytic marginalization of some of her most important insights.

Special acknowledgements, then to:

ANNA FREUD 3 December 1895 – 8 October 1982

*n*ote about *c*onfidentiality

The lesbian contributors to this book responded voluntarily to requests for information. All personal details have been changed where these could identify clients, their friends, partners, or children, group facilitators, or practitioners, except where this would invalidate their perspectives. Criticisms of non-lesbian practitioners are based on published work and may not represent their present views or therapy approaches. None of the women I work with in therapy is included, and I have omitted situations or identities which could lead to breaches of confidentiality. While this decision results in some inconsistencies, or the absence of certain important lesbian issues, it would have been more than unethical to include them.

These necessary changes can as easily mean that lesbians unknown to me might identify closely with the composite clients or the dilemmas discussed in the casework. This is far from my intention, although I am well aware of the commonality of lesbian experiences in a heterosexual world. I found myself in many of the examples featured.

Confidentiality works both ways. Because of the prejudice within professional therapy as well as in society, I ask that my privacy is also respected. I use the same name for all my therapy and writing work in both lesbian and heterosexual communities, and have been known by two other names, one for personal writings and another for legal issues or work unrelated to therapy. For instance, I have investigated cases of practitioner abuse and exposed exploitative practices in business through union work. All therapy clients, long-term colleagues and professional organizations know both, if not all, my names. Any attempts to associate current work with previous controversies, or disclosures of personal details, will be taken as vindictive and dealt with accordingly.

Val Young

introduction

Advice, guidance, counselling and psychotherapy represent an occupational domain in which good practice is inseparable from, and totally dependent on, the successful treatment of issues of ethics and equality ... Without a robust approach to ethics and equality, the standards would have no credibility and could not begin to improve practice in the field.

Consultants to the NVQ/SVQ Lead Body for Advice, Guidance, Counselling and Psychotherapy (Braun and Bell, 1995)

I quickly became a good, psychodynamic, client.

Lesbian contributor

What is it about equality that results in hostility, defensiveness, withdrawal, self-reinforcement and rapid reframing in professional therapy whenever the subject is mentioned? Why is the validity of anti-oppressive practice debated by social commentators, for instance to the extent that anti-racist initiatives in local authorities are likened to a 'witch hunt' (Phillips, 1994), and by therapy entrepreneurs who challenge the wisdom of equality-based practice as defined by the new NVQs? (National, and Scottish, Vocational Qualifications.)

Replacing 'equality' with 'lesbians' in the first sentence provides most of the answers, as well as more questions than a single text can even address – especially a practice guide which is the first in its field, a fact in itself evidence of modern therapy's 'equality complex'.

Contradictory events during the internal process of professionalization in counselling and the former radical schools require preliminary discussion here in the context of therapy's own codes of ethics. They provide clarification for many of the issues raised by contributors to this book, and to reports of discrimination against lesbians – clients, trainees, and practitioners – throughout modern therapy.

The most progressive change is formalized in a revision to the NVQ criteria for assessing practitioner competence published in March 1995. Active attention to equality – client-oriented practice – is now embedded in the standards to be applied to a wide range of counselling-related work, beginning with advice and guidance and, eventually, psychotherapy – a profound challenge to the traditional practitioner profile, especially in therapies where power differentials are created intentionally.

One of the most revealing professional initiatives, was the announcement of therapy's '4th Force' – the 'transracial/transcultural approach'. These subjects, background information, and a summary of the contents, are separated in this Introduction by sub-headings to enable selective reading.[1] However, the policy changes relevant to both future practice standards and the character of therapy are inseparable from the subjects of this book.

Content, style, and approach

Anti-oppressive principles are followed in several other ways in this book. The conventional practitioner-teacher perspective is inverted to create instead the more contemporary and accessible format of an experiential workshop or a self-directed counselling training course.

The purpose is to present as wide a range as possible of lesbian experiences and evaluations of therapy – negative and positive – and to explore in a series of session-length casework examples the themes raised in the first four chapters or in questionnaires and interviews during the survey (see Appendix). These will resonate also with many gay men, and with all women exploring the personal, social, and political meaning of lesbian identity.

The discussions include: the development of lesbian community counselling and support services, feminist perceptions of radical (anti-oppressive) therapy, and attitudes to lesbians in therapy (Chapter 1); general issues of equality between practitioners and clients in different disciplines and the relationships between differently-targeted oppressions (Chapter 2); the effects of heterosexist prejudice as 'counter-transference', in particular as internalized and expressed towards

lesbians by heterosexual woman practitioners (Chapter 3); and the negative and positive effects of other differences or compatibilities between
clients and practitioners. There are also comparisons of different therapy
experiences (Chapter 4).

Because all contributions were voluntary, there is no intention here to
prescribe a universal practice style nor to give the impression that every
possible 'lesbian therapy issue' has been included. The focus is on real
experiences of social and personally-targeted oppressions, and the ways
in which individual lesbians might respond and try to counteract the
consequent disorientation and effects on their sexuality, their personal
lives, their relationships, and their social and occupational options.

In order to bring therapy to life (in both meanings of the term) none of
the counsellors is perfect, and the examples include sub-textual 'assessments' and comments by both clients and practitioners. The difference
between participants in therapy is a matter of degree of self-knowledge
and self-valuation. (All ethical practitioners are also clients – of supervision, further training and, often, personal therapy.) Most of the
counsellors, and the supervisor, are defined as heterosexual women, since
this is the typical experience reported by lesbians – clients, trainees and
practitioners – except for those involved in a voluntary lesbian or lesbian
and gay support project or peer supervision group. The casework examples, of course, are fictional although the issues raised are real. Most of
the clients are composites of contributors. A short summary offers explan-
tions of the clients' experiences from the anti-oppressive perspective.

Anna Freud

The opening question of this Introduction – as students of Anna Freud will
have recognized – is a paraphrase of the understanding she developed of
defensive (self-protective) methods adopted instinctively by children and
by adults in hostile situations (Freud, A., 1936). This is the basis of the
anti-oppressive and client-oriented approach, outlined in the introduction to the casework examples. There are several other reasons for
acknowledging her work. One, because in modern therapy, a majority
women's occupation (see note 10, Chapter 2), all the important theories
are credited to men, even by feminists (Kitzinger and Perkins, 1993:25).
Two, this book is published in the centenary of her birth. Three, her

influence on psychoanalytic ideology and her importance to adult psychotherapy is barely acknowledged outside the USA, where in 1971 she was voted 'most outstanding colleague' in a poll of psychoanalysts *and* psychiatrists (Peters, 1979:xii). Four, she lived for all of her adult life – more than fifty years – as co-parent, partner, and colleague, with the child psychoanalyst Dorothy Burlingham. In different circumstances, she might have identified with lesbian feminism in her later years. However, she chose to remain faithful to her father's reputation and, in an uncharacteristic comment, criticized post-War feminists' 'wholesale condemnation' of psychoanalytic principles because they failed to note that 'the equality between the sexes for which they strive existed in the analytic movement from the beginning ... at all times women played an important role ... contributing to the psycho-analytic literature and as respected collaborators of Freud' (Freud, A., 1936:276).

It is right, in the first British practice guide written by lesbian women, to give credit to a woman-identified woman pioneer, especially since as a Jewish woman of her generation and in her early work as a Montessori teacher (Peters:22–27) she was uniquely placed to witness multiple oppressions and to observe their effects in young people in particular. The significance of the date of publication of the book, 1936, can hardly have gone unnoticed (Freud, M., 1957; see Chapter 5 and note 3, p. 196).

In addition, the 1990s post-feminist attitude to equal opportunities, barely different from when the concept was first introduced in the UK by the EEC and the United Nations (Arnot, 1985), is an expression of a general revival of 'family values'. In terms of therapy and women's and children's rights, this culminated in the 'false memory syndrome' campaign during 1994. Significantly, in terms both of opposition to therapy and of the anti-feminist backlash, this was almost a repeat of the outrage and denial which greeted Sigmund Freud's first revelation, a century ago, of the connections between sexual oppression and women's 'hysteria' (Freud, S. and Breuer, 1895).

Because these social attitudes are reflected in professional therapy, it is impossible to develop a practice approach or to discuss lesbian concerns without acknowledging that there are huge conceptual and historical barriers to dismantle, even though there are issues which are fundamental both to lesbians and to modern therapy – in the latter, at least in principle.

These include equality, equal opportunities, actively anti-oppressive working methods, empathy, ethics – in particular sexual ethics – awareness of entrenched cultural prejudices and in consequence self-prejudices; the inequalities, discrimination, marginalization, and dis-empowerment caused by them which create multiple forms of oppression; and a wider view of therapy as the creative application of individual and group resources to personal and social problems.

Sexism as heterosexism

There can be no question of the direct relationship between oppressions and personal problems; nor that women experience problems differently from men – and, often, quite different problems – as a result of the heritage of sexism (Dana and Lawrence, 1988). Issues of sexual identity, sexual expression in relationships, and friendships between women, remain paramount in therapy (McLeod, 1994). There is a clear connection between the early twentieth-century creation of 'gender disorder' theories and sexual pathologies of 'lesbianism' and the political oppression and control of women's lives, especially sexual self-identification, expecta-tions of social roles and behaviour, and occupational opportunities.

There is a wealth of lesbian and feminist writing which exposes the stereotyping of lesbian sexuality by establishment therapies that re-inforced existing cultural and religious prejudices against women and created new ones (Millett, 1971; Klaich, 1974; Cartledge and Ryan, 1983; Burstow, 1992). As late as 1971, British psychiatrists and psychologists were still trying to establish a 'gender disorder' theory of lesbianism (Chapman, 1989).

Homophobia is a product of sexism. The more explicit term heterosex-ism is used in this book to define the uniquely British combination of cultural, linguistic, racial, ethnic and Christian-centric values based on the stereotypical family ideal, the class system, and the paradoxical relation-ship between Church and State (incomprehensible to North Americans). This is expressed vividly in the gutter-press campaign of 1928 which led to the twenty-year ban of Radclyffe Hall's lesbian novel *The Well of Loneliness* (see Chapter 1). The political implications can be seen in the timing of this ban (and that of D. H. Lawrence's *Lady Chatterley's Lover*) – the year after all women won the right to vote – and the development of British psycho-analysis, which in 1927 elected to adopt the 'infant psychosis' child development theories of Melanie Klein instead of Anna Freud's (Peters, 1979:94; and see O'Connor and Ryan, 1993:158).

Power issues in therapy

All debates about equality are about power – the conceding of power or even rights to distressed and disempowered individuals and members of oppressed minority population groups. The new therapy professions, counselling especially, no doubt create their ethics and adopt social innovations (often from the USA) with the best of intentions, but, because they rarely seek the input of the minority population clients or practitioners affected, they are unaware of how patronizing and offensive these initiatives, statements or policy decisions appear. (Some are discussed in Chapter 2.) This is what makes the new NVQ/SVQ standards unique, and this was the first time that lesbian or gay service users and providers had been invited to participate in deciding ethics and standards.

Discussions about power differentials had already reached stalemate before the NVQs were proposed. There is confusion between necessary qualities such as personal strengths, self-reliance, knowledge, responsibility, or leadership, and the *abuse* of power and exploitation of vulnerable clients. Opinions are polarized. The 'expert practitioner' view soars frequently into the realms of self-reinforcing theoretical absurdity, rather like psychoanalysis. In the 'expert client' view, the practitioner (usually a counsellor) is a supportive though passive figure or companion on a personal journey, whose role is merely to offer feedback, summary, and 'unconditional positive regard'.

There is, as always, an alternative perspective, and that is to take such decisions out of practitioner-centred or 'interpersonal process' analysis and ask clients what they want, first establishing if they feel confident in making any choices, either about their lives or their therapy, and have enough information to do so. This is particularly the case when working with a client (or colleague) who is invisible in traditional therapy. Most writings (except the most recent texts, inevitably by Black practitioners or specialist disability groups, for example) assume that everyone is white, heterosexual, able-bodied, can see and hear,[2] is about 33 years of age, and brought up by a mother and a father in a vaguely Christian and usually middle-class household. (Therapy has yet to adapt to the fact that parents/caregivers play roles in character formation that often compete with those of television, siblings, sexual openness, the fear of HIV/AIDS, peer opinion, popular culture, addictive computer games, etc.)

Changes in practitioners' self-perception as either pseudo-parental authoritative or non-directive symbolic figures would require them to take full responsibility for ensuring that a client's vulnerability is never exploited. They would have to replace 'impartiality' (as many do), with an informed awareness of their own prejudices, the elements of oppression, and an understanding of the functions and methods of the social systems in which we live that *create* 'therapy clients'. Also, the client/practitioner dynamics have changed because of the widely-available information about therapy, and the self-help ethos. Modern therapy ethics require the perception of a client as an individual, from within her personal framework and her own social context[3] which, presumably, must include her cultural heritage. These concepts are so alien to traditional therapy that they conjure up a vision of the streets of West Hampstead littered with deranged psychoanalysts, deprived of the joys of 'transference'.

Lesbians, therapy and prejudice

Paradoxically, some psychoanalysts do explore professional prejudice against lesbians and (mostly) gay men, not in terms of oppression or counter-transference but because this is seen as a block to the development of empirical (pure) theories about 'homosexuality' (Denman, 1993). Possibly this is the only way that radical practitioners can present political ideas to this anachronistic occupation. However, there are several new critiques of this entire body of work, especially the assumptions that all manifestations of heterosexuality adhered to a stereotypical norm and that all homosexuality is therefore perverse (Chodorow, 1994), and of the theories about 'lesbianism', which were developed with the apparent intention 'to discover more and more diverse forms of pathology' (O'Connor and Ryan, 1993:24).

If lesbians are classified in psychoanalysis solely as clients with a psycho-sexual pathology, they are invisible in modern schools outside feminism, especially in counselling and clinical psychology – by policy, not oversight – and other views about lesbians are prejudicial, insulting, conflicting, stereotypical and uninformed. (See Chapter 1.) This is in sharp contrast to initiatives in voluntary organizations, such as Relate, and other care sectors, in particular sexual health, and in mental health service user advocacy organizations. MIND introduced lesbian and gay support services during 1994, has publicized the discrimination against women in the psychiatric services (Gorman, 1992; MIND, 1993) and researched private sector counselling and psychotherapy standards in the context of anti-oppressive practice (Wood, 1994). MIND also held a 'lesbian, gay and bisexual' mental health conference in June 1995.

In the modern schools, lesbians (where they are remembered) are classified solely as clients, and then categorized according to the institutional beliefs about clients and their concerns and theories of homosexuality. Few practitioners receive training on lesbian or gay issues (Moon, 1994). For example, a clinical view is that an adolescent exploration of lesbian sexuality is an 'identity crisis' (Proctor, 1994:294) or a 'phase' (296), although a lesbian can come out at any age. In behavioural schools or those in which lesbian or gay affirmative approaches are new (such as modern psychotherapy), and where there is no specific training, the sole 'lesbian-and-gay' concern is believed to be coming out – the first sexual self-identification (Annesley, 1994). There are several theories about the 'stages' followed during this process, although Hitchings (1994) also discusses relationship issues (and see Davies and Neal, 1996). Coming out is, in fact, 'an ongoing process of negotiating psychological, personal, social, and political boundaries' (Heenan, 1994:284). Classifying 'lesbian-and-gay-and-bisexual' issues together and as 'sexual minority' issues, which is common, is marginalization and very misleading.

Lesbians have been studying, and practising openly for at least fifteen years – many advertising in city listings magazines as well as lesbian, women's and gay media. Still, the situation in modern therapy is little different from that in classic psychoanalysis, where lesbians and gay men are considered unsuitable candidates, or must practise discreetly (Ellis, 1994), or must write critical articles under pseudonyms (Denman, 1993).

The rare openly lesbian practitioner faces a number of 'professional and personal risks' (Heenan:284) such as isolation and anxiety about coming out (worsened by discrimination from other practitioners). This can lead, especially though not exclusively in analytical schools, to ' "temporarily" adopting a heterosexual identity albeit while celibate or asexual' (285). She risks 'attacks on her professional integrity', and more often (in the humanistic fields) 'a complete disregard of her sexual relationship or lifestyle' and an 'ongoing daily practice of negotiating the internal, private and external, social impact of her sexual orientation' (286).

Hitchings (1994) adds an important statement (121):

> When working with gay men or lesbians, irrespective of whether or not the psychotherapist is gay or lesbian themselves, a therapist needs to have explored their own sexuality and at least to some degree have transcended the sex-role stereotypes offered to us in our society.

The decision by the British Association for Counselling to turn down an invited proposal for a training guide on lesbian issues, the active exclusion of a lesbian study group, and most recently a lesbian and gay group, in the British Psychological Society (see Chapter 1), and the de-prioritizing of women's sexuality concerns, also render heterosexism invisible. This means the failure to address essential subjects: practitioners' sexual prejudices, unresolved sexuality issues, and sexual orientations (a term which does not apply solely to lesbian, gay or bisexual people) and an understanding of the direct connection between patriarchal sexual politics and other forms of oppression. (See Chapter 2.) This raises urgent questions about the quality of services offered to all women clients, and the level of adherence to training criteria.[4]

Hitchings' chapter on 'Psychotherapy and sexual orientation' appears in what seems to be the first official handbook (Clarkson and Pokorny, 1994) of the UK Council for Psychotherapies, which has an Intercultural Committee. So there is a section on culture with good chapters on gender, race, and working with survivors of the Nazi Holocaust, as well as 'sexual orientation'. There are no separate chapters in this section on disability or class, and power issues are discussed several pages later (p. 384). (The British Association for Counselling, from its foundation, has had a disability issues sub-committee, DISC, which is planning a 'reader' on counselling issues for publication in 1996.)

Omissions

For several reasons, subjects which practitioners might expect to find in a text on lesbian therapy have been omitted from this book. This is either because they are covered elsewhere in lesbian, gay and feminist writings or are more effectively addressed within lesbian communities and, for instance, in writings on helpline work (Macourt, 1989), on bisexuality (Off Pink Collective, 1988; Jordan, 1994), or in political critiques (Kitzinger and Perkins, 1993; Jeffreys, 1994).

For example, there is no chapter on the first coming out, although the order of the casework examples follows a wider coming out process. This is also because all the contributors identified as lesbians (or gay women or dykes or women-oriented women) and, in particular, to challenge the perception that lesbian women's sole concern is sexuality or sexual relationships. While these issues are fundamental to identity, one of the reasons that many lesbians work with, or would like to work with, lesbian practitioners is to avoid all problems being identified with their sexuality and further pathologized. They may be experiencing additional prejudice from both heterosexual and lesbian or gay communities, because of a more visible difference from the stereotypical norm, such as race, ethnicity, disability, health, age (Young, 1995, 1996) or cultural/class characteristics (and sometimes all of these). Economic, domestic or mental health problems are made more difficult for a lesbian because of her limited options, for instance support from local lesbians should she want to move to another district.

The controversy around issues such as partner violence and SM is discussed in a courageous new British book (Taylor and Chandler, 1995) and is both political and conceptual. There are important questions still to be asked, in particular, whether the psychiatric, psychoanalytic and social stereotyping of lesbian sexuality still results in some lesbian women believing they are 'mad, bad, and dangerous' and therefore trapped in victim/abuser behaviours and isolated within their problems. Also, whether women told that they are 'mad, bad, and dangerous', or are persistently abusive, decide that they must be lesbians, rather than, as may be the case, women with unresolved sexuality issues who might otherwise be abusing their children. (See Elliott, 1993.)

Such notions are confused by categorical statements such as one in the O'Connor and Ryan text (p. 251): 'Homosexual identity is particularly vulnerable to . . . doubts, disruption, possible heterosexual fantasies . . . indeed, it is often reported that many more lesbians have heterosexual fantasies than heterosexual women have homosexual ones.' They give as one source a book published in 1971 (Wolff). The likely reason – sexist heterosexist imprinting (Tweedie, 1975) – is explored in Chapter 4 by a composite client who took heterosexual SM fantasies to a non-lesbian practitioner. The extent of lesbian fantasies among heterosexual women was revealed by Friday (1975) and Hite (1976).

There is more to say on the recycling of abandoned or discredited theories in (family) therapy which have appeared also in US lesbian and feminist texts. Lesbian, and gay, relationships are invariably perceived from a heterosexual perspective (Kitzinger and Coyle, 1995). Issues which could apply to any relationship are re-defined as lesbian. Examples are merger, attachment to a mother-figure, co-dependency, cycles of abuse, gender-specific roles, and of course SM sexual practices and 'lesbian battering' (see Chapter 1).

Work with these issues requires an open mind and the framing of discussions in the context of internalization of heterosexist values, in particular issues of power and control (dominance/submission), bearing in mind that lesbian women are probably more often victims of heterosexual, male, and family violence, psychological and emotional abuse, and exploitation by heterosexual women 'exploring their sexuality'.

Therapy's '4th Force'

Questions about racism in the British Association for Counselling (BAC), raised by members of the RACE Division (see note 5, Chapter 2), were 'resolved', magically, by an article in the first issue of the journal *Counselling* for 1995 entitled 'Counselling culture and race'.[5] The following extract appeared under the heading 'BAC Reference Library – selected references in counselling practice'.

> This complex arena is a developing field in the profession's literature, predominantly in the USA where substantial research, development, and writing is occurring ... This concern for improved and sensitive practice in the context of transracial/transcultural counselling is being hailed as the 4th Force in psychotherapy (after Analytic, Behaviourist, and Humanistic theories) ... the [reading lists] also specify literature on race and culture as distinct areas ... for detailed knowledge is required of these phenomena before combining them with the activity of counselling. (p. 31)

The purpose of Equal Opportunities policies, introduced in the 1970s, was to remind providers of services and charitable organizations (such as the BAC) that they were created for a 'transracial/transcultural' society and that there is legislation which details rights of access to services, at present only in terms of gender and race discrimination.[6] This was the reason for long-standing anti-racism initiatives among counsellors (including the writer of the article) and the eventual formation of the RACE Division (Race and Cultural Education in Counselling, not mentioned in the article).

Three approaches are missing from the list of theories – feminism, surely the most fundamental to equality and 'transcultural' understanding; 'inner child' work with abuse survivors; and, less formalized but as important to an entire generation of women, addiction recovery. Perhaps none of these counts as an official 'approach'.

The article also overlooks the fact that the most 'substantial research,

development and writing occurring in the USA' is on sexuality – specifically, lesbian, gay and bisexual sexuality (in a multicultural context), the
emotional and psychological consequences of prejudice and discrimination, lesbian and gay youth concerns, relationships, and social issues.

The University of Amsterdam Lesbian and Gay Bibliographical service
(there for fifteen years) lists over 50,000 papers, 5,000 books and 300
magazines. The Lesbian Information Service in Lancashire (which has
been there for almost ten years) lists almost 7,000 professional papers,
most of them in therapy, mental health, and social services fields. (See
Resources, and references where relevant in the text.)

How can 'transcultural' therapy be addressed solely in terms of race and
ethnicity? Surely attitudes to and different cultural mores about gender
role behaviour and sexuality are essential to the 'detailed knowledge'
counsellors apparently need for working in a multicultural setting? (Presumably, the author means white counsellors. It is likely that
correspondence on this issue will appear in this journal for several
months.) While it is positive to see white people taking responsibility for
racial equality issues, it seems that several years must pass before the
overarching cultural values which apply to all forms of oppression are
understood. (For more insightful writing on culture see Jacobs, 1995.)

It is difficult to know how much authority can be read into such articles,
as often decisions which appear to be policy are contradicted later. For
example, a puzzling statement appeared in the BAC's 1994 Annual Report
(Chair's Report) regarding the NVQs/SVQs. 'This has been a controversial
exercise . . . We entered this work almost from a position of defence . . . we
are now in a positive and influential position. BAC is, rightly, central to the
definition of counselling and the development of standards.'[7]

Shortly afterwards, articles appeared in *Counselling* which examined
psychoanalytical concepts (November 1994) such as transference and
counter-transference, psychodynamic theory, and 'client psychopathology'. The impression that counsellors wanted to learn psychotherapeutic
methods was confirmed in an article about the relationship between
counselling and psychotherapy (another continuing debate). Sexual ethics arose again in a discussion of a male counsellor's attraction to a female
client. A similar earlier article drew correspondence from men and women
asserting that female counsellors (especially older women) would not
have such problems of sexual attraction to (presumably) male clients.

The last word on equality must go to a leading humanistic psychotherapist, innovator, and prolific author, John Rowan (1995). He writes (in
the same journal): 'In the current issue there are several people who do

not know what counselling is about, as if it was some great mystery . . . it annoys me even more when the NVQ Lead Body doesn't seem to know what it is about. Let me explain . . . '

National and Scottish Vocational Qualifications (NVQs/SVQs)

At the beginning of 1995, the NVQ/SVQ Lead Body added psychotherapy to its 'advice, guidance and counselling' remit (ACG&PLB). The Standards of Competence were being ratified by the Employment Department as this book went to press, and were due for publication at the end of 1995. It is not possible therefore to confirm whether they will become formal qualifications or obligatory, though this is the intention. Applying first to the advice and guidance sector, and counselling-related work in various care and business fields, they are being introduced to 'therapeutic' counselling during 1996 and in due course to psychotherapy (a task of unimaginable proportions).

They are relevant to this book for several reasons. First, they provide a model of equality-based and *actively* anti-discriminatory practice applicable to a wide range of work: individual, couple, and group therapy (including self-help groups), project work, the training of volunteers, and several other possibilities. They also provide a set of standards by which therapy clients can evaluate the practitioners' attitudes, skills, and willingness to address power differentials.

Second, the practice principles and approach discussed in this book are almost identical to those defined in the revised equalities elements of the NVQs/SVQs, although the Standards are not described as 'anti-oppressive'. This apparant coincidence is not entirely surprising, since the research followed the same procedures (obviously, on a vastly different scale) and this practice style is considered normal in voluntary sector projects and, for obvious reasons, lesbian and gay projects. (See Chapter 1.) It is from this counselling 'frontline' that the Standards have been developed. In the case of the Lead Body, there was a long, painstaking process of consultation with different counselling sectors, training and adult education centres, and representatives (clients and practitioners, service users and providers) across the cultural range of UK society, and – precedentially – lesbian and gay groups, including in Scotland, where the scheme is administered by SCOTVEC.

There is an Ethics and Equality Group, a Minority Ethnic Network (620 organizations contacted) and a Disabilities Network (400 organizations contacted).[8] The Lead Body therefore is not a remote quango but an Equal Opportunities initiative involving hundreds of people, including those best-placed to define what oppressive practice feels like – counselling clients and community project service users, many of whom have been traditionally marginalized by mental health and formal therapy services and given discriminatory or disempowering treatment.

Third, the input of the lesbian contributors to this book, including those with a background of community support, helpline and counselling work, helped to form the practice approach described, which emphasizes that if there is a 'lesbian approach' to therapy it is an equality-based approach applicable to a wide range of therapy-related practice in multicultural settings.

The revised Standards arrived too late for the casework section to be annotated, so the main changes – unique in the whole NVQ/SVQ system – are detailed here. They are also new to professional therapy. (The following is taken from Braun and Bell, 1995.) The purpose of these qualifications is to ensure that Equal Opportunities policies are applied throughout training and practice, so that individuals 'have an equal right to achieve their full potential' and to avoid discrimination by structure, institutions, and individuals, with 'the consequent loss to society of their skills and abilities'. The ethics include: the maximizing of opportunities and enabling people to implement their own choices, achieving the greatest good, causing the least harm, fairness, and acknowledgement of the variance between professional roles and in different sets of circumstances. As the report states, 'good practice is inseparable from, and totally dependent on, the successful treatment of ethics and equality' without which 'the standards would have no credibility and could not begin to improve practice in this field'.

Ethics and equalities principles are embedded in the Standards, instead of being tacked on as separate policy statements or added as 'token litanies'.[8] The Standards of course relate to every aspect of practice competence. It is only the revised equalities elements which are detailed here.

The fundamental revisions specify the addressing of power differentials between practitioners and clients, 'this shift in power reflected at all levels within the standards'. The responsibility is given to the practitioners, for example:

1. Enable potential users to determine the use they will make of the service.
2. Agree ways of working with clients.
3. Enable clients to agree their issues and concerns.
4. Offer referral opportunities to clients.

Measures of competence ('performance') include the need for 'options to be discussed with potential users to enable them to determine their preferred course of action'. Also (and this is the key to traditional practitioners' concerns), 'clients' wishes about ways of working are sought and taken into account in agreements made'.

Part of 'communication with potential users' includes the criteria: 'Differences between the practitioner and potential users are acknowledged internally by the practitioner and the implications considered'; and 'Where the practitioner is unable to have an unbiased approach to the potential user then appropriate advice or referral procedures are sought'.

The purpose of the NVQ Standards is 'to remove overt statements of anti-discriminatory practice and to place trust in the immediacy of the performance criteria to ensure that issues of ethics and equality are adequately reflected'. Practitioners involved in the field trials are reported to have welcomed this new approach.

In the general conclusions to this report, the authors (Lead Body consultants) state that among the essential processes used in devising the standards were 'being sensitive and alert to the potential for oppression and discrimination' (in the content and format of language used to describe competence); and 'trusting to feelings and perceptions of discrimination and abuse as much as to "expert" practitioner statements of professional practice'.

In summary, the sole authority is the client. The anti-oppressive approach used in this book includes the understanding that a client creates her own 'therapeutic methods' and that these should be identified and encouraged by the practitioner.

A good definition of the practitioners' role (in counselling) comes from the Lead Body.

... the standards include the expectation that practitioners should internalize prevailing codes of practice, recognize their prejudices, and work effectively with differences between themselves and potential users ... client-centredness is emphasized by shifting the focus of outcomes of practitioner actions or behaviours to outcomes for and/or empowerment of the client.[8]

The NVQs/SVQs provide the clearest definition of what Equal Opportunities means in practice: 'the avoidance of stereotypical judgement and assumptions; avoidance of oppressive language and culturally imposed inequalities; and positive representation of client groups in the concepts, language and images used in printed materials'.

Among the criteria for assessing a practitioner's competence, according to the agreed codes of practice (Braun and Bell:6) is the requirement that a 'practitioner demonstrates a willingness to hear the client's own perceptions of her/his experience in relation to race, gender, class, age, sexuality, religion and physical abilities'.

The following chapters explore the reasons why, for so many lesbians in therapy, such concepts are not only idealistic, but actively resisted by traditional practitioners and many of the new entrepreneurs to whom 'professional' means academic, competitive, androcentric and, of course, heterosexual.

Author's perspective

The appearance of the revised equalities elements of the NVQs/SVQs provided a valuable formal framework within which to document lesbian women's experiences of prejudice and discrimination in therapy – as clients, trainees, and practitioners. It is thanks to the publisher's flexibility that details could be included (even though this results in some inconsistencies in the main text). It is possible that the presentation of the new Standards to the main counselling and psychotherapy organizations will result in changes and improvements. However, we record experiences of oppression to ensure that they do not happen again, and all the contributors' views remain valid for them and, probably, for hundreds of other lesbians in therapy at all levels in its strange hierarchy.

The impetus for this book came from my own experiences of prejudice in formal psychotherapy and related training courses (in London), and, subsequently, from my challenging of perceptions of lesbians within the various fields, which is the only way to identify the prejudicial views that remain hidden by 'flag statement' codes of ethics and Equal Opportunities policies.

I worked for most of my adult life outside the UK and have lived in eleven countries (including Australia, South East Asia and Melanesian countries, and, briefly, India). Living and studying in London was a cultural challenge, especially since I began my course (in humanistic psychotherapy) as lesbians and gay men were campaigning against Clause 28.[9]

Work in a very supportive lesbian and gay project compensated for the prejudice, misunderstanding, and denial of sexual politics issues in formal institutes, and for my mixed experiences of personal therapy and supervision. The contact with lesbian women in therapy throughout the UK (including Northern Ireland) during the research for this book helped me to recognize that the personal discrimination I have experienced is due, not to my idiosyncratic 'Aussie' character or my other cultural differences (there are cultural expectations of counsellor behaviour too), but to the nature of British society and of therapy. Sydney is, of course, the home of Mardi Gras, the most extravagant and gender-bending lesbian and gay festival in the world, as well as being a city in which individuality, challenge, assertiveness, new ideas, open communication and insistence on equal personal rights are welcomed and almost expected.

I have identified as a lesbian since 1966 (when I was caught out and packed off to a psychiatrist like so many of my contemporaries) and emigrated to Australia in 1967. My parents were Indian-British and Irish-Jewish and both of them would be defined now as new middle class. I am able-bodied.

I work as a women's specialist in therapy (in a non-profit practice) and, usually, as a volunteer counsellor at a lesbian and gay project. Other experience includes media and communications work (arts, health, and education), arts projects and cultural exchange, teaching, training, and (in the UK) workshops for trainees or practitioners on equalities issues, and equalities work within lesbian and gay communities. I do other writing on women's and lesbians' therapy issues, usually in books (in the past under other names) and reviews or satirical articles in counselling magazines.

This book proved difficult to write, since it is the first one and I do not consider myself an expert on lesbian therapy issues. Because of the constant changes in the private sector therapies, it was hard to know what was going on or what the continual adaptations to different external pressures – the EEC, the media, academia, the health service – would mean in practice for lesbians. In many respects the professionalization process feels like the masculinization of re-birthing.

I know I am not the only lesbian or feminist to have joined this occupation, following years of volunteering, feminist activities and other related work such as body therapy, at the peak of social awareness of women's sexuality issues, to discover that everything soon changed. It is a struggle to be listed as a women's specialist on the national register, since entries are classified by school or approach.

Prejudices which target lesbians and gay men hide the system of sexual secrecy about abusive heterosexual behaviour that campaigns like the 'false memory syndrome' are designed to strengthen. However, the trainee and practitioner organizations Pink Therapy and the Association for Lesbian, Gay and Bisexual Psychologies, founded in 1994 (see Resources), are already creating positive changes. Many of the lesbians and gay men producing new writings in this field are members of one or other organization. I hope, too, that there will be more therapy-directed information on the subjects omitted from this book, especially for young lesbians, and for lesbians who remain isolated within their problems or 'psychiatric' labels, and who avoid non-clinical therapy because they cannot find themselves in its publications, or because academic lesbian-feminists consider therapy and the self-help 'culture' anti-political, or because they are far from, or unaware of, lesbian support projects.

Now that there are courses (mostly in London) which have established sexuality programmes or have a tradition of being feminist-oriented and lesbian and gay 'friendly', this is a possibility. Tellingly – perhaps because of the 'North/South' divide – many of the more radical counselling initiatives come from the Midlands, the North and Scotland. Even so, most lesbian women find themselves 'the only one' on the course and, if they are supported, they are the ones who raise lesbian and gay issues.

As a final synchronicity (as Jungians might say) and considering that many lesbians are still trying to lay to rest the ghost of Stephen Gordon who haunts psychoanalysis, a British company[10] announced that the nation's second favourite English Rose, Emma Thompson, had agreed to star in a proposed film version of The Well of Loneliness. All we can do is persevere and insist on defining lesbian identity in our personal and individual ways.

Val Young
International Women's Day, 1995
Oxfam International Year of Women
UN International Year of Tolerance

NOTES

1. For information on the availability of audiocassette versions of this and other lesbian and gay titles, please contact Cassell.
2. There are now some courses for deaf people who want to study counselling, contactable through the British Association for Counselling. Some books on therapy (though not specifically for blind, visually-impaired or print-disabled people) are available in Braille and/or audiocassette versions from the Royal National Institute for the Blind (RNIB).
3. Issues of social context are covered in the codes of ethics and practice published by the British Association for Counselling and the UK Council for Psychotherapies.
4. Training criteria for BAC/UKCP recognized courses (a relatively new scheme) include requirements for training on sexuality issues, social context, and an understanding of the social systems in which we live, regardless of the 'model' or practice approach being taught.
5. *Counselling*, vol. 6, no. 1, February 1995, p. 31. Published by the British Association for Counselling.
6. Sex Discrimination Act 1974, and Race Relations Act 1976. The campaign for rights of access for disabled people was continuing throughout 1995.
7. BAC Annual Report, published by the British Association for Counselling, September 1994.
8. *Networks*, no. 4, December 1994. Published by the Lead Body for Advice, Guidance, Counselling and Psychotherapy. Secretariat, 40A High Street, Welwyn, Herts AL6 9EQ.
9. Clause 28 became Section 28 of the Local Government Act 1988. It bans local councils, and any funded organizations and schools, from intentionally promoting 'homosexuality'. This is the first time that lesbians have been included in law.
10. Kudos Productions.

Part One

therapy from a lesbian perspective

Therapy presents a confusing image to lesbian women. The most extreme examples of self-consecrating theories – which both were influenced by and reinforced social and political prejudices – are known to be sourced in British psychoanalysis. Because the frameworks contrived by the 'classic' schools are so complex and thickly-textured, the heterosexist source of these damaging stereotypes – every lesbian woman's heritage – has been identified only recently (O'Connor and Ryan, 1993). The structures, terminology, mode of thinking, and the assumption of universal non-perverse heterosexuality on which all theories of 'lesbianism' are based makes challenge difficult for anyone outside analytic circles, as well as explaining why lesbians and gay men officially are excluded from practice or, if they do, must deny their sexual orientation (Ellis, 1994).

The lesbian (and gay) sexual pathology, gender-disorder, and perversion theories were devised to reinforce the cultural stereotypes and heterosexual ideals (Chodorow, 1994) and enabled psychoanalysis to gain acceptance by the medical establishment (Klaich, 1974). Since the theoretical framework which includes 'homosexuality' as a pathology is fundamental to the whole of psychoanalytic thought, which appears almost to be dependent upon it, as O'Connor and Ryan point out it is hard 'to think differently about lesbianism' within this framework (p. 235).

All psychoanalytic structures and concepts, which are apolitical and have no concept of oppression, therefore are at their base heterosexist. No aspect of them can be adopted by modern schools without considering the implications to models of personal development, sexuality and sexual orientation, the relationship with external authority figures, or theories about the interactions between clients and practitioners.

The virtual invisibility of lesbian concerns in the modern schools – especially professional counselling and most of clinical psychology –

means that there is no middle ground. So being a lesbian in therapy, as a client, trainee or practitioner, is often disorientating and, at worst, a re-experience of the same types of discrimination and tokenism experienced in wider society.

Because of the principles and ethics developed by counselling, in particular, during the 1980s therapy was one of the few occupations in which being a lesbian was an asset. In the progressive and liberationist years, therapy was also about relating the different aspects of an individual to each other – a considerable advance on the traditional separation, by establishment treatments, of mental health, 'neuroses', psychology (conscious and unconscious), behaviour, illness and childhood issues – in psychoanalysis, classified solely in terms of sexuality and gender.

Yet the impression given now is of an apolitical heterosexual profession, reverting gradually to theory-based working, which marginalizes minority concerns, and has prioritized its own status over its codes of ethics and the concerns of its primary users.

Some positive experiences of therapy, reported by lesbian contributors, are included at the end of this chapter. Other discussions which follow suggest that professional therapy is yet to address the most deeply entrenched of all prejudices.

Heterosexism is sexism: negative judgements on – or the invisibility of – lesbian sexuality issues affect all women. Theories deny the reality that all lesbians define themselves in individual ways, and may not want their sexuality to be the focus of therapy. Self-prejudice experienced by heterosexual women results in distancing from lesbian women and their insights and experiences, or over-concern with sexuality issues, and the classic lesbian nightmare of being involved with a heterosexual woman 'exploring her sexuality'. Therapy practitioners are not exempt from such interests. Of greater general concern is that, where patriarchal values are given priority, other forms of discrimination are very close behind. Where the process of marginalization – of any minority population group or individual – is not understood, or remains unacknowledged, other forms of discrimination will also be taking place. Worse, these are being validated through competitiveness, the academic requirements for course access, and recognized 'models' for training institute and practitioner accreditation. The reduction in opportunities for those who support the principle of individuality, and the right to self-definition for themselves and their clients, is a strong move away from humanitarian and holistic principles and 'personal potential' ethics.

The two organizations involved in professionalization – the British

Association for Counselling (BAC) and the newer UK Council for Psycho-therapies (UKCP), are assumed by health service and other employers to be the standard-bearers of ethical therapy. They supply resource lists to individuals, referral services or libraries, publish course recognition criteria (yet to be universally adopted) and accredit or register practitioners. The BAC, which has had a media relations officer since the beginning of 1994, is widely assumed to be the authority in counselling – which was, of course, its intention and is stated in the aims published in each issue of its quarterly journal. However, membership cannot guarantee ethical responsibility.

While there are existing networks separate from each other for people who know how to find them, there is no 'professional' lesbian or gay group within these organizations, nor in the British Psychological Society. This means that there is no way for the hundreds, possibly thousands, of lesbian practitioners or trainees to contact each other, and no way for people who want to work with a lesbian practitioner, supervisor or trainer to contact them. Perhaps it does not occur to professional heterosexuals that lesbians have anything to offer. Most lesbians are unable to come out, or, except in cities, advertise themselves as lesbian practitioners, even in many women's centres. Those who do experience different levels of misunderstanding, silencing, discrimination and isolation (Heenan, 1994) and cannot find the level of support which a heterosexual practitioner would consider her due. Some lesbian practitioners are prevented from earning a living.

Unless modern professional therapy is able to address the difficulties lesbian women experience in heterosexual, and heterosexist, society, it cannot describe its service to potential clients as equality-based. In addition, when it assumes lesbian concerns are solely 'sexual minority' issues or a component of 'lesbian-and-gay' issues, it is failing to recognize the innumerable other forms of marginalization that lesbian women experience, which may be more disempowering for them or, alternatively, give them a greater sense of roots and identity. All lesbians are individuals, and many of them understand therapy better than therapy understands itself – a benefit (if it can be described as such) of living life always from a dual perspective. There is another reason too.

The development of the lesbian population in the past twenty years – a population at least as large as therapy practitioners, and possibly much larger – is a model of therapeutic self-empowerment in anybody's terms. While the community services (discussed below) are for lesbian women or gay men (some are for both), a considerable number of lesbian practitioners come from this background. The assumption, then, that lesbians in therapy are unprofessional, or not even there, is an undervaluation of this unique form of collective empowerment, as well as of skills, self-reliance, creativity, and resourcefulness – the very same qualities required of a therapy practitioner.

The therapy perspective of lesbians (Part I)

An informal survey by the author and several of the contributors to this book revealed that there was no consistency in contemporary attitudes towards lesbians, either in therapy or in feminist writings. As so many contradictory opinions were found, typical attitudes from different sources are given here.

LESBIANS IN THERAPY ARE:

1. *Not in therapy*

The authors of an otherwise excellent study which set out to challenge the stereotyping of women by the mental health system did not include any lesbians because they 'could not find' sufficient case studies (Barnes and Maple, 1992:4).

2. *In therapy only as clients*

(a) All practitioners are heterosexual (see 3 below).
(b) All psychoanalysts are most decidedly heterosexual, and therefore non-perverse. Lesbians and gay men are unfit to practise, first, because of their 'psychopathology' and, second, because they would be unlikely to understand a heterosexual client's point of view(!) (Ellis, 1994).

3. *Have no particular or different needs in therapy*

All counsellors (being heterosexual) are capable of working with lesbian clients. Such matters are dealt with in training. A book on counselling with lesbians wouldn't be appropriate for a training guide series.[1] The British Psychological Society has twice turned down a proposal for a lesbian group and (at the end of 1994) for a lesbian and gay psychology group.[2]

4. Are therapy's ideal clients

All lesbians suffer from a gender disorder based on pre-linguistic paranoid-schizoid ('psychotic') infant delusions, due to having failed to negotiate the Oedipus Complex and wishing to merge with their mothers.

Even respected British critics of psychoanalytic theories of 'lesbianism' collude with this perception. In one 'clinical' case study, O'Connor and Ryan (1993) report that ' . . . the relentless terror' in the client's dreams 'coincided with a sexualising of the transference, coupled with increasing paranoid feelings . . . [her] recurrent phantasy of maintaining her "lesbian" (*sic*) self served to protect her from breakdown' (p. 98). There are innumerable other examples, such as that lesbians are violent, practise SM, or are alcoholics, and that all such problems are *products* of lesbian partnerships and symptomatic of each other (Taylor and Chandler, 1995).

Most of the 'family systems' or 'dysfunctional family' theories, exposed as sexist by feminists, have been recycled onto lesbian relationships – such as 'merger', dependency, self-victimizing or colluding with abuse (Jeffreys, 1994) – and have been heavily criticized by British lesbian feminists (Kitzinger and Perkins, 1993). All the expressions or behaviours attributed to all women under the general heading of 'hysteria' or 'mental illness' remain associated with lesbians. Black lesbians, especially, experience severe and punitive psychiatric discrimination (Montsho, 1995).

In 1971, a group of doctors from the Maudsley Hospital in London asked for lesbian volunteers from the network Kenric to offer themselves (naked), urine samples provided, for examination. Samples of cells were taken from inside their cheeks. They were measured, weighed and photographed. They also answered a psychological questionnaire. Needless to say, the doctors' hope of discovering a genuine gender disorder were dashed (Chapman, 1989).

5. Do not experience male violence in their families

The editors of an otherwise superb book on family therapy in the context of violence against women included lesbians solely as victims of violence by their lesbian partners (Renzetti, 1993).

6. Should not be in therapy

The lesbian feminist authors of the first British book on lesbian therapy and psychology decreed that lesbians in or practising therapy, self-help, or recovery groups, were anti-political, because therapy individualized problems and solutions, took lesbians out of the community and dis-tracted attention from collective aims. Lesbian feminist therapy was especially dangerous and damaging (Kitzinger and Perkins, 1993:26).

7. Must not say so if they are

The authors of the British challenge to psychoanalytic theories of 'lesbian-ism' did not, or could not, identify their sexual orientation except in one very oblique, easy to miss, comment (O'Connor and Ryan, 1993).

8. Represent solely minority issues irrelevant to therapy studies

The director of a humanistic therapy training centre, whose own training and several years of practice were in mental health settings, on refusing a series of offers for workshop trainings on lesbian and gay issues, hetero-sexism awareness, and anti-oppressive therapy, stated that there were too many 'so-called experts' who dealt only with 'minority concerns' and were therefore 'not objective'. Such issues that arose in training or supervision were dealt with 'quietly and simply'. Anti-oppressive therapy 'had over-tones of political control and was therefore contradictory to the spirit of counselling'.[3]

9. Cannot possibly be lesbians if they are famous or eminent

Anna Freud, voted 'most outstanding colleague' in a 1971 US survey of psychiatrists and psychoanalysts (Peters, 1979:xii), lived for more than fifty years as co-parent, partner and colleague with Dorothy Burlingham. They founded the London wartime nurseries and the Anna Freud Clinic. How-ever, she could not have been a lesbian because she was 'much too much her father's daughter ever to have a sexual relationship with Dorothy' (Sayers, 1992:159 – unsourced comment).

SOME RESPONSES

1. Examples of lesbians' experiences with mental health services were included in Out for Ourselves (Dublin Lesbian and Gay Men's Collectives, 1986:162) and in Inventing Ourselves (Hall Carpenter Archives, 1989). A long list of references and resources is included in How Can We Help You? (Macourt, 1989). Kate Millett's experiences in the USA and Ireland were published in The Loony Bin Trip (1991). There are, in any case, enough

lesbian stereotypes in psychiatric and psychoanalytic textbooks to at least be challenged. There are dozens of resources: lesbian and gay centres, helplines, and women's centres, including one round the corner from where one of the authors of the study works (in Leeds).

Several practitioners in my survey worked with lesbian clients and colleagues. Almost everyone who responded to the survey had been in therapy herself and knew others who were practising, studying, or experiencing one of the many hundreds of therapy schools and styles. There is a demand for lesbian practitioners, pointed out in the O'Connor and Ryan study (1993), and shown by the waiting lists for counselling in voluntary organizations, and mental health service users' support projects. MIND began to address this need late in 1994, following the year-long Stress on Women campaign which reported discriminatory treatment of women already marginalized by society, and often sent for psychiatric care because of their responses to this stress (Gorman, 1992). There is a particular need for lesbian counsellors with personal experiences of marginalization both in society and in lesbian and gay communities.

The Kitzinger–Perkins study pointed to an entire therapy 'culture'. A young lesbian reported that in some city circles therapy was a prior requirement of relationships, to ensure a good level of intimacy. Most lesbian practitioners studied as a result of their own varied experiences of therapy (most of them with heterosexual women practitioners). So there are lesbians in therapy, and several of them are survivors of the mental health system and workers in this field.

2. See above. Two training centres in London are known to be run by lesbian women. Several lesbians work in counselling and non-statutory psychotherapy training centres as academic staff or guest regular lecturers. There are private therapy centres, lesbian and gay services, networks and an equivalent number of holistic and body-centred therapy practitioners who advertise in women's, lesbian and general media, and have done so since the early 1980s and possibly longer.

3. Recent surveys show that most counsellors and psychologists: (a) know nothing about lesbian issues; (b) don't want to know; (c) think they know all there is to know; (d) treat lesbians the same as other women clients; (e) never ask what it feels like to be a lesbian; (f) know nothing about lesbian culture or community, support services, or lesbian 'minority' issues (that is, further marginalization of lesbians from minority groups); (g) work often with lesbian clients, especially on 'coming out' issues (Moon, 1994; Annesley, 1995; Kitzinger and Coyle, 1995).

4. Come to the next Pride demonstration!

5. See lists of sexual abuse survivor groups listed in appropriate media, at helplines, or women's and lesbian/gay centres. For details of young lesbians' suicides, and the reasons for their depression and isolation, contact the Lesbian Youth Information Service. Also, see the CHAR survey of reasons for homelessness among young women of all sexualities (Hendessi, 1992:13) and *The Lesbian Victim of Sexual Assault* (Orzek, 1989).

6. Every lesbian has the same rights as anyone else to seek to achieve her own best level of well-being in whatever ways she chooses. She has the right to the support of her peers, other lesbians or women who experience similar personal difficulties, and to use culturally appropriate accessible language which is neither pathologizing, alienating, nor excluding of her. Therapy is 'politics for individuals' (the general consensus of contributors to this book). Modern anti-oppressive practice, especially feminism, is a natural development of the progressive, self-empowering political movements of the 1970s and 1980s. It is traditional therapy which is 'anti-political', not its troubled clients, and it is capable of changing its stance: practitioners have considerable support throughout their careers, a massive pool of readily available information, and the willingness (and ethical expectation) to challenge their own perceptions, presumptions, and prejudices. In theory, anyway.

7. Heterosexist prejudice prevents lesbians working in therapy from being open about their sexuality, just as in society. Some consider their sexual orientation irrelevant to therapy practice. Some lesbian practitioners have been victimized once they came out. Lesbians working in women's projects report tokenism, silencing, the expectation that they will work with all clients, that they are experts on lesbian issues, and that they must support the centre workers and policy before either themselves or their clients. Apart from six London training centres named by contributors (though there may be more) lesbians are usually isolated in training. Lesbian issues are never discussed unless they raise them. Lesbian practitioners, who work with heterosexual supervisors or peer groups, often feel prevented from discussing lesbian clients' concerns, especially around sex, and the particular boundary issues in lesbian communities.

8. See discussions on heterosexism, the value of the collective lesbian experience to therapy as a whole (this chapter) and ideas on therapy practice, throughout this book.

The general impression is that there is a limit to how much self-empowerment professional therapy can take. In every respect, lesbians are the limit.

Lesbian therapy and collective empowerment

Modern client-oriented therapy approaches, and self-directed styles of training, share their origins with feminism and the liberationist and civil rights movements. Because there is no single school of feminist therapy, all of the radical schools are defined as being founded by men (Kitzinger and Perkins, 1995:25). The exceptions, paradoxically, are in psychoanalysis (though mainly child psychoanalysis) – Melanie Klein and Anna Freud. Given that women are in the majority in therapy – almost 70 per cent in the most recent survey of counselling membership – this assumption stretches credulity. It may be men who promote themselves, found training centres, and think up new names for what are almost identical approaches, but all the ethics and professional codes are based on identifiably feminist and equal rights principles.

The anti-oppressive approach defined in this book takes its politics from feminism. However, the understanding of therapy as a social ideology can be found in the earliest psychoanalytic writings of Sigmund Freud and, in particular, Anna Freud (see introduction to the casework examples). The approach as applied to the casework was developed from the lesbian experience of founding a self-identified and collectively therapeutic population group. Additional insights came from several of the contributors. The principles are based on the recognition of social and political causes of individual problems; and equality between clients and practitioners, in every respect. It is a *social* therapy: lesbian women most often live, or want to live, in social settings, and therapy can be considered as a resource for expanding their world or their role within it. The limits to the participation of lesbians in the wider society are caused by past and present oppressive factors which also have become internalized and are thus in conflict with her personal potential and her autonomy. In this sense, therapy is politics for individuals.

Individuals do not fit into theories, especially theories which ignore the phenomenal political and cultural changes of the past thirty years and, in particular, the revelations, by thousands of women, of the real meaning of 'family values'. The years of sexual liberation become the era of sexual abuse disclosures. HIV and the threat of an AIDS epidemic have affected everyone's perception of sexual identity and expression. It is reasonable therefore to state that any theory of personal development or ways of relating, or of sexuality or 'psychosexual' problems, devised before, say, 1988, is now redundant.

Any practitioner who works in an actively anti-oppressive way will be aware of, and may have been involved in, anti-racist and anti-sexist initiatives without equating these issues with lesbian (or gay) rights.

Because of the pathologization of their sexuality in psychoanalysis, and their treatment by psychiatric services, lesbian women have been among the strongest critics of oppressive and sexist theories and practice since the 1970s (Millett, 1971). The postwar distortion of Sigmund Freud's non-judgemental perception of homosexuality and bisexuality, written in 1905, was exposed in the context of attitudes to lesbians since the foundation of Western society (Klaich, 1974). An exploration of the effects of silencing and isolation on the lesbian psyche provided early evidence of internalized heterosexism (Abbott and Love, 1972).

Lesbians' different perspectives and experiences – political, academic, and personal – gave feminism and the gay rights movement additional evidence with which to challenge social policy. Radical therapy in the USA addressed lesbian and gay issues from its beginnings, and, significantly, included a report that, in 1968, the worst epithet which could be applied to Women's Liberation was 'lesbian'. 'The sisters ... faced labels like commies or tramps with equanimity ... but they broke down in tears when they were called lesbians' (Shelley, *Radical Therapist*, 1974:151). The article ended with the comment 'Hostility towards oppressors is healthy. But the guardians of modern morality, the psychiatrists, have interpreted this hostility as an illness, and they say this illness causes, and is, lesbianism' (152). Several feminists have identified the source of myths and stereotypes about women's 'madness' or 'natural emotional instability' (Chesler, 1973).

So, for more than twenty years, the connections have been made between sexism/heterosexism, establishment therapy's stereotypes, ideals of mental health, diagnoses of madness, and 'lesbianism' (Burstow, 1993). In the UK, this information, and insights from the consciousness-raising groups of the late 1960s, led to the development of the then-revolutionary women's self-help groups.

New approaches were evolved, and a definition of anti-oppressive therapy from that time is as sound today, and as relevant, as when it was created in one of the first self-help groups, Red Therapy. It is especially applicable to lesbians.

'It's a pity we called it therapy', wrote Sheila Ernst and Lucy Goodison, authors of *In Our Own Hands*. 'Real change would come from *combining* our political activity ... with the ideas and experiences coming from discussion and consciousness-raising groups *and* with the feelings and emotional energy we can tap through therapy' (1981:4). (Original emphasis.)

Their practical guide to self-help began, as all good therapy should, by addressing issues of gender, class, race, taboos on expressing feelings, attitudes to the body and sexuality specific to different cultures, the fears and guilt experienced by survivors of persecution, and the discriminatory treatment in psychiatric hospitals where working-class people were considered 'unsuitable' subjects for therapy, and given instead electro-shock or drug treatments (p. 5). Later women's writings have shown this same, and worse, discrimination applied on the grounds of race (in particular), age, and sexual orientation (Barnes and Maple, 1992; Wilson 1993; Burstow, 1992; MIND, 1993; Montsho, 1995).

The lesbian perspective at that time was acknowledged as crucial to any sexuality debates and discussions of oppressions, and, ironically, this was before feminism had taken on board Black women's issues (Mason-John and Khambatta, 1993:11). In those days lesbians self-identified in their writings on women's sexuality (Cartledge and Ryan, 1983).

Therapy became integral to the development of lesbian communities. The 'collective coming out' of an entire population of perhaps three million lesbians from every sector of society is unique in British history and is a model of self-empowerment and co-operation between diverse groups and individuals. The opportunity to be visible was also therapeutic for so many closeted lesbians. Already skilled at self-organizing, lesbians formed networks, helplines, and befriending groups, and studied counselling and the feminist, humanistic, or 'alternative' therapies. Some – like so many other people – set up in practice without qualifications. Until trainings became accessible and affordable, many lesbian women were, in any case, excluded from them. If Red Therapy and self-help groups could invent their own approaches, then anyone could.

There was (and still is) a continual interchange of information, flowing freely between political groups, formal therapy and mental health work, helplines and community projects, rights organizations and, most recently, sexual health. Lesbian volunteers, some of them newly-out, learned – as they do today – by experience and from each other, by inviting comments from service users, and by applying equality-based relationship ideals to supportive practice. Lesbians denied opportunities elsewhere, or who had spent years in psychiatric care where they were sent by enraged parents, found empowerment in being enabled to develop their personal qualities and skills in a variety of essential work: support, outreach, training, administration, group facilitation, telephone/Minicom counselling, technical work, management, fundraising, and much more. Others worked with feminists in women's crisis or support projects, or with gay men, and still do. However, not all lesbians have access to an organized and funded community centre, and this remains the case today.

For many of those involved in befriending, support, helpline, or counselling projects, the experience of being a member of an oppressed and stereotyped minority community meant an increase in sensitivity towards other people, and enabled deeper communication and empathy.

Lesbians who are interested in supportive and empowering work and who value diversity and individuality are committed to equalities practice and to full access for all lesbians – and women who believe that they might be lesbians – to centres and events. Progress is sometimes slow, but attendance at a large event – a good example was the 25th Anniversary Pride festival – demonstrates the multicultural and multi-ability make-up of the lesbian and gay population, and the enjoyment of that diversity.

Politicized lesbians, like feminists, for many years have addressed issues around race, disability, class, ethnicity, political views, religious beliefs, sexuality and, most recently, sexual health. Some groups, often developed by helpline workers, address problems such as partner violence or addiction (see Taylor and Chandler, 1995). There are formal counselling services in the larger, funded centres, all of them operating independently from statutory or voluntary sector health or care services, though supervisors are sometimes external. This strong tradition of counselling and commitment to mutual empowerment has meant that many lesbians from this background who study therapy, either to formalize their skills or learn more, decide to make this a career. Several of the contributors to this book came from this type of background, including women's crisis centre work. This lesbian energy, and the ability to find creative solutions to problems, appears to be unstoppable.

There is, therefore, a massive resource of experience, knowledge, expertise and insights on all of the 'professional' issues being addressed by modern therapy. These include ethics, equality-based practice, boundaries, client-oriented practice, the capability of working with a wide range of issues and social problems, and an understanding of the causes of individuals' problems. Lesbians have something to contribute about every possible 'therapy' theme: alienation, isolation, self-motivation, commit-ment, risk, trust, negotiation, assertiveness, self-expression, resourcefulness, identifying and challenging prejudicial attitudes and behaviour, individual empowerment, skills development, managing change, or coping with crisis. They also have much to say on problems which affect women in particular – depression, eating distress, or self-harmful behaviour. Most of all they have plenty to contribute to the issues which dominate therapy, and are probably every client's fundamental therapy issues: autonomy, sexual identity and purpose.

It is highly offensive that this perspective is ignored in therapy, and that, when lesbians are remembered, they are perceived solely as clients and stereotyped according to the views of the majority heterosexual practi-tioners or their organizations.

Among the many lesbian survival skills are reclaiming stereotypes and a sense of humour. Several lesbians – clients, trainees, and practitioners – report wasted weeks wondering what the practitioner or supervisor *really* thinks and knows, or 'teaching' her or him about life as a lesbian. Perhaps all lesbians interviewing therapy practitioners (etc.) should wear large T-shirts emblazoned with Certified Psychotic, Unresolved Oedipal Issues, Merged with Mother Substitute, Female Paedophile, Female Homosexual, Socially Diseased, Sex Addict, Violent Alcoholic, Gender-Confused, Invert, or No Sex Except When In A Definitely-Doomed Relationship With A Heterosexual Woman Exploring Her Sexuality And You're Next. All the theories and assumptions could then be dealt with, and dumped, in the assessment session. An inverted perspective is, in any case, useful, since it is often only by a series of psychological acrobatics that a lesbian can understand what heterosexist therapy is all about. (See Chapter 2.).

There is ample evidence of an increasing tendency in therapy to problematize ordinary concerns and to study or develop theories about them. The interest, in entrepreneurial counselling, in psychoanalytic theories and practice principles, and the use of expressions such as 'client psychopathology', are of particular concern to lesbians and gay men. (See *Counselling*, November 1994.) Any theories are disempowering if clients do not relate to them, and any therapy which concentrates solely on psycho-logical concerns is far removed from the body-conscious and 'whole person' therapies of the 1980s.

For example, the BAC – the same organization which turned down the (invited) proposal for a book on counselling with lesbians at the end of 1993 – published a volume entitled *Psycho-Sexual Problems* by Dr Elphis Christopher. According to the BAC mail-order brochure (August 1994) this book covers 'the various aspects of heterosexual difficulties, homo-sexuality (*sic*), lesbianism, sexual minorities, sexual offences and sexuality, and disabilities' – all in 84 pages.

Well – perhaps a book on counselling with lesbians which also explored issues such as practitioner prejudice and lesbian practitioners' boundary issues didn't quite fit into the training category. So Psycho-Sexual Problem must be added to the T-shirt list above.

For those concerned about the origins of these theories, and the relationship between heterosexism and other forms of oppression, the most illustrative piece of writing, which in a few words explains the British cultural establishment attitudes, is the *Sunday Express* diatribe against Radclyffe Hall's *The Well of Loneliness*. This resulted in the twenty-year ban of the novel in the UK (Hall, 1948). It says more, in its way, than an entire library of lesbian feminist exposures of different oppressions. It is timely to reproduce it here, in view of the proposed British film of the book. Students of psychoanalysis may care to compare the content of the editorial with the theories of lesbian sexual pathology being developed around the same time – one year after all women were granted the right to vote on equal terms with men.

The Well was banned (in the UK only) within two months of publication, following one of the most extraordinary trials in literary history, when the publishers Jonathan Cape, who withdrew the book on the Home Secretary's instruction, shipped in copies printed in Paris (Klaich, 1974).

The ban was because *The Well* did not condemn lesbians – not because it was 'obscene'. There were more than 300 pages before there was a hint of sex, and other books with a 'lesbian' theme came out around the same time. Virginia Woolf's *Orlando* was considered a 'sex-change fantasy' and another, now lost, classic, was the send-up of the whole sorry saga, *The Sink of Solitude*.

The editorial emphasized the close connections between Anglican religion, heterosexism, British linguistic chauvinism, racism and nationalism.

The paper called on 'the Christian Churches' to destroy this 'doctrine' because the 'pestilence [of homosexuality] is devastating the younger generation ... and wrecking young souls ... the plague is stalking shamelessly through great social assemblies'. The 'unutterable putrefaction' forced upon society the task of 'cleansing itself from the leprosy of those lepers ... This seductive and insidious piece of ... perverted decadence ... and depravity .... The battle has been lost in France and Germany but it has not yet been lost in England ... Literature, as well as morality is in peril.' ... And so on in the same vein.

Despite scores of contemporary writers (many of them lesbian or gay) appearing as witnesses, the ban went ahead. The book sold phenomenally well in fourteen other countries. Out of date by the time it appeared here, it was still on the 'adults only – by request' shelves in public libraries in the early 1960s. It probably did more harm than good: it established yet another set of lesbian stereotypes. The irony was that Hall had described her heroine Stephen Gordon in medical terms popular at the time, in the hope of gaining public sympathy, as a biological 'freak' and 'God's mistake'.

The war against lesbians continued in popular psychology books, based on pseudo-psychoanalytic theory. An example is Frank Caprio's *Female Homosexuality* – the first widely available book on the subject (1954). This added a few more 'neuroses' to the list: seducing and enslaving young girls, hypochondria, alcoholism, insane jealousy, nervous breakdowns, drug addiction ... lesbians seem to be 'very sick individuals indeed'. Sexism ruled: 'Lesbians seem to hold on to the belief that life without love of some kind is meaningless ... lesbianism is contrary to women's basic needs ... women unconsciously (*sic*) prefer to fulfil their maternal role and to be loved by a man.' And perhaps the final, unmitigated truth about the roots of heterosexism – 'however *brilliant and talented some lesbians might be* their emotional life is childish and immature' (my italics).

Clients' rights in therapy

As long as lesbians considering therapy options remain aware that, most of the time, they will be working in the context of heterosexism, they will feel more able to challenge a practitioner's assumptions. No client should need to do this, nor to 'teach' a counsellor or psychotherapist about themselves. However, practitioners are not perfect – which is why their codes of ethics require them to be in continual supervision, and to be committed to personal development and further training as necessary.

Difficult as it may be in practice, clients do have the right to question and complain if therapy is not working, since it is often the case that the responsibility for this lies with the practitioner. (See Casework examples.)

To conclude on a positive note, several of the lesbian contributors to this book reported good experiences of therapy. Some representative comments are included here to demonstrate that a therapy room is a place to focus on individual needs, and to take a rest from political or academic debate, challenge, and confrontation. What they are describing is being treated as equals, the fulfilment of ordinary human needs, and a shift in perception from needs to rights. This is another aspect of therapy which defines it as politics for individuals. (Identification is as given by contributors.)

Older lesbian, parent, and worker – out four years

> I think I had a good therapist – I was lucky. Therapy gave me emotional support, strengthened and facilitated change, stood by me, in fact. I wanted a male therapist to enable me to work through difficulties with men – not sure a woman would have worked for me.

Middle-class, able-bodied, out for ten years

> At the moment, I love it – sometimes I've hated it. My therapist is firmly grounded as a Person-Centred practitioner and this is important to me and is a shared value base.

Woman, parent, creative, bisexual thirteen years, lesbian five years

> Overall, I feel very positive. Therapy has been a good and life-enhancing experience for me. Through it I came to believe that I had the right to love women, and to have that right respected by others. I have learnt that I am not the bad and useless person I thought I was. Rather, I have abilities and many good traits. In short, I have the right to live my life in all its facets, to love and respect myself and others.

Black lesbian, Jamaican and white (British) descent, artist

> What was good about therapy – the first time, long ago – was feeling that someone was interested in me as a woman and shared my feminist views. All my lesbian friends were white, I was very career-minded and some of them resented that – it wasn't sisterly. I liked the body work but in the end she was unable to support me in terms of my racial identity issues. The second time was much longer, four years, and this was fantastic – lots of exciting techniques like visualization and clay modelling and drawing, but spontaneous – unusual for me. I discovered a completely new person underneath a lot of rationalization. But nothing lasts forever, and when I realized that she never once asked me what it felt like to be Black I lost my confidence in her. But, for

myself, I came out of it much stronger because of what she gave me. She said it was OK to feel like that because it meant that I respected myself as her equal.

White, middle-class, middle-aged, Christian, left-leaning, single – has identified as gay woman, rather than lesbian, all her life

I initially wanted six sessions to work on a specific item of interest ... I'm still there over five years later. It has been an exhilarating journey of discovery, including the odd shipwreck here and there. The key to successful changes is the integrity and commitment of my therapist – her not inconsiderable skills come second to the quality of the relationship.

Scottish lesbian, out for ten years, Canadian-born, one son

I've had different therapies – groups and one-to-one. The group was hard work, and stressful to listen to other people's pain. But I learned a lot by listening, and it was very empowering to be able to share my insight to what another woman was saying. I stopped feeling stupid and scared, and was able to talk about women feeling like victims all the time. In private therapy, it was the opposite. She didn't say much, so I could think and just be myself, and experience what it was like to be able to dream a little and let things work out by themselves. It was important as I am always busy and work in a noisy place, so it was therapeutic to be peaceful and just realize things.

White, non-UK, a lesbian for sixteen years

My most important relationship with a therapist was very powerful and empowering – massively important to me, and changed my life. I have had some experiences that have 'not worked', most notably, an initial appointment with an eminent 'psychotherapist' who refused to work with me because my doctor's letter was 'inadequate'!

White lesbian, 28, abuse survivor, student

The best thing was that it lived up to my expectations. What it said in the books was what I got. To have my feelings validated, to be able to express them without criticism, to understand why I had feelings and how this supplied the meaning for me of my experiences, to work out what my needs were, to feel 'held' and allowed to be powerful without her collapsing! To find out I wasn't the person who first went into therapy, and to still be accepted for who I am. I really feel she loved me, the first person in my life to do that.

Menopausal dyke, recently bereaved, out everywhere, confused

What started as bereavement counselling – several friends died of AIDS within a few months – became mid-life crisis therapy, then spiritual re-birth therapy, then I don't know what else. Half the time I felt I was connecting with her on a very deep level, at other times I was off somewhere in another universe. My dreams were amazing and I was terrified a lot of the time. But the great thing was that she was calm through all of this, very skilled, always un-fazed, and what was most important, she understood every single crazy and spaced-out thing I ever said! A genius.

White (European), 56, grandmother, lesbian twenty years or more

Therapy was about stopping being Mum, Grandma, feminist superwoman, all that. I wanted to reclaim my childhood sense of myself, some ordinary, non-political joy and spontaneity. She was much younger than me, which I was worried about at first, but then I thought, what the hell, and could be as silly as I liked. I went through different ages – two, nine, 13, 18 – saying or doing the things I was never allowed to do, that no girl of my generation was allowed to do, like having a tantrum about nothing, being irresponsible, talking about sexy feelings, hating getting married and doing housework, really disliking my first child, grieving for the loss of that girlhood. Therapy is about realizing that whatever you think you lost is still in there, somewhere, and all experience is worth validating.

NOTES

1. During 1993 the British Association for Counselling (BAC) requested in its journal, *Counselling*, proposals for its new Guidebooks series on 'topics which need experience over and above that which would normally be expected of a generic counsellor', the Guidebooks to give 'essential information to counsellors faced with a client who raises a particular issue in which the counsellor has no experience and little knowledge'. Topic suggestions included 'cross cultural' issues. A lesbian BAC member (also an established author and conference speaker) wrote suggesting *Counselling with Lesbians*. The Information and Publications Manager replied (29 July 1993): 'So far we have no one offering to write on "Counselling Lesbians" so I will discuss it with members of the Publications Sub-Committee . . . I do hope you are keen to take this project further'; and invited a detailed proposal using the format suggested. This was duly submitted with samples of writing, etc. The reply from this same officer (4 October 1993) stated: 'There was a lot of concern about this as a suitable subject for a Guidebook. As you point out in your proposal, Lesbians are humans and should be treated

as normal people.' (The writer did not in fact use these words.) 'A well trained counsellor should be doing this anyway. It is not the object of the series to do the job of the trainers but to fill in specialist information. The general consensus of the Publications Sub-Committee was that this is not a suitable topic for the series.'

The proposal covered a range of issues similar to those discussed in this book (such as lesbians as members of a multicultural and multi-ability population, sexist/heterosexist issues for counsellors, need for knowledge of lesbian community concerns, issues between lesbian counsellors and clients, etc.). (Copies of this correspondence, and the Guidebook proposal, are held by the author.)

2. The proposal for a 'Psychology of Lesbianism' Section in the British Psychological Society (BPS) was reported in several publications, including *Feminism and Psychology*, vol. 2, no. 2, 1992, pp. 265–8 and 269–70; vol. 3, no. 2, 1993, pp. 282–3; *The Psychologist*, vol. 9, no. 1, 1993, pp. 19–20; *Self and Society*, vol. 21, no. 1, 1993, pp. 7–9; and Pink Therapy *Members' Newsletter*, January 1995. See also Chapter 2, References.

3. Excerpt from letter (17 June 1994) to a lesbian trainer who had on several occasions offered to her former training institute various workshops for staff or students on lesbian, gay, and heterosexist-awareness issues, prejudice-awareness, and anti-oppressive practice, within the guidelines of the BAC and UK Council for Psychotherapies (UKCP) Training Course Recognition Criteria, and statements on intercultural issues. The institute concerned is recognized by both these organizations. The lesbian trainer would have accepted refusal on grounds such as incompatibility of therapy approach or the availability of more experienced lecturers on these subjects. However, one statement in this same letter caused particular concern: ' ... we have not asked anyone to offer the kind of thing you are offering, because this approach, i.e. anti-oppressive practice, does not fit in with our way of working ... BAC and UKCP ... do not prescribe what to teach as long as the students are made aware of the issues involved – and the staff are free to choose the manner that we do that ... ' The lesbian trainer was continuing to argue the issues as this book went to press. (Correspondence held by the author.)

The relevant excerpts from the Training Criteria which relate to Codes of Ethics and Practice and policy statements are:

British Association for Counselling:
The Recognition of Counsellor Training Courses, 6, Theory, iv

The social systems in which we live and the ways these affect client development and counselling practice. [The term 'social systems' is taken to include such factors as race, culture, gender, sexual preference, politics and ethics.]

Code of Ethics and Practice for Counsellors B.2.6.3:

'Counsellors will take all reasonable steps to take account of the client's social context.' This is understood to include the factors detailed above and religion, age, and the wider economic, political, educational, organizational and institutional systems.

UK Council for Psychotherapies:

Training Requirements, 2: The Minimum Curriculum
2.2. Acquisition of a critical understanding of the relevance of studies in human development, psychopathology, sexuality, ethics, research, and social science.

(Minimum) Ethical Guidelines for incorporation within Codes of Practice for Training Organisations and Trainees:
2.3. Teachers will respect the diversity of trainees and not to discriminate on grounds of difference.

Ethical Guidelines (Code of Ethics and Practice).
1.1 ... Each organisation will include and elaborate upon the following principles in its Code of Ethics.
1.2 ... Psychotherapists should endeavour to use their abilities to their client's best advantage without prejudice and with due recognition of the value and dignity of every human being.

Race Policy Statement [excerpt]: ... inner (world) and outer (external processes) must be viewed together, at once a political and psychological enterprise. Without perspective on the psychological processes employed in the service of prejudice in individual and institutional racism, we [psychotherapists] are ill-equipped to act for constructive change. Without perspective on the social, economic, and political processes which produce the individual, we are equally ill-prepared for therapeutic or political activity of any sensitivity or relevance.

Intercultural Committee Report to Annual General Meeting 30.11.93: ... the Intercultural Special Interests Group ... decided to extend its brief to look at other areas of discrimination ... [and] felt that though different areas of discrimination needed to be attended to specifically, there were strong overriding themes in terms of difference and the anxiety it creates, and destructive ways of dealing with this ... we would like to consider all aspects of equal opportunities. It is clear that certain groups of people experience discrimination and we want to take responsibility for making sure that the Council is ... developing a psychotherapy practice which is appropriate and helpful for all members of the community. Conditions which we are particularly concerned to take responsibility for include the elderly; differences of gender; sexual orientation; class; religion; disability, both learning, physical and sensory disability; the unemployed and poor people. We would approach these from a political, philosophical and ethical viewpoint ... in certain cases, we would need to create workshops or structures whereby theoretical matters can be discussed.

the equality complex

Clients are the people for whom therapy was originally intended, and both meanings of this statement are the focus of this chapter. The fundamental power differential between practitioners and clients, which creates situations fraught with possibilities of abuse, has been continually challenged by feminists, and by several practitioners in the modern schools. But the structure of most therapies reinforces power differentials. This chapter makes a direct connection between professional therapy's present 'equality complex' – its perception of clients – and its attitudes to lesbian women.

Therapy's inability to resolve the 'lesbian problem' is based on the same set of values, inherited from psychoanalysis, which has created an industry dependent on the regular creation of 'new' approaches and the continuing existence of 'clients'. The social reality is that there always will be people who want personal support or guidance, or resources for identifying their own means of self-empowerment. The radical therapies addressed this issue by aligning themselves with the progressive politics of the liberationist years, especially feminism. They were 'guided self-help'. Anyone could learn the principles, communications methods, and techniques, and adapt them to their own methods of achieving their optimum level of well-being, either individually, in couples, or in mutually supportive groups. (See Chapter 1.)

But the radical therapies are now professions, and firmly 'apolitical'. They define themselves by specific models (approaches and sets of theories) and even 'client-centred' schools focus on what the *practitioner* does. Counselling is a new field of academic study, and has crossed the borderline between itself and psychotherapy. These moves have increased the divisions between practitioners and clients, and between the grassroots, anti-oppressive practitioners and the academically minded entrepreneurs. They have set up competitiveness between the different schools – 500 at the last count, although they are not so very different from each other. They have also increased the division between heterosexual people and everybody else.

The answer to all questions of ethics, practice methods, or criteria for practitioner competence, is to identify who will benefit from any changes. Today's approaches and training course recognition requirements have been developed in part as a result of negative reports by individuals or their organizational advocates, supported by the popular media, which, it should be acknowledged, enjoy any anti-therapy story. There are benefits from emphasizing the negative, which is what public watchdogs are for, but the ambitious therapy practitioner is more of an expert on the needs of vulnerable people than the average journalist – even the 'impartial' reporters of *The Independent*,[1] and finds ways of re-framing the most stringent of criticisms.

As a consequence of the 'mind-bending seducer' stories (many of them true, as several surveys proved), the essence of good practice has been distilled into codes of ethics and the new National Vocational Qualifications standards (NVQs/SVQs: see Introduction). However, not all the internal critiques have had positive results.

The definition of a professional – ethical – practitioner, is now a matter of public record. The UK Council for Psychotherapies has a national register, and counselling is due to follow – at present, its resource lists (local and national) rely on members of the associations filling in their directory entry forms. Some counsellors do not want to be listed, possibly because there is another division now, between 'accredited practitioners' and 'non-accredited' (or lapsed) practitioners.

Choosing a therapy, or a practitioner, is more complicated for potential clients than before. One method is to choose by the school or model, as this is usually how different practices are described, in the registers or listings, even though most people choose by a sense of rapport, the individual practitioner's experience or specialism, by personal recommendation and, often, by referral from a professional in another field. Choice is considered a crucial element in starting therapy but, in reality, few people who are vulnerable or in distress have confidence in their ability to make appropriate choices. (See Chapter 3.)

Most of the 'new' schools or practice approaches overlap with each other, and many are imaginatively retitled derivatives created for professionalization purposes – including bizarre variations of 'integrative' therapy – often authenticated by tagging 'Freud' onto the list of founding fathers. (They are always 'fathers'.) There is even a school of 'reality therapy'.

The fundamental criterion for choosing a therapy (if there is a choice) is the individual practitioner's perception of 'clients'. This will follow the diktats of their school, and shed light on their perception of lesbians. Even where there is no specific policy or theoretical base, practitioners have their own agendas. Organizational Equal Opportunities and 'non-judgemental' ethics can hide a multiplicity of prejudicial beliefs. The Sex Discrimination Act is, after all, only twenty years old, and there are very few 20-year-old practitioners.

In addition, therapy, being a social microcosm, is not frozen in time. The recent overhaul of training and practice standards has made practitioners much more aware of what they are doing and of the meaning of the codes of ethics, but life goes on for the counsellor, her lover, her children (if she has them), her own counsellor (if she has one), the counsellor's supervisor and the supervisor's cat.

Attitudes to lesbians fall into three broad categories. The psychoana-lytic view is summarized in Chapter 1. In 'clinical' psychology, where most clients are 'neurotic', experiencing behavioural problems or 'phobias', or, sometimes, 'the worried well', a lesbian's therapy issue is perceived as coming out (that is, her first awareness of her sexual orientation). In counselling and the former radical therapies (outside feminism) lesbian sexuality is invisible. A lesbian client is perceived as equal either to any other women or to gay men, as evidenced by references to 'lesbian-and-gay' issues (see Introduction).

There is no certainty about any of these attitudes, of course, since there is no official lesbian policy statement from any professional organization, except the British Psychological Society (see Chapter 1).

These attitudes are particularly relevant when a lesbian wants to focus initially on a serious and health-threatening problem. A frequent concern is 'Will the practitioner imply that the only way I can resolve my problems is by becoming heterosexual?' That is, does the fact of being a lesbian make her more of a *client*?

When all clients are mad, sick or stupid, lesbians are madder, sicker, and stupider. At the opposite pole, all clients are fine, equal to each other and to the practitioner, and responsible participants in their own therapy, which is 'self-directed' or perhaps feminist (MacLeod, 1994). Here, les-bians' sexuality is their own concern and no longer the cause of all their problems, though it may be a problem in relationships. These tend to be treated like any relationships, except if they are abusive. Then they are perceived as 'abusive *lesbian* relationships'. For example, 'lesbian battering has been defined as a pattern of violent or coercive behaviour whereby a lesbian seeks to control the thoughts, beliefs, or conduct of her intimate partner or to punish [her] for resisting the perpetrator's control' (Renzetti, 1993:188).

There are several other levels of assumption in equality-minded counselling officialdom. One is that all trained practitioners should be able to work with lesbian clients (see Chapter 1). Another is that the corporate or practitioner view is the same as everyone else's in society.

Paradoxically, the diametrically opposed therapies – 'classic' psychoanalysis and 'client-directed' counselling – share some highly significant official beliefs. One is that there are no lesbian practitioners, trainers or innovators, nor is there any validation of lesbian contributions to therapy as a whole.

Another is that both schools are 'apolitical', although in quite different ways. Another is that practitioners know best – not always about the client's issues, but about how to 'do' therapy. Most unexpectedly, at their extremes, both types of practitioners say that they are merely 'mirrors', and work only with 'what the client brings'. (The difference is that analysts interpret and have pre-conceived theories: at least, that *used* to be the difference.)

So how can a lesbian considering her therapy options make a genuinely informed choice? Well, by using the same techniques as she found effective when making any other kind of life choice. If she feels unable or unqualified to do this, a well-proved method is to ask other lesbians. (See Chapters 3 and 4.)

Coming out from behind the looking-glass

The patronizing view of clients as a species separate from practitioners is endemic, even in some feminist therapies (McLeod, 1994; Dana and Lawrence, 1988; and others). The alternative – that the client is a responsible, equal partner in the process – is also confusing for lesbians who want active support or guidance. Each school has its own policy, and a potential client may not understand the intricacies of different approaches, nor what they mean in practice. That is, the school or the practitioner makes the decision about the approach, not the client.

If a lesbian says to a counsellor, for example, 'I know you consider us to be equals, but I want you to give me more feedback and ideas', will the answer be: (1) psychoanalytic – 'Mm-hm. Do you want to say more about that?' or (2) non-directive – 'Do you mean you feel starved of ideas, or that you don't believe you have any ideas of your own?'

Suitable ripostes for frustrated clients might be:

(1) 'No. I want you to tell me what *you* are thinking.'

(2) 'No. I don't believe that *you* have any ideas.'

(See 'Jane's' and 'Lotte's' experiences, Chapter 4.)

In terms of (2), if a practitioner is present, therapy cannot be 'client-directed'. An explanation of this double-bind can be found in *The Art of the Obvious*, an exploration of what children's specialist Bruno Bettelheim *really* said. (Bettelheim and Rosenfeld, 1993.)

Because of the traditional perspective – client = mad = lesbian – therapy cannot be therapeutic or anti-oppressive or helpful without a complete rejection of this perspective.

Because lesbians first became visible *solely* as clients in psychoanalytic case studies – some of them a form of intellectual pornography – modern therapy needs to address this and perceive lesbians as people (clients, trainees and practitioners) from whom it can learn the truth about its theories. 'Impartiality' can be equally demeaning and pathologizing, since lesbians cannot know exactly what practitioners are thinking. If their attitudes are heterosexist, how can she learn to identify these same attitudes outside therapy sessions if the practitioner is unwilling to discuss them?

The major conceptual barrier is that therapy stands on one side of a two-way mirror (where lesbians are invisible) and perceives all lesbians as shadowy presences on the other. Occasionally they are invited to cross the boundaries, in the interests of Equal Opportunities, to talk about 'lesbian-and-gay' issues, but only in the confidential and supportive setting of a training workshop, where the ethical requirement of being 'non-judgemental' also means being non-judgemental about practitioners' prejudicial attitudes.

This disorientating situation offers advantages, paradoxical as this might seem – principally because therapy is full of paradoxes. These are most easily detectable by an observer who, being invisible, can float through mirrors, barriers and lead bodies, be any size at all, and appear in any chosen manifestation. Everything becomes logical and purposeful when examined from both the inside and the outside and (not the least) from an inverted point of view. This is of course a normal manoeuvre in lesbian life, although most lesbians choose to stay – or have to – in one position or another.

Therapy relies on an individual's ability to find personal meaning in unintelligible events and to identify constructive approaches to life's major problems. (Both are standard lesbian survival skills, but the clinical practitioner discussed later in this chapter would no doubt consider that my penchant for such creative detecting is because the first piece of music I heard while being breast-fed by a panic-stricken mother (or who knows, a nurse or a bottle) was the *Enigma Variations*, at full volume to drown the sounds of an air-raid.)

Collective lesbian insight into the invisibility which Dolores Klaich identified as a Conspiracy (1974:10) has led to a clear understanding of where its present paradox originated. How did 'Equal Opportunities' cease to mean 'equality'? The answer lies, as it so often does, in a fable.

The therapy client as snake-in-the-grass

Early in the women's movement, a reportedly true anecdote attributed to the USA comedy writer Jean Kerr,[2] made its way to the UK.

In the story, a tearful and indignant small boy was telling his Mom he'd been cast as Adam in the school play, a radical feminist version of an ancient Bible legend. Said his baffled Mom, 'But – sweetie, darling – Adam? That's the *lead.*'

'Yeah', said the boy, warmed by her support. 'That's what I thought. But *the snake has all the lines.*'

I don't know a neater illustration of the Equal Opportunities predicament, the moment when a sense of impotence overwhelms practitioners faced with the deepest of their prejudices in the shape of a new client, whom they must permit to 'speak' uninterrupted, unjudged and uncriticized. Deprived of their traditional values, and perhaps lost for words, they must assume a pose of unconditional positive regard and try to imagine themselves within a framework or context which is, in their experience, alien. None of their squirmings, of course, must be noticed by the client.

In supervision, they might get angry about this ethical compromise of their authenticity (a 'person-centred' ethos) and, like the columnist Melanie Phillips (1994), decide that equalities policies are in fact discriminatory, as they prevent the smallest comment about the most appalling behaviour of 'minority' people.

Leaving aside the question of whether Eve was re-cast in this school performance as the innocent victim of male chicanery (or perhaps a lesbian), the boy clearly saw himself as a new type of scapegoat, upstaged by the beastly, wriggly, leathery, poisonous snake – the true originator of Original Sin and probably into SM to boot. Adam, out of the spotlight, didn't even get to be funny any more.

In real life, the snake would get fed up with being amusing proof of how unprejudiced the producers were, and slither off into the grass to set up a snake-only drama therapy group. The rest of the cast, hiding their anxiety about the danger beneath their feet (as everybody knows, snakes always assume that everybody else is a snake too), would have searched frantically for a solution. Do snakes like apples?

Indulgence is a good and soothing ploy, so eventually the snakes would have been invited to come out to say a word or two or workshop an enactment of a little epilogue all of their own making – the alternative story of who got kicked out of the Garden of Eden and why. But the play would still be called *Adam and Eve* and the snakes would still be the amateurs. Because of their skin-shedding talent, and their membership of at least three animal minority groups,[3] they would remain too unpredictable to be considered possible employees – well, they are *different* and sort of androgynous. Who knows what they might get up to behind the scenery in between acts?

The wild applause from audience and cast would be due to the fact that the snakes could act at all, let alone stay together and present a collective point of view. And if they weren't grateful for being given the opportunity to glisten?

Well – that's another story, to be told shortly.

The concept of equality has a specific meaning in each of the dimensions of therapy.

In working with clients, equality is about accepting the unexpected, validating personal views, and recognizing each perspective of an individual as an aspect of her whole, in terms of knowing, and feeling comfortable with, the diverse or contradictory aspects of personality. The principle of any creative endeavour is that the combination of apparent opposites, with the right catalyst and appropriate energy, can produce a new solution to an old problem or an entirely new interpretation of something formerly believed to be unarguable fact.

Equality applies to the relationship between client and practitioner in which the client's authority, rights, and particular needs are recognized or identified and valued, with the acceptance that their needs will change as the therapy progresses (if it progresses). 'Contracts' are negotiated, 'alliances' are established, and boundaries are defined. In reality, therapy is based on a complex interchange of information, during which both participants learn that it is never as simple nor as one-sided as it appears.

Why is the non-average, that is, the minority individual perspective, so important to therapy? In any enterprise which has an image to maintain and funding to secure, conformism is the basic organizational principle. If minority concerns are in vogue, then minority interests will be the organization's central concern. Progressive organizations recognize that efforts to conform to the majority image are self-defeating. Here, 'minority' concerns – individualistic views and experiences – are understood to be more about reality, spontaneity, creativity, survival and growth than the fiction of constructed theories. In terms of therapy, the majority of clients (and, probably, practitioners) have experienced different kinds of oppression in varying degrees and, therefore, have the most important perspectives and are of the highest value. In addition, they represent the 'public' to which the organization relates.

It is from 'minority' experiences – individual struggles for self-definition in oppressive societies – that practitioners learn about basic truths and survival skills. The awesome determination to develop autonomy and overcome the most hostile external conditions, the creativity required for negotiating obstacles, and the compromises made in expressing that individuality when limits are imposed are the primary causes of the symptoms of conflict and frustration which in so many cases become problematic and self-defeating. The same characteristics appear in problems as in creative and self-healing abilities. (See Chapter 5 for explanations of these and other anti-oppressive principles.)

Most practitioners are people of integrity, and perceive therapy as both a useful and socially progressive occupation, an opportunity to learn about possible solutions to basic human dilemmas. As therapy is society in miniature, practitioners and planners continually face these same dilemmas, although with considerably more resources and support than their clients. During the recent professionalization, most of them have been under considerable pressure to conform. For a lesbian practitioner, these factors are made ten times more complicated. As one counsellor asked, 'In an occupation designed for misfits, what happens when they try to fit them into categories?'

Because of their work, they are presented with additional options to consider. These include the needs of their clients, their own professional survival and development, their personal needs and individual creativity, their contribution to therapy as a whole, and the continued growth of therapy as the industry which provides them with a living.

Therapy has its own cultural stereotypes of practitioners to maintain, so the last of the practitioner options became the first priority. Inevitably, the clients – the 'floating' population – became the last priority: policies cannot apply to people who may never arrive, so Equal Opportunities became abstract.

During the professionalization process tradition won over multi-culture, and all the island-race stereotypes re-emerged. It was, after all, the fiftieth anniversary of D-Day. Upper lips were stiffened (for practitioners must be seen to be capable and not downhearted) and everyone hoped for the best. Rationalization was the order of the day, sleeping dogs were left to lie, and care was taken not to frighten the horses or to be seen by the neighbours shouting in the streets. Everyone minded their own business, while peeping through the curtains to see what the Joneses[4] were up to, thereby failing to notice that their paths were littered with banana skins. The spirit of the Blitz re-emerged and everyone pulled together and dug in, while others went in search of the wounded. Sex once again became a private function. And politics? Well, everyone's entitled to free speech, or advocacy if they are unable to speak for themselves (except lesbians), but helping the distressed is good old-fashioned Christian charity and is another form of political correctness.

However, equality principles are built in to the ethics which underpin the new NVQs, so 'competence' now includes a measure of ability to adhere to equality-based practice. Equal Opportunities policy is there because of the recognition that people perceived as 'different' from the assumed majority have traditionally experienced routine negative dis-crimination – personal, social and political. This discrimination can be based on a fact of birth, beliefs, ability, attitudes, personality or behaviour. It was (and still is) purposeful – the denial of basic rights to anyone perceived as varying from the stereotypical norm. That is, oppression.

The function of equalities policies is, therefore, to *actively prevent* neg-ative discrimination and its consequences to individuals, families, groups, and entire communities. This means that the responsibility for imple-menting and upholding these policies lies with the people who hold the authority, make the rules, offer services, training or work, and who have the means of ensuring the provision of equal rights and full access and information for all potential service users, as well as staff or trainees. This is not charity, largesse or indulgence. It is law – external in terms of gender and race, internal in terms of organizational policy. When members choose to join an organization in order to claim its benefits, they also accept its rules and principles – the codes of ethics and practice.

In such a human enterprise as counselling or psychotherapy, equalities rules must be applied to every aspect of practice, training and organization. The people who are offered, or who ask for, therapy are the people in whose interests the rules were created. The practitioners' responsibilities here are clearly defined.

Equality policies are often interpreted passively or simplistically, and are as often misinterpreted. Equal Opportunities are cancelled out when an organization fails to emphasize the most important message of all – that the *service providers* have the responsibility for finding out, and being able to empathize with, exactly what feels prejudicial, judgemental, dis- criminatory and oppressive to the service users (and, of course, to themselves).

This also means, at least, that they must identify their own prejudices, know when they are expressing these and behaving oppressively and exploitatively, and ensure that they learn how to stop themselves from doing so. This self-responsibility is now required on 'recognized' courses, voluntary on others, and now formalized in the NVQs/SVQs. The new codes of ethics and practice in counselling and the new psychotherapies apply to client work, training, supervision, and to organizational methods and approaches to policy changes, accreditation schemes, events and publications. However, codes of ethics, like any other aspect of practice, are open to interpretation.

Logical trivia and schizoid intellectualizing

Evidence that some counsellors were finding equalities practice stressful and disempowering began to appear during 1990. Workshops were offered for white counsellors to explore their heritage of learned racism, their white identity and their separation from Black people (Thorn, 1990). It took a further two years for a race equality division to be established.[5]

Shortly afterwards, a new publicity group proposed an image-creation charter and membership drive. Its aims included 'increasing awareness among Jo(e) public' and 'increasing the profile/professional image of the BAC'.[6]

That equalities issues were a low priority was evidenced again in the same edition. The Ethics committee invited debate on the length of the 'cooling off period' after which a counsellor could 'engage in sexual activity with former clients without it being considered unethical'. Counselling as a *dating* service?

This sticky issue dominated the next two years. Surely twelve weeks was enough, said some. Letters and honest sharing poured in. One man wrote a long article about how he had worked through *his* sexual attraction towards a 'flirtatious' and 'sexually attractive' young woman client and made this and her 'self-objectifying' central to *her* therapy process. A woman counsellor sympathized. Commending his openness, she observed that male counsellors 'were at a greater disadvantage in the therapeutic process than female counsellors' because 'the majority of women . . . especially older women . . . would not have the problem of their own sexuality intruding (*sic*) into the process'.[7] A male counsellor agreed, thinking it 'obvious that most older female counsellors would not have been sexually aroused by a client's "flirting" '.

On a different, though related, tack, one correspondent asked the editor to explain why a 'client's experience' article had been rejected as being 'too subjective'. Suggested the editor, 'it may be worth re-submitting the article . . . I'm sure that we still have a lot to learn from "clients' subjective experiences" '.[8]

While the new codes of ethics now state how long the 'cooling off period' must be (sometimes forever), these random examples of practitioners' attitudes remain typical, and a similar personal analysis of a male counsellor's sexual attraction to a woman client appeared in the November 1994 issue of *Counselling*, described as 'eroticized counter-transference' (see Chapter 4, note 4). This is clearly not an isolated phenomenon. One woman's experience of long-term sexual exploitation in a therapy relationship was described in the humanistic quarterly *Self and Society* (issue 4, vol. 2, 1994), confirming the findings of several professional surveys. There are questions to be asked about why debates on the length of the 'cooling off' period continue (including in the November 1994 issue of *Counselling*). There are sensible ways around such ethical dilemmas if the attraction is genuine and mutual, such as not seeing each for a year, experiencing a period equivalent to the length of the therapy as friends and equals, or making a written or witnessed agreement, for instance with the counsellor's supervisor present.

This suggestion came from a lesbian couple who met in therapy, although neither was aware of any sexual attraction at the time. They met by chance a few months after the therapy ended. The former client is now studying therapy herself.

Do counsellors find it so difficult to live up to their own ideals? Everyone has their own areas of prejudice and self-prejudice, and personal or occupational limits, and one of the functions of professional associations is to provide guidance on how to uphold their stated principles and training or practice ethics.

The question is not the length of time that must elapse before having sex with a former client, but whether counsellors are able, or even willing, to examine their own sexuality issues from the beginning of their training, so that these do not 'intrude' into the client's therapy.

This is implied, though unstated, in the requirement for continual personal, as well as professional, development, and is included in the BAC training criteria. A brief check of courses which do not discuss lesbian and gay concerns revealed that sexuality workshops, when they are offered, are about the development of *gender* identity. This is, of course, where the homosexual 'pathology' theories began (Chodorow, 1994).

A racism awareness workshop is not meant to be an opportunity for white counsellors to comfort themselves for their difficulties in being non-racist. Therapy is not a mass market product to be flung at 'Jo(e) Public' in the hope that some of it will stick. As for the chuckly idea – to consider featuring 'a client's subjective experience' – surely every training or casework article should *automatically* include the client's perspective?

This book's efforts to question the issue that older women (any women practitioners) are less likely to be sexually aroused by 'flirtatious' clients are discussed in Chapter 3, which reveals the power of internalized heterosexism in relation to therapy with lesbian clients, and in part explains the invisibility of lesbian issues in the modern schools. The subject of male counsellors' (or similar) relative 'disadvantage' in this respect has been covered reasonably well elsewhere (every piece of feminist writing in the twentieth century, for example) and this familiar defence is best summed up by the title of the article which prompted so much discussion on sexual ethics: 'Therapeutic journey through the Garden of Eden'.[9] Some male counsellors are now demanding recognition of their minority status (see note 10).

In the face of such blatant, even self-congratulatory racist, sexist, and Christian-centric attitudes, the additional issues of ageism and practitioner-oriented public relations appear comparatively marginal. They are not. On the contrary, they are central to the perspective of this book.

For women – and around 70 per cent of counsellors are women, according to a BAC survey,[10] ageism has long been understood as a point of convergence for a great many other forms of discrimination against women (MacDonald and Rich, 1985:102–6).

Older women are sexless, therefore (presumed male) clients are safe from the temptation of unethical sexual activity. Women's sexuality issues will not be a problem, nor interfere with the therapy process. Good. That means lesbian clients are safe, too (but see Chapter 3). There are, by deduction, no older lesbians. And there are, naturally, no older lesbian practitioners. To put this into perspective, the postwar baby-boomers who became the majority population which demanded the equality legislation of the late 1960s are now around 50 years of age. In 1991, one in six people was over 65, and in 25 years' time, this figure is expected to be one in five (*General Household Survey, 1991*).

So, in addition to heterosexism, professional therapy needs to consider its own internalized ageism (in fact, an element of heterosexism).

Each type of oppression can be seen to be linked to all the others. The first common element is that the oppressor (the most privileged person) always finds justification and seeks support, and the victim is always seen as the cause of her own victimization. Clients, then, become blamed for practitioners' behaviour or attitudes. This is the basis of 'counter-transference', and it will not be long before someone invents a new version of it which proves that it is always the (woman) client who seduces the (male) practitioner. (The concept of counter-transference is discussed in Chapter 3 in terms of its heterosexist origins.)

Heterosexism and multiple oppressions

All forms of oppression can be seen to be sources of prejudicial attitudes towards sexuality, and women's sexuality in particular, which is why the promotion of 'transracial/transcultural therapy' (see Introduction) as a separate 'school' appears to be a cosmetic device to eliminate accusations about racism in counselling.

Black women have exposed the racist stereotypes inherent in sexism which are the legacy of slavery – myths about 'exotic' sexual appetites and 'animal' passion – 'designed to justify the rape and abuse of African women who were used as breeders to supply labour for plantations' (Agana, 1994:158; and see Mason-John, 1995:ch. 1).

In Australia, such babies were taken far away from their Aborigine mothers to be schooled in white values and a lifetime of servitude. The destruction of Aborigine culture (and virtual genocide) followed. This ancient race had high standards of morality and mutual respect, and the most strict of incest and sexual behaviour taboos and marriage laws (Freud, S., 1914). The impact of colonization 'on a nation of people whose cultural and spiritual values were radically different to the [British] colonizers' destroyed these taboos which were integral to the culture and the survival of the nation, and changed the basis of gender, family, and tribal relationships (Greer and Breckenridge, 1992:189).

Jewish activists, among them radical psychoanalysts, have exposed the sexual elements of racism, ethnicism, and religious oppression enforced by the Nazi anti-Semitic propaganda which led to the destruction of half of the Jewish population of the world. Wilhelm Reich, who, with colleagues, exposed the manipulative psychology behind the relatively new concept of 'fascism' (1946), was also a pioneer in identifying the sanctification of woman-as-mother, for instance, by the nauseatingly sentimental Mother's Day tributes by Nazi writers in 1933 (p. 57).

Reich explained that the tie to family authority was established by sexual inhibition. The mutual tie of mother and child, enforced by social role expectations and laws, 'forms the barricade to sexual reality and leads to an indissoluble sexual fixation and an incapacity to enter into other relations' – the real 'Oedipus Complex', he believed (p. 56). In addition, 'in their subjective emotional core, the notions of "homeland" and "nation" are notions of mother'. Reich quotes one of Goebbels' 'ten commandments' from the 1932 Nazi almanac: 'Never forget that your country is the mother of your life' (p. 57).

Reich believed that the 'fixated tie' to a mother-figure cannot be explained biologically. He claimed that it is a 'social product ... a reactionary social force'. In consequence, his writings, and those of his colleagues, were added to the Gestapo hit list in 1935 (see Preface, (1946:xviii) in Reich, 1970).

When white feminists exposed male-dominated psychiatry's pathologization of women's ordinary feelings (Chesler, 1973) Black women showed that a comparatively higher proportion of mental health patients were Black women. Montsho (1995:207) believes that 'as many as 60 per cent of Black lesbians [in the UK] have had, or will have, some experience of the mental health system during their lifetime'. There was also a rush of psychiatric admissions of older women, the menopause and ageing also being considered 'sicknesses' (Barnes and Maple, 1992: MIND, 1993).

All these discriminatory systems are locked together, and operate as different components of the same mechanism.

There is, however, a further obstacle in therapy, and a major one. It is one of the simplest and most widely used methods of silencing dissent: the implantation of an idea which arouses one of our deepest fears.

Masterminding modern therapy

There is one facility revered above all others and, in the West, valued more highly than wisdom: logic. The single facility which distinguishes us from our instinctual selves is the one we fear losing the most: our mind. It is what makes us individuals, what gives us a sense of ourselves, and a conscious memory from which identity is formed, and is, collectively, our best adaptive skill. 'Intelligence' means 'using information' and is an essential means of survival, development, self-empowerment, independence, and social progress.

The passive oppression of withholding information (also obscuring it) is extremely effective, as so many lesbian women have discovered since 1928, and lesbian therapy practitioners are discovering now. The 'forbidden fruit' of Biblical legend was, after all, from the tree of knowledge, and the snake is an ancient symbol of the unconscious, knowledge, female energy, healing, and much more (Chetwynd, 1982:363–6). This author, in his compilation of mythological and modern European imagery, also refers to sexual symbolism as 'the creative life of the mind, especially creative imagination' (p. 366), an idea which could encourage re-thinking on sexual fantasies.

In Chapter 3 a composite contributor, 'Jay', discusses the imposition of heterosexist ideas in fantasy and demonstrates also how much more effective than withholding information is the active suggestion of the idea of madness, and the double oppression of labelling difference, dissent and protest as another kind of madness – for example, 'female hysteria' and, particularly, pathological 'lesbianism'. ('Pathological' means 'sickness', but is widely interpreted as 'diseased mind'. 'Psychopathology' refers to particular 'diseases' of the mind, as in 'psychopath'.)

The idea of going mad – 'losing our minds' – is terrifying and controlling, as so many lesbians know. It is connected to the milder fear people express when they say that someone or something 'is doing my head in' (for example).

Labelling a group of people or an individual 'mad' or even 'illogical' or 'irrational' is the most effortless way of generating prejudice against them. The Greek dramatist Euripides – an early dissenter – knew that 'whom the gods wish to destroy they must first make mad'. A student of the Greeks, a Jewish philosopher searching for further explanations of civilization's discontents, made several discoveries about the nature of oppressions but was prevented from broadcasting the most important. Fatally ill, depressed and disillusioned, he left us an observation: that 'culture[11] is something which was imposed on a resisting majority by a minority that *understood how to possess itself of the means of power and coercion*' (Freud, S., 1927:4–6; my italics).

We now have confirmation of that philosopher's musings, and understand even the most subtle forms of coercion.

Much of therapy relies on definitions of 'psychopathology' or 'disorders', and (for example) psychoanalytical vocabulary makes all 'psychological' problems into forms of minor madness, and the sole responsibility of the individual – repression, suppression, depression. All of these, however, mean the same thing, and are reactions to the same type of force – oppression. Because of its 'non-judgemental' ethics, modern 'equality' therapy may no longer describe clients as 'mad'. However, it still writes of them as 'different' – either charmingly, as rather sweet, lost, dim and inadequate adult children; or viciously, as stupid, resentful, difficult to work with, trouble-making, and their own worst enemies.

This is even in humanistic therapy – not, as would be expected, the self-aggrandizing psychoanalysis.

The quotation below is from a piece of writing, published in September 1994, by John Rowan, former radical person, leader of the humanistic, innovative, integrative, transpersonal school of psychotherapy, author of many books, once a partner in a feminist therapy training school (interestingly called The Serpent Institute) and principal voice in the previously 'new age' whole-person approach. He has been closely involved in the formation of the UK Council for Psychotherapies and is the epitome of unconditional positive regard. We may take what he says as 'Gospel' and there is barely a professional issue on which Mr Rowan has not stated his position. (See Introduction.)

Members of the Association for Humanistic Psychology have been the most responsible in addressing practitioner abuses, the politics of therapy, and the exploitation by cultish training 'gurus' of entranced and dependent students. They also fund the UK journal *Self and Society*, which more often features the client's perspective than the practitioner's, and explores the wider social and political factors that influence therapy today, including lesbian, gay and bisexual concerns.

Rowan writes a regular 'Trivia' column in an AHP membership bulletin.[12]

In the September 1994 edition, he tells of a man who neglected a deep, serious and dirty wound until, one day, it became inflamed.

This was caused by an accidental knock, and he was forced to seek surgical help, but 'for one reason or other [Rowan writes], I can't remember why – it was impossible to use any anaesthetic, and it hurt'. So he fled, bandaged the wound himself, knowing it might flare up again.

Then the man told his friends: 'Medicine is no good. I went for treatment and all they did was make it worse. They are a load of rogues and incompetents. And I heard later that the surgeon had an affair with one of his patients, so that goes to show what a bunch of shits they are.'

Rowan's conclusion for this doubtless fictional tale? 'People in psychotherapy and counselling sometimes pull out halfway, too.' Left, presumably, with open and suppurating wounds, inexpertly cared for, which only a skilled therapist could heal. (A similar attitude was expressed towards lesbian clients who walk out of psychoanalysis: O'Connor and Ryan, 1993:24.)

I doubt if 'counselling' would welcome being implicated in such a suggestion. Nevertheless, the credibility of its 'non-judgemental', classless and (previously) non-academic image began to be strained by the inclusion in its quarterly journal of an academic, well researched, and theoretically sourced article, written by a senior clinical psychologist, Alex Hossack.[13]

He discussed a 'defensive intellectual-schizoid' client, defined as 'describing his problem in the manner of a neutral observer ... for [him] life often *feels futile and meaningless*'. (My italics.) So, it turned out, did therapy, which the client, Lucian, had tried several times before. Lucian was described as 'a well-dressed, droll, rational and articulate man' whose experiences twenty years before, with LSD, frequently came back to disturb an otherwise uneventful and emotionally austere life (which nevertheless included marriage, children and lecturing in computer studies). The practitioner, Alex, pointed out that 'therapy at an emotional distance is inadequate *for the facilitator*' (my italics).

To demonstrate Lucian's 'neurotic obsessional defences' (his 'safety net ... of academic debate'), the practitioner instanced a refusal by Lucian to engage with his suggestion of guided imagery, that is, to fantasize himself lying on a warm beach. Lucian responded with comments such as 'Don't be silly, how can I, I'm here ... why should I imagine it?' He said that, even if he could imagine a beach as safe and comfortable, 'I'm not there, I'm here, so it's impossible to feel it'.

This example was offered 'to help the reader appreciate the defensive position of the client' (and the difficulties experienced by the practitioner). While this practitioner was no doubt over-worked, frustrated, and doing his best – including persisting with therapy sessions in order to offer a safe, predictable routine – his idea of safety, a beach, was at odds with Lucian's ideas of safety. One of these was Lucian's need for intellectual debate, and, in particular, to talk non-stop about his bad trips. The solution sprang out of the pages. The man was terrified of losing his mind. What he wanted was for the hallucinations to *stop*. What the practitioner proposed was another form of hallucination.

The practitioner seemed unable to perceive the client as an equal, only as a patient. He was 'sane' and 'logical' and the patient 'mad'. He wanted to give him 'therapy' and the client wanted a safe, predictable, and realistic form of human contact. The practitioner said that he could not get past the client's 'rationalization' of everything, but continued himself, in the article, to rationalize about object-relations theory and breast-feeding issues. This was, perhaps, his training, and quite probably the approved approach in clinical psychology.

Lucian himself – as clients always do – actually told the practitioner what made him feel safe when his hallucinations occurred: 'If I can touch something, I can hang on. I find myself grabbing the seat of the car, and lick it, it tastes, it's an *old* car, and I can smell the leather. I am holding on to the window, the cool air rushes in. I can feel it, I *must be real to feel it.*' (My italics.) Did Alex find this man an old, smelly, leather armchair, big enough to curl up in? Was the window open so that he had plenty of cool air? It does not say. Often, therapy is about ordinary human consideration and common sense.

Therapy is *for* clients, and clients must be allowed to contribute their own ideas about what is therapeutic for them, and even make their own rules. And, yes, therapy does 'still have a lot to learn' from clients' 'subjective experiences' – and from their objective ones, too.

These examples were chosen because they are from publications in two fields – counselling and humanistic therapy – which many lesbians associate with modern, equality-based practice.

The need to dovetail the different discriminatory therapy attitudes (which affect all clients) within the lesbian perspective is because it is lesbians who most often carry the stigma: client = mad = sick = sexually deviant = trouble-making = stubborn = ungrateful and, yes, 'schizoid'.

If Rowan's view, quoted earlier, is that people who avoid pain and therefore 'healing by expert hands' become dismissive, critical and defensive, then he has illustrated both the psychology of prejudice and his true belief about the cause of practitioners' current problems: ungrateful clients. We have returned, full circle, to the 'client as snake in the grass'.

Rowan has also drawn attention to some other essential questions. Why should therapy need to be painful at all, and if it is, why is there no 'anaesthetic'? What could this 'patient' have done to help *himself* cope? If he 'walked out', this was a clear statement that he did not want any more pain, and that he was far too sensible to allow his wound to be messed around with by a surgeon who could not think of an alternative form of anaesthesia. There are already enough questions about the ethics of gain from other people's pain. To denigrate even a fictional client for preferring to take care of his own wound as best he could must also be saying something about the heartlessness of the 'doctor' concerned.

As a final comment on 'object relations' theory – which a follow-up article (May, 1994) on Lucian's case again recommended – it is worth sourcing one of the leading British experts in this field, who appeared in the list of references.

Guntrip (1983) says, for instance, 'Prostitution and homosexuality are clear cases of schizoid compromise in their evasion of the full commitment to the real relationship of marriage'.

In the first book to analyse the 'ghetto' nature of lesbian relationships – *Sappho Was a Right-On Woman* – the authors identified the dual identity of oppressed and closeted lesbians as 'sane schizophrenia' (Abbott and Love, 1972). Yet therapy still talks about lesbian merger, dependency, 'sexualized transference', object relations, and much more (O'Connor and Ryan, 1993). A more relevant example of 'object relations' is the way that oppressors objectify, often sexually (as discussed), their victims to justify their actions.

The following chapter explains some of the consequences and the reasons for such pathologizing, infantilizing, and prejudicial views.

Notes

1. A. Taylor, 'It felt as if he had seduced me', The *Independent*, Health section, 1 September 1992. This feature, prompted by the therapy abuse survivors' group PROPAN (Prevention of Professional Abuse Network), was followed up by a series of articles in that newspaper, other dailies, and radio and television broadcasts. This huge media anti-therapy campaign, which peaked with the 'false memory syndrome' reports during 1994, may have been prompted by a survey report in the Consumers' Association magazine *Which?* (December 1991). Of 450 therapy organizations and 100 CA members polled (213 organizations replied), 162 thought there was a need for greater

regulation of therapists and 63 per cent said that there were therapists who had sex with their patients. The report concluded 'it seems likely there are real dangers for consumers from unprofessional therapists'.

2. Jean Kerr is a US humorist and screenwriter, for example, *Please Don't Eat The Daisies* (MGM, 1960) starring Doris Day and David Niven.

3. Snakes, who can live in water, trees, or on land, are said to represent the fish, bird, and mammal worlds. They also have symbolic meaning in mythology.

4. Ernest Jones was the founder of the British Psychoanalytic Society and Sigmund Freud's principal British biographer.

5. One of the founder members of the British Association for Counselling's RACE (Race and Cultural Education In Counselling) Division wrote a strongly critical letter about the marginalization of racial and cultural issues and the fact that out of 12,000 members, only 150 – 4 per cent – had joined RACE. The letter pointed out that issues of race and culture 'cross all work settings, all clients, and all counsellors', adding that 'most counsellors skim the issues and few trainers feel comfortable dealing with issues as heated as racism. How can we be faced with issues of multiculturalism, but choose whether or not we participate in groups such as RACE?': Natasha Aruliah, letter, *Counselling*, vol. 5, no. 1, 1994, p. 8. The RACE Division was founded in 1992, with its inaugural meeting on 9 May in London. And see 1992 Chair's statement (Mansour Jumaar), vol. 3, no. 4, p. 215.

6. S. Hutton-Taylor, 'Which headline would you like to read more about?', *Counselling*, vol. 3, no. 4, 1992, pp. 195–7.

7. Letter from Elizabeth Tindle, *Counselling*, vol. 3, no. 2, 1992, pp. 67–8; and response letter from John Lees, vol. 3, no. 4, p. 198.

8. Editor's Note in response to letter from Janet Christian, *Counselling*, vol. 3, no. 2, 1992, p. 68.

9. P. Thomas, 'Therapeutic journey through the Garden of Eden', *Counselling*, vol. 2, no. 4, 1991, pp. 143–5.

10. British Association for Counselling Membership Survey, *Counselling*, vol. 4, no. 4, 1993, pp. 243–4. The figures were surprising. For example, 73 per cent are married/cohabiting (sexual orientation not given), 49 per cent live in the South East (compared to 30 per cent of the UK population), 45 per cent are in the age range 41–50, and 69 per cent are female. Only 2 per cent of the survey (500 from over 1,000 questionnaires) are registered disabled. Women make up 85 per cent of counsellors in Relate, and male colleagues recently bemoaned their minority status and the inability of the women to encourage them to find a male identity as counsellors: *Counselling News*, issue 17, March 1995, pp. 18–19.

11. The German word *Kultur* is more accurately translated as 'Society'.

12. J. Rowan, 'Trivia: going halfway', AHPB *Newsletter*, 1994. (Association for Humanistic Psychology in Britain.)

13. A. Hossack, *Counselling*, vol. 5, no. 4, November 1993, pp. 277–80.

REFERENCES

Comely *et al.* (1993).
Freud, S. (1927).
General Household Survey 1991. London: HMSO, 1993.
Neal (1993).

heterosexism and counter-transference

Among the psychoanalytic concepts becoming widely used in counselling and non-clinical psychotherapies are transference and counter-transference. The first is said to be what the client does by the fact of being in therapy, and as a natural part of her therapy process. Some theories take this phenomenon as the *whole* of the process, and essential to its effectiveness. The second is what the practitioner does, during sessions, and primarily *in response* to the client's 'transference' – her demeanour, behaviour, comments or expressions of feelings.

Neither set of feelings or responses is considered to be 'real', that is, solely to do with the personality or approach of the practitioner. The client's feelings or thoughts are metaphors for the way she has related, since infancy, to other important or authoritative people (or figures) in her life – most often, parents. The practitioner's responses are echoes of what the client's powerful 'others' felt or thought. So, if a male practitioner feels like hitting a woman client who is being battered by her male partner, that is 'counter-transference'. If the woman behaves in a way which to the practitioner appears to be 'inviting' his rejection or abuse, that is 'transference'. This extreme is common also in 'systemic' family therapy theories which assume that women are responsible for their own abuse and are 'drawn' to violent men, an example used here to draw attention to what 'counter-transference' really means – heterosexism and the creation of power imbalances within this system, including in therapy.

The purpose of this chapter is to invert the view that this assumed two-way process is instigated by the client or even necessary. Counter-transference – heterosexist projections and assumptions, the norm of life – is precisely what lesbians go to therapy to confront.

In therapy practice, the first stage (as described in Chapter 2) is the *separation* of client from practitioner but this distinction is already in place long before anyone considers therapy (and is possibly why so many lesbians reject it).

It is an extension of similar attitudes in society – class structures, prejudices, stereotyping and marginalization – since a key element in oppression is to separate people (1) from their autonomy – independent thought and feeling and awareness of their own needs, for example; (2) from society as a whole; (3) from members of their own minority population, or particular needs group, who could offer support, friendship, information, validation and opportunities for self-development; (4) from their own chosen partners and/or their children.

The 2,000-year-old Christian heterosexual stereotype is the stuff of dreams, myths and modern fiction – supposedly, a woman's deepest desire (Luke, 1993:69–70). The reality, as feminists have shown, is the projection of the sexist male fantasy of women in bondage – emotional, psychological, physical and sexual – and thus available for men's sexual desires, as well as their emotional needs and domestic requirements (Eichenbaum and Orbach, 1984; Burstow, 1992; Hansen and Harway, 1993).

As Jill Tweedie, author of *In The Name of Love*, a summary of feminist revelations (1979), wrote of women's masochistic sexual fantasies, these are 'a result of generations of psychic repression ... and many men act out their fantasies in real life' (1975:4). The heterosexist fantasy – the bonded woman sex slave – has been exposed often by feminist analysts of abusive relationships.

Browne (1987) identified the stages and the elements of 'seduction' of adult women, and of children, include: separation/isolation, entrapment, control of information, disempowerment, secrecy and silencing, increasing vulnerability and disorientation, feelings of humiliation, fear (including fear of loss, a consequence of the loss of self – autonomy, needs and values), dependency and, consequently, abuse. These are also features of every type of exploitative act throughout history.

Almost identical elements are found in the classic long-term therapy relationships which feminists, anti-therapy campaigners and responsible practitioners have worked so hard to expose. In consequence, the modern codes of ethics and practice are designed to address each of the potentially abusive elements, including client *and* practitioner dependency, and the issue of power.

At the very least, a client must be enabled to experience *safe* dependency (a normal relationship need). This is possible only if the practitioner is responsible enough to hold and balance the constantly changing power differentials, and to ensure that the client has taken her power back at the end of each session. This is the principle behind the ambiguous, 'client as expert', non-directive modern counselling style, although the means of achieving it have been defined only recently in the NVQs/SVQs.

The idea of encouraging transference, then, is contradictory to ethical aims. The idea of using counter-transference as a 'therapeutic tool' – well, this terminology sums it up. What many practitioners describe as 'boundaries', especially in analytical schools, are the deliberately erected 'veils' which encourage fantasy, a technique used for centuries. 'A veil offers nothing in place of the truth. Hence its power to incur projections' (Luke, 1993:59). The client is at risk of being manipulated into a 'transference' and dependency which can take years to 'work through' and, most significantly, can dominate her life *outside* therapy sessions.

Anyone who has 'fallen in love' with her counsellor, and then started an affair with someone very like her might want to consider the connection between the end of the affair and a sudden shift in her perception of herself in relation to her counsellor (or to the therapy). For example, she might become increasingly aware of the counsellor's mistakes. Alternatively, anyone who has experienced the type of therapy which prohibits other support, for example a self-help group, and has felt increasingly dependent on the practitioner, may want to consider the effects of this intense and exclusive relationship on her feelings towards her partners, friends, children, work or study – that is, everything in life which is meaningful to her. Anyone who hates, resents, or envies her counsellor ('projection of feelings and fantasies about mother') might want to ask what the counsellor is doing to draw so much attention and energy towards herself and, in any of these situations, what she might be doing to invoke such powerful feelings, some of which can dominate a client's every waking thought – and even her dreams.

In many cases, at least with the wisdom of retrospect, a lesbian can find some value in these experiences, or something learned about power-based and isolating relationships, or recognition that the dream image of wonderwoman is, in fact, herself. The question to ask is: how much choice was there for the client about the practice approach, or was the choice solely the practitioner's own?

For isolated or newly-out lesbians, especially those who find that their feelings are often dismissed or misjudged, therapy can be the first experience of genuine equality and unconditional love and is, in consequence, self-validating and empowering. This is a good therapy experience (and reported by several lesbians now themselves in practice) but, for most, it is an ideal, 'the invisible chasing an illusion', as one contributor said. The personal nature of the 'therapeutic alliance' is essential. Most of the contributors who had a choice reported that they chose by instinct – a sense of rapport, a warmth, a personal liking, a trust in her experience and skills, or, as one lesbian said, 'the first valuable feedback I'd ever had'. (See Chapter 4.)

There is a wide assumption in therapy that women are (a) capable of making the decision about whether or not they want therapy (MacLeod, 1994:95); and (b) equipped with enough information about therapy to have useful criteria for their choice of practitioner (for example, BAC Code of Ethics, 2.2.12, 1993).

However, the most extreme of negative reports by contributors were the results of the practitioners' setting up and then mishandling both the lesbian clients' 'transference' and their own heterosexist 'counter-transference'. In all cases, the clients concerned were in serious distress and could not have been expected by any sensitive person to be in positions to make choices about therapy, nor to feel confident in their abilities to make appropriate choices about any aspect of their lives.

This is, after all, often why people go to therapy, expressed by opening statements such as 'I've got a problem and I don't know what to do', or 'I'm confused about some memories I've been having lately', or 'Everything seems to be going wrong and I don't know which way to turn or what to do for the best', or 'I can't seem to make up my mind about anything. I feel stressed out and anxious, and I find myself making long lists of pros and cons about every little decision, or asking everyone I know what *they* think I should do'.

One contributor, Djuna, stated: 'Techniques and approaches like transference and counter-transference can be useful, but they can also be abusive. Problems can be prevented if the practitioner explains to the client what she wants to do and why, instead of maintaining the client's existing state of disempowerment and disorientation through the whole therapy.' Another contributor, Joanna, added: 'Counsellors resort to theories and techniques when *they* don't know what to do. Isn't that a sort of counter-transference?'

In addition to theories and 'interactive' models, therapy has its own 'corporate' counter-transference. Feminist-based self-help language is (for instance) about getting angry, being assertive, self-help, survival, recovery or healing, self-esteem and empowerment. It often uses terminology, such as sharing, relating to, negotiating, or group support.

Therapy language can be demeaning and pathologizing, such as projection, acting out, neurotic, or paranoid. Client 'psychopathology' is another increasingly popular term. It seems appropriate then to explore:

The Psychopathology of Everyday Therapy

(With apologies to Sigmund Freud[1])

This book's philosophy is that clients are the best teachers of good therapy practice, and the survey questionnaire invited lesbians to 'speak for themselves'.

The following 'discussion' is based on interviews with three white lesbians, two of them now practitioners. This is followed by 'Jay's' story and then by comments from a lesbian psychotherapist. (Identification is as given by contributors.)

PARTICIPANTS

1. **Djuna**, a white lesbian born outside the UK, has a 'work-related' disorder which affects her upper limb nerves and muscles ('RSI') and is registered as disabled. She has experienced therapy individually, with a lesbian counsellor, in women's and lesbians' self-help and led groups. After a long break, she began therapy again with a woman who identifies as bisexual, whose name she was given by an abuse survivors' charity. Her memories of childhood abuse began to return during an experience of (Gestalt) therapy when she was 23.

2. **Pat**, unusually, came out as a lesbian during her therapy training, and her memories of abuse returned during her 'training therapy'. Her course prioritized practitioner self-knowledge, self-reliance, and individual development; and (also unusually) concentrated on all aspects of sexuality and was very supportive of lesbian and gay trainees. The course had developed in parallel with the centre's therapy work with abuse survivors and its trainings for professionals in this field. Like Pat, many of her co-trainees had worked previously in body-oriented therapies, and, also like her, some had been sexually abused as children. She was drawn to the ethos of the course, which includes the development of firm personal and professional

boundaries, a 'whole' self-aware, responsible, and well supported practitioner within them, and, of course, openness about personal sexuality issues or concerns. In terms of the survey for this book, Pat's experience is unique, in coming out as a lesbian, remembering abuse during therapy, being in training and working as a (body-oriented) counsellor, all at the same time. She stated: 'Heterosexism creates an environment of secrecy around sexuality issues – whether about abuse or coming out, so the healthy, positive information gets repressed along with the denial of sexual abuse.'

3. **Joanna** has been living as a lesbian for twenty years. She took a counselling skills course initially to help herself to understand and recover from a shattering experience of therapy, which concluded by her taking an overdose and being hospitalized. She believed this to have been an expression of a 'desperate need to be taken care of'. Fortunately, she was saved from further psychiatric intervention by her partner, who took her home immediately she could be moved. Through her skills course, she found a 'wonderful' heterosexual counsellor and was able to renew her faith in herself. This experience, combined with being in a therapy group, led her to take professional training.

In the group, and during her training, there was a continual expectation that she, the only lesbian, could answer all the group members' or trainees' questions, 'except that they would always ask me *outside* the group – they would never bring their issues into the group, which was what it was for. I had to deal with their heterosexism'. She now practises part-time as a generalist counsellor, with people of all sexualities, and continues her other work, which includes advocacy for people with learning difficulties. She was previously a volunteer at a lesbian and gay centre in the nearby city, but gave this up because of her belief that work and social life should be strictly separate. She now feels isolated as a lesbian counsellor.

She explained: 'I would feel uncomfortable in social settings with *any* client, as this experience was personally detrimental to me as a client in my therapy with a lesbian counsellor.'

Since sexual abuse is one of the most extreme expressions of heterosexism, the issue which each of these lesbian women wanted to discuss was abuse in therapy, and the types of practitioners' behaviour and incompetence which disempower lesbian clients. For simplicity, Djuna, Pat, and Joanna are placed in conversation with each other.

DISCUSSION

PAT: I was sexually abused by a body therapist. I mean, I had sex with him, and my supervision group facilitator told me that he had been unethical and abusive.

DJUNA: I know a body therapist who says she is sometimes turned on by her clients. That's bad, isn't it? Should she be allowed to practise?

JOANNA: Sexual feelings do occur sometimes. The essential point is to recognize our responsibilities to clients and not abuse them. Supervision is the place to work through these and other feelings of closeness which can result from very deep contact.

PAT: There needs to be more honesty about sexual attachments between clients and practitioners – I mean from the practitioners' side – it's sexual attraction. Many therapy practitioners I know have dropped their body work. Massage, for instance, is nurturing. It's difficult to reconcile these different approaches. And I think body therapists should have counselling training to learn about boundary issues. Sitting back from body work evolves naturally, and for me it was a professional decision. However, I don't want to be defined solely by my sexuality, and the therapy work I do isn't solely about sexuality – it's humanistic, about the whole person.

DJUNA: Therapy is about healing from sexual abuses ...

JOANNA: And other types of abuse, emotional abuse ...

PAT: I'm an abuse survivor, and I know now that good therapy *can* help the healing process.

JOANNA: You had a total 'coming out' experience.

PAT: Yes, there are so many parallels. The secrecy number in the family, numbing off from my body, cutting off needs and feelings, always feeling different from other women – a real crisis of survival. Everything to do with sexuality felt out of my control and chaotic. The main thing for me was the isolation, the desperate need to *tell* someone, and the fear of what might happen if I did.

JOANNA: That sounds just like my first experience of therapy, except for the sexual abuse, of course, and particularly of how I felt about the counsellor.

PAT: Like acting out sexually with older men in power positions or who are there to help you?

DJUNA: So should lesbians avoid therapy? And groups?

PAT: Well, childhood survival techniques do work – self-isolation, to get space and to work it out. Privacy is crucial ... but that isn't *living*.

DJUNA: But it's risky: I saw a straight counsellor a few times, and she came on to me. A lesbian in my self-help group had a similar experience. One counsellor had also flirted with lesbians on the management committee of the centre. At other times she was hostile. It's a lie about 'predatory lesbians'.

JOANNA: My really bad experience was with a lesbian counsellor.

DJUNA: Predatory?

JOANNA: No, very charismatic, warm, very open about her life and about her sexuality ... that came from feminist equality principles. I saw her after attending a sexuality workshop – a difficult experience for me. I would meet her outside the therapy, at events and demos and lesbian workshops, and I couldn't cope, though I thought it was great she was there, a really involved lesbian ... and I was overwhelmed because she brought so much of herself into sessions.

DJUNA: If you've been abused you are very vulnerable and desperate for help. You assume professionals are trustworthy – we have to, because we have no confidence in our ability to make choices. We don't have the skills to select people. We need guidelines on how to do that, or we get abused again and again. That's my experience. What is 'trustworthy'? And there's that middle-class heterosexual thing, that we shouldn't question their ability or challenge them.

PAT: You never told anyone?

DJUNA: Oh, yes, in the survivor group we reported her to the management committee of the centre, but she denied it, then she left. They said she was ill. I'd also been harassed by a straight woman at work, so I knew what it was. The group fell apart.

JOANNA: I fell apart after the therapy ended. We had become – well, not *friends* exactly – I can see that now, but at the time I thought it was real. One day she told me she was going away, and that was it. She just went. That's when I took the overdose.

PAT: How did that happen? How did you get so obsessed with her? And how come you became friends?

DJUNA: I was dumped like that. My mother died, while I was in therapy. The counsellor cut me off. She couldn't handle death and grief. That was ten years ago. I hope things are different now.

JOANNA: How did you cope?

DJUNA: Read a lot of books, did some Gestalt, joined the incest survivor group, the one that ended so badly. The facilitator was so lesbophobic she flirted with all the dykes. But when we complained to the management committee, it was the usual thing. Heterosexual women don't want to address the issue of female abuse. That's why it's dumped on lesbians, we are blamed for it ... like we are the ones doing the chasing, or hoping, or that we're imagining what they do ...

PAT: How did you protect yourself after that?

DJUNA: I didn't. I'd been abused a lot – also physical abuse in my family. I didn't know how to protect myself or what to protect myself from. I was completely disempowered.

JOANNA: So, it's all about power.

DJUNA: Yes – straight women suddenly getting power as therapists. And lesbians were only learning about it then. We didn't even have enough power between us to keep the self-help group going, to cope with each other's pain. Everyone wanted to be 'the counsellor'. It's very hard to give up the little power or self-control that you have and let yourself be vulnerable, because our experience is that this always leads to more abuse.

JOANNA: So, how can a lesbian tell if a counsellor is OK? Agreed, we all want 'healing' of some kind, but the charismatic healer type – that was my worst experience.

PAT: The lesbian counsellor?

JOANNA: Yes. Her boundaries were non-existent. It felt like she was pumping her power and her sexuality into me. When I was at my lowest place – dependent, obsessed with her, in real pain – she didn't know what to do. She couldn't be strong for me. So she got out her Louise Hay[2] book and said . . .

DJUNA/PAT: 'How about trying some affirmations.'

JOANNA: Yes! It didn't really go with lesbian-feminist separatist sexuality issues! She said affirmations would 'cure' me – not of my pain, but of my feelings for *her*. I felt like killing her. That was the real abandonment. Maybe that's why she kept up the friendship afterwards. Practitioners have to understand that therapy is a relationship unlike any other. This 'equal sharing' sisterhood thing can be very dangerous.

PAT: It was *your* therapy. What did you really want?

JOANNA: I was depressed and needy and open to abuse. Looking back, I wanted meaning and a real connection with myself as a lesbian, as a woman.

The sexuality workshop I'd been to churned me up. It was very disturbing – that's the reason I went to her for therapy.

PAT: Instead, you became suicidal.

DJUNA: Before I had therapy again, I read some books and I talked to other lesbians, and the first question I asked her was about her supervision. I wanted to be sure that I got her attention and that she was supported in her support of me. I mean, I pay her. Not much, since I'm on benefits, but I pay what I can. I check all the time, like, 'Am I being taken for a ride?' Once I worked with a woman whose only training was co-counselling, which is a mutual, non-paying method. Who can check up? They have their names at lesbian helplines. They exploit us. They know we don't want to go to a regular shrink.

PAT: It's good you asked about supervision. Supervision and further training, is essential. We're all people. I'll never stop 'working on myself', I expect.

JOANNA: A counsellor needs to be really strong at times. My second counsellor wasn't charismatic – quite remote, really, but not backing off, not cold. She was consistent with that – strong and containing. She has always encouraged me to claim my own power, to see that what I admire in others I have in myself. The first part of therapy was getting over the other one.

PAT: Maybe you're a closet charismatic!

JOANNA: Oh, sure, yes ... I'm a survivor. I tried to overstep her boundaries once. She got angry. So I learned: 'I'm allowed to get angry too if people do that to me.'

DJUNA: She's the opposite of the other woman, your first counsellor.

JOANNA: Yes. And I found out she didn't have supervision.

DJUNA: But they don't have supervision every day. What's *their* responsibility? What's 'professional'?

JOANNA: The opposite of our experiences!

PAT: What, then, Djuna? You're the only one here not a counsellor. What would your criteria be?

DJUNA: It's how they cope when things are hardest for us. What we have said happened instead was – they detached themselves, like grabbing at techniques, or saying 'do affirmations', or terminating the therapy. Or they get really into it, merge their own feelings with ours, encourage the dependency – that rescuing thing you had, Joanna – they encourage the intensity, what you called your 'obsession'. That's a very offensive label.

PAT: ... which is how I was sexually abused by the body therapist. He took advantage of my 'acting out'.

DJUNA: And if you confront them or complain, they just exit. Denial, detachment, evading responsibility. That's the test, would they abandon you?

PAT: How much of this is about lesbian sexuality? Djuna, you said when straight women come on to lesbians ...

DJUNA: Happens all the time. I don't know if they want to be lesbians or if it's this guru-rescuer thing, the power to convert you to heterosexuality, make you into their image of a whole, healed woman ...

JOANNA: Or, they don't know what to do or how to ask about lesbian sexuality, like the women in my group.

PAT: But we are also talking about an abusive lesbian here.

JOANNA: No practitioner should be allowed to work with *anyone* unless they are comfortable with themselves, heterosexual or lesbian. Politics is one thing – my lesbian counsellor didn't have supervision, so she got her political wires crossed. Maybe she didn't have any training. There are some short counselling courses which recruit lesbians, and they teach only basics. They know we've got no money. That isn't *therapy*. The process of therapy is about personal empowerment, and for practitioners that means developing your own qualities. Conservative beliefs like theories or 'skills development' are synonymous with power, authority, and control. These issues *must* be addressed by all practitioners. A course that claims to be 'professional' and teaches only basics ... that's disempowering for the trainees. They're not equipped.

DJUNA: Power ... that's very addictive.

JOANNA: I think my first counsellor, or the non-counsellor, was playing out her old self through me. I never met any of her other clients at these demos or meetings. Maybe I was the only one! I certainly *felt* like I was really important to her.

DJUNA: And you said, lesbians don't get support in training.

PAT: My centre was unusual. There are five or six schools in London which do at least address lesbian and gay issues.

JOANNA: You're privileged in London. I'm sure my training experience is typical. The only lesbian on the course. I'm the only lesbian counsellor I know in the whole region. It's very isolating.

DJUNA: So, that type of counsellor, lesbian or heterosexual woman, maybe through that kind of isolation, hasn't resolved her own issues. They are turned on by our sexuality, especially if we are more obviously sexual than they are.

JOANNA: Yes, there's that expectancy that counsellors are all like the sexist ideal of a 'nice' woman.

DJUNA: Nonsexual.

PAT: Right. That was a basic issue on my training, sexist oppression, women's stereotyping.

JOANNA: I've been thinking – my lesbian counsellor – she could relate to me *only* as a lesbian.

PAT: Yes. The stereotypes, when you go in the door, 'Lesbian!'

DJUNA: That's what *heterosexual* women do.

PAT: There's internalized heterosexism among lesbians too. That separatist thing, I think it hides a lot of unresolved issues. People think, whatever you're really like, that lesbian sex is chains, angry, butch, into SM. I used to think like that, then suddenly I met all these completely normal lesbians. Everyone was wrong about us. I'm so much more comfortable with myself – my whole self – now that I'm a lesbian.

DJUNA: So whoever the counsellor is, lesbian or heterosexual woman, if she's not comfortable with her own sexuality ...

PAT: Or has some *external* image of what a lesbian is supposed to be, say separatist or feminist ...

JOANNA: And is charismatic and thinks she's here to heal the world; or is heterosexual and likes power over lesbians ...

DJUNA: That's heterosexist counter-transference.

The reality of counter-transference

Are all feelings or thoughts towards therapy practitioners 'transference'? Or are they genuine feelings of closeness to someone who is trusted with secrets, or normal frustration at being misunderstood or getting the wrong type of responses? And what about the practitioner's *own* transference, that is, her personal feelings or beliefs, preconceptions about clients in general and lesbians in particular, her self-image as a counsellor and her expectations of what clients can achieve in therapy? Are these part of what is described as counter-transference, that is, 'professional' feelings and therapy tools? Or are they prejudice? The only measure of the reality of these interactions is the affect on the individual client and the progress, or otherwise, of her therapy.

The experiences described above are not unusual and, incidentally, challenge another view – that the typical therapy client is in her thirties. Lesbians are often 'sent' to therapy when they are very young – for example, when they first come out. Others, like Djuna, opt for therapy because it is available, and, as she points out, it is difficult to keep self-help groups going unless they have an established structure, or evolve from a facilitated group. Since the 1980s, therapy for women has been more of an interchange between different styles, for example a mixture of approaches used in non-facilitated self-help groups, formal one-to-one or couple therapy, and in co-counselling. This latter is probably the only therapy which does not have vocabulary such as 'counter-transference', though it does have an exercise for exploring 'transference'. It is also useful as a skills-base for self-help and for resolving relationship issues (Ernst and Goodison, 1981:50–56; Cartledge and Ryan, 1983:67–88). The main consideration, however, is: if therapy clients are also in groups and re-negotiating boundaries, and learning 'therapy' language and skills, are concepts such as 'transference' now irrelevant? Is this why some practitioners discourage clients from exploring other resources?

Heterosexist oppression is purposeful. Whether or not it is described as 'counter-transference', it can occur even in situations such as therapy, which is assumed to be benevolent and validating. Sexuality or sexual orientation is of course not the only difference which affects a therapy relationship (see Chapter 4). However, part of heterosexism is the 'practitioner knows best' attitude – when the decisions about how to approach lesbian issues are made by the practitioners, according to their personal or professional attitudes, ideals or principles, expectations, training and theories, or stereotypical assumptions. Therapy, as Djuna in particular experienced it, and Joanna with her first counsellor, becomes actively anti-therapeutic and oppressive in ways which are subtle and so not immediately apparent.

As 'Jay' explains, it took her a long time to connect what was happening in her life to her therapy. This is a long example, as 'Jay' is a composite of three lesbian contributors who had a similar confidence in their counsellors, and no identifiable 'transference', nor was 'transference' discussed. They were selected from several similar therapy reports because of the focus on issues of particular concern to lesbians – heterosexism, sexual abuse, and SM fantasies. (See also Casework example 6: supervision).

JAY'S STORY

I didn't think of myself as a victim of heterosexism or homophobia in my therapy. I thought it was me, or bad luck. It was very hard to believe anything negative about my counsellor. She was a lovely woman – warm, generous, and *always* there for me. I felt she loved me, but it was never one of those 'maybe she's a lesbian' things – just a nice, gentle love. I didn't fancy her.

I felt that she liked me as a person, too. That was very therapeutic, and I did think 'I wish I could meet lesbians like that'. She was really special. She was also very skilled – I mean she was a 'natural'. I bumped into her once in a bookshop, and I was amazed that her conversation was exactly like in the sessions. So she was one person, a real person.

She had a lot of techniques she used, and I didn't like all of them but I was ready to try anything. I'm a practical person, so she would get clay and building blocks and things, kids' stuff, but I liked fiddling with it and making things to represent people or parts of me, whatever. I learned a lot doing that.

She was always concerned because I didn't feel equal to her, and she gave me lots of assertion tips. I was in awe of her – I couldn't imagine anyone getting the better of her! And here she was, this great woman, on my side. Perfect.

So, what went wrong? To start with, I lost my job – I was working for a city company that supplied plants and flowers to big office buildings, indoor gardens, roof gardens, or special displays they hired for functions, trees and things. The company got asked to do some TV commercials – much more money – but I got the sack. Well, I got 'squeezed' out, as they say in the city. Then I split up with my partner, Tina. A lot of gay men we knew had died or were dying of AIDS. It was a terrible, terrible time. My new 'assertiveness' wasn't working. I got legal advice but they couldn't prove sex discrimination, so that was it. All this, and some other problems I was having, took up nearly two years of therapy and I still hadn't got to the point.

Why I wanted therapy was because I couldn't have sex without SM fantasies, actually heterosexual fantasies. At the time, I thought I was the only lesbian in the world like that – so it was a bit of a crisis of identity, you might say. It killed off all my sexual relationships, because I used to be 'out of it' and my girl friends didn't like that. I thought 'Am I *really* a dyke?'

What happened with Tina was we went to a gay festival and they showed lesbian erotic films including some of SM acts. She wanted to go, right then, and I wanted to stay. When I got back we had a terrible fight, not physical, but nearly – I sort of grabbed her, I was completely out of order. We both got upset and scared and hugged each other, then I sort of blurted it out that I had erotic fantasies when we were in bed. I'd never told anyone before. That was it. She left.

I did tell the counsellor this was my therapy issue, but I couldn't, I just *couldn't* tell her what it was about, no details or anything. I just said SM fantasies. The thing is, I told her this too, I would never actually want to *do* it. I'm a total hypochondriac, and I can't stand any little ache or pain. I hate being stuck in an office or in a lift – I'm an outdoors person, though I don't mind a greenhouse – that's different, there's plenty of light. So I'm not an SM person, no way.

I began to get the feeling that she thought I must really be straight, and she was waiting for me to work this out. I thought that's what she meant when she said I should feel that I was equal to her.

I did have sex with men when I was younger, but that was blokes saying 'if you don't you must be a dyke' – usual things. I always looked like a dyke, anyway, like a lot of women in my family. We're all big, strong, hard-working people.

I missed some periods – stress, I suppose, and I was bingeing a lot then. She asked me if there was any chance I could be pregnant. She must have seen how shocked I was and she covered it up – made some joke about virgin births and 'psychological re-birthing'. Re-birthing was the big thing then. People did it weekends.

Or she thought I was really a man. I'm very butch, but it's a 'look'. It's not really me, but I don't want to look different to other dykes I know. It would look like I was posing. So I started to wear more butch things to sessions, my brother's old biker's gear and suits and things, and she never said a word.

Bit by bit my confidence in myself as a lesbian was worn away. I get a *lot* of hassle from people, family too, except my brother. I'm a big, fat dyke and my hands are always dirty. The more out I was, the worse it got. One of my ex-girlfriend's mother banned me from the house. I used to do some gardening for her, and get cakes and pies and things – she liked people with a healthy appetite. She said it was because of the next-door neighbours.

But my counsellor never once said 'You're getting a lot of prejudice from people'. She kept telling me to be myself, but I didn't know what 'myself' was. I got more and more angry, then one day, I thought, sod it, I don't have to see her ever again, and I told her about one of my fantasies, a sort of bikers' orgy, except my brother swears they don't have them. Really heavy. She smiled, sort of knowingly, and went and got me a book about sex games and said I could borrow it. So there were some of my fantasies, and everyone in the bloody book was straight – married couples. I gave it back the next week and didn't say anything. I wouldn't talk about it. I got really depressed after that.

The message was, I was obviously straight, I mean heterosexual, and in terms of sex I was whacko, completely kinky. Anyway, I got some new fantasies out of the book. I was on my own, and so I – well, I got hooked on the whole thing. There was a joke going around, something like the ultimate self-deception is faking orgasm when you masturbate. I think for lesbians it's being alone in a big bed making love to yourself with a heterosexual SM orgy in your head. That's a closet – with no way out.

There was a late night show on TV one night about sex addicts and after that I joined a group, sex addicts anonymous. I was the only one who wasn't having sex with anybody, but they didn't mind. Most of them had been sexually abused, men and women, some of them by both their parents – there's a lot of child porn photography done on these big housing estates. So, at the age of 38 that's how I found out I was sexually abused.

When I told the counsellor, she said she thought that might be it but she was waiting for me to tell her in my own time. We both cried, and I asked her why she did, and then she told me she was abused too, about the same age I was. We got really very close after that, but she didn't tell me anything about her abuse and I didn't want to hear about it anyway. She was good like that. She gave me some more books, but only two of them had anything about lesbians. Then I found a therapy book, which was really good [Gil, 1988].

I started to do my own therapy. I made it up with Tina. She felt bad for leaving me and now that she could understand, she was really nice to me, really sweet. But we don't have sex – yet. She said 'Why don't you join a women survivors' group?' The sex addicts one was too much for me. People really did do the things I made up in my head. In this new group, from what other women said, I knew my therapy was over. There were two other lesbians in the group, and we'd all heard that counsellors think if you're a lesbian it's because you were sexually abused. The other women all laughed. They said 'Well, we're not, so what's that about?' They were very supportive to us. But I still needed someone there for me. It was all a bit overwhelming.

I had some sessions with a children's counsellor. I was her first adult and her first lesbian. She was great. She told me she had to put away all her 'anatomically correct' dolls because they found out that children would want to fit them together anyway, and some workers had been accused of making children identify abuse that hadn't happened.

She thought they should be given the benefit of the doubt, and she said it made her feel useless, which is why she was now working with adult survivors. She was involved in some campaign to raise awareness of child abuse through adult stories. So I told this woman 'that's me, an Anatomically

Incorrect Doll'. She laughed a lot and gave me a big hug. We cut out bits from medical magazines and I made a really rude picture – a gender bender.

I do voluntary work now. I'm making a vegetable garden at a children's home, and I've gone vegetarian – lose some weight. We're all looking forward to our first home-grown vegetable stew. I'm going to do training as an abortion counsellor, and what I'd like to do is sexual health advice work for young girls. You're not allowed to, but I'll do it anyway. I've applied for a job at a project for homeless teenagers. I don't suppose I'll get it. But if I do I'll start a lesbian group, and we'll talk about all the things no one ever told me about – prejudice, sex, abuse, dreams, fantasies … whatever comes into anyone's head. And then we'll work out where it all comes from. Whatever happens, I'm still a lesbian, and no way would I ever want to change that.

'Jay' connected several of the problems which came up during the therapy to the counsellor's inability to understand her point of view as a lesbian. It is not solely the negative feelings which are prejudicial 'counter-transference'. Some relationships between clients and counsellors become very close and affectionate, and one of the reasons that all practitioners must now have supervision is so that these positive feelings do not interfere with the client's therapy. Feminists often report that sexist expectations can be based on the best will in the world, and the same applies to heterosexist expectations expressed by therapy practitioners.

Lesbians such as 'Jay' who have heterosexual fantasies (positive or destructive) come from the same social environment as heterosexual women (who, it should be said, also have lesbian, romantic, or SM fantasies). These are not necessarily about being sexually abused as a child – they can be what Jung described as 'the collective unconscious' – more accurately, heterosexist myths embedded in the psyche.

Counsellors whose image of 'successful therapy' with a lesbian client is that she is really a closet heterosexual may be expressing an inner conflict of their own about their unexpressed lesbian selves. Several contributors reported curiosity from their counsellors, and odd comments about 'cross-dressing' or use of political language (see Chapter 4).

When a lesbian who is clearly content with her sexual identity is discouraged from expressing herself as a lesbian in therapy, the repercussions on the rest of her life can be very serious.

A lesbian psychotherapist explained:

'From the example of "Jay" it would appear to me that once a client has become dependent on a practitioner, and feels very close to her in a good therapeutic alliance, lack of discussion on what her lesbian identity means to her can result in her expressing this part of herself – the parts she feels that the counsellor can't accept – outside the therapy.

'So, was the consequence that "Jay" unconsciously ignored the ordinary restraints of professional work, such as conversation subjects or manner of dress, which we all have to conform with? Was she being a lesbian first and a worker second? It shouldn't matter, but in a commercial company which relies on good relationships with buyers there is obviously a lot more prejudice or expectations of behaviour. That's reality.

'Counsellors may not be judgemental about things like dress, but if a client changes her appearance dramatically, or starts to emphasize a particular aspect of herself, she's trying to make a statement, to tell the counsellor something important. I mean, how blatant do you have to be if you want to say "I'm a dyke"?

'The woman who wanted to see erotic lesbian films – perhaps some sex therapy would have been useful, about how to make sex more erotic and mutually enjoyable without alienating one or other partner. Do lesbians feel comfortable talking about their sex lives or sexual needs with hetero-sexual counsellors? I don't know. I think it would have been helpful for the woman with SM fantasies if her counsellor took the focus off the problem part of this and asked her what she *did* enjoy about sex, what she needed, so that she could have good sex without resorting to fantasies, and what was blocking her from being completely in her body. That's standard psychosexual counselling.

'This approach would also validate the norm of lesbian sex. After all, we are not any more "anatomically correct" or "incorrect" than heterosexual or bisexual or asexual women! And how do lesbians appear themselves in their fantasies? Do they have an ideal body size or shape? That should be a basic question.

'I sympathize with heterosexual women who are unable to discuss sex openly with another woman – of any sexuality – and I imagine this means that they have internalized a lot of negative sexist thinking about their bodies. It's very sad, and I suspect that the sort of stories lesbian clients tell may not be so very different from stories that other women tell when they go to therapy wanting to explore their sexuality and meet with the same sort of blank response. I don't know how anyone can feel comfort-able practising in-depth therapy without a good understanding of sexuality. It seems to me the most important subject for anyone.'

In the following chapter, lesbians discuss the effects on their therapy – positive or negative – of differences, in addition to sexual orientation and gender, between themselves and their practitioners, and compare experiences of contrasting styles of therapy.

NOTES

1. Sigmund Freud, *The Psychopathology of Everyday Life* (1901, reissued London 1914; Pelican pb, and SE, vol. 6): his most popular work, and his first 'textbook' for non-professionals. In it he explains the origins of the 'Freudian Slip' and its various manifestations, and shows that all such 'errors' are purposeful and rational. A very revealing document about a truly original (if eccentric) mind.
2. Louise Hay is a US New Age therapist who also self-publishes several books, booklets and tapes. These give emotional and psychological sources for several forms of illness, and affirmations for healing. The income from them is rumoured to be around $1 million *per month*. (See Bibliography.)

whose therapy is it, anyway?

The counsellor's role is to facilitate the client's work in ways which respect the client's values, personal resources, and capacity for self-determination. (3.1)
Counsellors are responsible for working in ways which promote the client's control over her own life, and respect the client's ability to make decisions and change in the light of [her] own beliefs and values (2.2.3).
Counsellors will take all reasonable steps to take account of the client's social context. (2.7.3)

Code of Ethics and Practice, British Association for Counselling[1]

Ethics, equality, reality, and rights

The codes of ethics and practice in counselling and psychotherapy are designed to protect the people who use therapy services from judgemental, pathologizing, incompetent or abusive practitioners. They spell out the practitioners' responsibilities, as well as defining some of the types of behaviours or attitudes which are unethical.

The codes which apply to counselling differ in wording, though not in principle, with those published by the UK Council for Psychotherapy,[2] and are more specific in terms of practitioners' wider responsibilities. Both sets of codes are underpinned by Equal Opportunities policies. The British Association for Counselling (BAC) ethics are quoted here, first, because they are more widely known and acknowledged (for example, by statutory employers), because the BAC has over 12,000 members, and because, unexpectedly, they state that 'it is not possible to make a generally accepted distinction between counselling and psychotherapy' (3.2), an issue which may be resolved by the new NVQ/SVQ standards of competence (see Introduction).

The codes identify the values on which therapy is based. These include integrity, impartiality and respect, and, most of all, equality.

Integral to 'ethics' is the expectation that practitioners (including volunteers and trainees on placement) are responsible enough to apply them to situations not specified in the codes. Supervision is one of the ways in which they can identify what might be experienced by clients as exploitative, judgemental, prejudicial, coercive, biased or neglectful of their needs.

What is most important about these codes is that they inform therapy clients of their rights. There are complaints procedures which oblige the organization concerned to investigate any reported breach of ethics. In one sense they have a limited value, since any practitioner who is the target of a complaint needs only to resign his or her membership. At present, none of the codes (except those relating to points of law) is covered by legislation, but they give any lesbian considering therapy a good idea of what to expect – or, at least, what the ethics committees define as good practice.

The fact that supervision is obligatory, and that many practitioners are also required to be in therapy themselves, at least while they are training, emphasizes two important points.

The first is that practitioners, supervisors and trainers are human. They make mistakes and have gaps in their knowledge (see Casework examples). All practitioners have had clients who have suddenly withdrawn following an insensitive remark, or who have terminated their therapy abruptly. Often, the practitioner does not know why.

The second is that practitioners have problems of their own. They are expected to be aware of this and to make every effort to find support in resolving them, and to keep them out of their work with clients. It is unethical, and often abusive, to expect clients to know about these problems (except where illness or bereavement requires sessions to be changed); or, worse, to attempt to resolve them in a therapy session. This applies all the way along the line: supervisors and trainers also have supervision.

Practitioners, in addition to knowledge gained through training and experience, have considerable support and access to a massive library of information. This includes professional publications, fact sheets, conferences, further training courses, and special interest groups.

In contrast, a client is unlikely to have any support during the period of her therapy, although, if she is able to read them[3] and interpret the jargon, there are scores of guidebooks available.

Whether or not a client feels reassured or intimidated by the practitioner's apparent position as more knowledgeable, more 'evolved', or more powerful, the level and quality of support and information available to a practitioner creates between them the greatest difference of all. This difference is an issue of huge significance, yet is unaddressed by the codes of ethics.

Most lesbian clients face this difference – however it is perceived – with the additional awareness that the practitioner is most likely to be a heterosexual person. While this is not inevitably a disadvantage, it is considered irrelevant by many practitioners, some of whom would never reveal any personal details to clients, especially in schools where it is assumed that all practitioners are heterosexual.

Most people (therapy clients or not) *do* perceive a difference between counselling, therapy, psychotherapy, analysis, psychology, psychiatry and all the other types of practice, including alternative therapies, which are available today. Why do the codes of ethics fail to address the question of how a practitioner can define to a potential client exactly what s/he does and how the client can evaluate this? Could it be because the same professional organizations which have worked long and hard to provide meaningful definitions, measures of competence, training criteria, and so on, have now confused all of them by the statement that there is 'no generally accepted distinction between counselling and psychotherapy'?[4] Or perhaps it is because the only people who *could* state what these differences mean in practice are the people who have experienced them – that is, the clients. But, as usual, this is not how the distinctions are made. (See, for example, Rowan, 1995.)

Whether the approach is described as 'counselling' or 'psychotherapy' the basic choice is between anti-oppressive working – that is, therapy tailored to meet each individual client's particular needs with due and *informed* regard for her 'social context'; or a practitioner-centred 'model'– that is, one based on learned theories or techniques which the practitioner applies (with differing degrees of flexibility) to all clients. This distinction often can be more important than comparisons between different theoretical schools – they are, in any case, far less different from each other than they appear to be.

It is more useful to ask the practitioner what the basic outcome is perceived to be. For example, 'behavioural' therapy is designed to focus on a specific type of usually self-harmful or self-limiting behaviour, with the target of changing it. This might simply be re-learning, while someone familiarizes herself with whatever causes anxiety; or a specific series of changes directed at, for instance, damaging eating habits. Some of these work well, although they rarely address the original cause of the problem. Therapies which have 'cognitive' or 'analytical' in the title include the understanding that knowing more about the problem enables a client to change her self-limiting behaviour. These approaches are inaccurately described as 'therapy', since one form of behaviour can easily change to another if the *cause* remains unidentified or unaddressed. They are behaviour-modification.

One lesbian explained: 'I was an alcoholic and also had problems around food – my binges were usually booze and burgers or a pie and a pint. I recovered, but I couldn't cope with people, and I got just as hooked on movies. I spent all my money and time on renting video movies. I would have preferred the kind of therapy which helped me to understand why I did it.'

No therapy client could be expected to know what therapy will mean to her in the long term or what all the differences in approaches mean, although she does have the *right* to know. If she has a choice, her ability to make the appropriate one depends on so many factors that it is hardly surprising that most of the time the choice is made on a sense of good personal rapport.

Lesbians who have a good knowledge of different therapies, or who have had some sort of therapy before, may be in a better position to make an informed choice than a lesbian new to the whole idea of therapy, or who wants immediate help in a crisis. There are of course other factors which limit choice. A lesbian in training, for example, may be required to work with a practitioner from the same, or a compatible, school, or who is on the trainer's referral list.

In almost every case, the differences between a lesbian client and her therapy practitioner will have a considerable effect on her experience of therapy and its outcome. The differences outlined above complicate the question of whether or not a lesbian practitioner is likely to be more effective than a heterosexual woman practitioner. Lesbian practitioners, in any case, come from every 'school', and many don't prioritize their sexuality.

The differences which were reported as most significant for contributors to this book were gender, sexual orientation, race, class, and beliefs – theoretical, religious or political. What is even more significant is that where differences created problems, they created the same *types* of problems. Yet there is no requirement in the codes of ethics to make these differences clear, or discuss them, nor to enable a client to deal with them.

Some schools consider such discussions therapeutically inappropriate. Again, the NVQs/SVQs may result in changes to these codes, since acknowledgement of differences is now a measure of practitioner competence. (See Introduction.)

Politics, power and practitioner prejudice

Political awareness, power and therapy are defined differently by everyone. However, the Equal Opportunities policies are statements that therapy is designed to empower (within realistic social or personal limits) people who traditionally experience oppressions – that is, prejudice and negative discrimination.

How 'politically aware' do therapy practitioners need to be? What is 'political awareness'? Everything that happens in society affects people who become involved in counselling or therapy. Most practitioners are well aware of this, just as they are that certain social factors (and subsequent media coverage) will create an increased demand for their services – and new trainings – while others will reduce it. In the same way that a single good idea or positive social change can alter an individual's entire perception of life, a single bad idea can filter through from a Government department to a training centre, from a trainer to trainees, from supervisors to practitioners and from practitioners to their clients. The cumulative effect is considerable, and because oppression works in the way that it does – slowly and, at first, unobtrusively – the effects often go unnoticed until problematic symptoms appear. What applies to an individual client also applies throughout the interconnected elements of the counselling structure.

While therapy is said to be apolitical, 'political' is not always defined. Where it is, it is seen to be something separate from a 'clinical' issue.[5] The 1970s comparisons – 'radical' or 'establishment', even feminist – have disappeared.

Therapy can be defined as political, or politically aware, when it recognizes the direct connections between politically motivated social oppressions and individuals' well-being and ability to make choices about their lives.

One illustration of the perception of therapy as 'politics for individuals' is the following excerpt from an interview with a lesbian feminist, based on the standard practice of asking a client to identify her therapy needs.

She said 'I assume you mean what I see as my political *rights*. These would be self-definition, autonomy, a realistic degree of self-empowerment, acceptance of me as an individual, and the opportunities to express my abilities. For me, this would be doing political work.[6] As I am disabled, I am concentrating just now on better access for me and women like me to places where lesbians can meet and talk and plan things. For other lesbians it might be raising kids or doing arts or just hanging out without fear of being harassed or beaten up. I wanted to talk to a lesbian counsellor, but the one I like lives in a place that doesn't have wheelchair access. She promised to let me know when a room comes up at a women's centre that will be able to accommodate me. I'm also trying to find a disabled counsellor.'

What this lesbian described as her political rights are, of course, basic human needs (plus her particular needs), and are identical to those of all clients in counselling or psychotherapy – or so the codes of ethics imply.

Another illustration is in answer to a question that potential clients are often asked, about other therapeutic experiences. Usually, this means previous therapy or self-help groups, although the development of political awareness can be equally, or more, therapeutic, especially for a lesbian. A woman aged 19 described her experience in this way:

'At first I wasn't aware of anything except feeling awful. I was lonely, I didn't know what to do or who to talk to.

'I thought I was a hopeless case, the only woman in the world with this problem. The people I was close to – my sister and my oldest friends – were embarrassed or upset if I talked about myself.

'They thought there was something really wrong with me. One friend said I must be going crazy, and I should get some help. So I looked up some helpline numbers in the library, and got dialling. Things became a lot easier then. Though I was still scared and worried, at least I had a better of idea of what was going on for me.

'I told my sister and my friends what I was doing, but this made it worse – now they knew for sure I was sick. I believed everything other people said about me – I always had. My sister said I was just trying it on to get attention, because I'd seen it on the telly. Everyone was against me – classic paranoia!

'Anyway, there I was telling everything to this complete stranger. Weird. We didn't have much in common, but it all poured out of me, stuff I'd forgotten about, going right back to my childhood, from when I was about nine years old. I didn't have much choice except to trust her – there wasn't anyone else, and I didn't have anything else to lose. She seemed to be strong and to know a lot. She told me about places where I could get more support, or meet women like me, but I didn't do anything about that because I sort of fell in love with her.

'Part of that was I was sure she was the only one who had all the answers. She had ways of dealing with other people which she told me about, and I copied her, but after a while these didn't work for me. Then I found my own ways of dealing with things, and this was much better. I wasn't as hopeless as I thought. I went to some of the places she'd told me about – not great, but it was a start and I didn't feel quite so stuck with myself.

'Then I fell out of love and we laughed about all that. I knew we would never be friends but I didn't like to say. I wanted to be off out of it, to be more independent, and to take care of myself. It was very hard realizing there was nothing for me at home any more. But that's the way it is – now I'm going to get a life.'

Any counsellor, and anyone who has been in therapy, would be able to relate to many elements of this woman's story. Except that she wasn't talking about counselling or therapy.

Most lesbians will have immediately identified with what this woman was saying. While every experience of coming out – or of therapy – is unique, the similarities between the processes are striking.

This is hardly surprising, as one of the purposes of therapy is to enable a client to 'come out' as herself, in whatever ways she feels are right for her. If she defines herself as a lesbian and chooses an independent life instead of living with restrictions in her birth community, or disapproval and misunderstanding from her friends, she is making a strongly political statement. She is also giving up her roots and the benefits that this community could offer her.

One of the consequences of the omission of the lesbian perspective from therapy is that this crucial relationship between coming out and the therapy process is rarely, if ever, understood. The symbolism of the story above, of a lesbian determined to define herself in her own way and live independently, is also an illustration of the importance to any individual of autonomy. In some cases, this is felt as more important than life itself – an oppressed life, for many people, is no life at all. As discussed earlier, many more lesbians than is realized commit, and attempt, suicide. (See Chapter 1, p. 30).

Therapy's 'apolitical' stance often means that 'equality' between practitioner and client can be an avoidance of examining practitioner prejudice and a client's experiences of oppression.

One lesbian, named Lotte here, gave this book its title. She described her therapy as 'one long guilt trip'. She spent all her time 'trying hard' to be a 'good client' and to follow the counsellor's suggestions – to relax, identify her needs, and be spontaneous about expressing her feelings in ways other than 'crying a lot', in particular showing her anger.

When asked why she felt guilt-tripped she said, after long considera-tion, 'I think the counsellor had an equality complex'.

The counsellor was also 'trying hard' – to work in an anti-oppressive way, which is how she understood her codes of ethics and practice, and according to her own training, which she described as 'humanistic and client-centred'. She gave Lotte a copy of the codes, and a fact-sheet titled *Counselling and You.*[7]

This explained that in counselling sessions, a client is encouraged to explore various aspects of her life and her feelings about these, talking about them 'freely and openly in a way that is rarely possible with friends or family, to a person who neither judges nor offers advice. Bottled-up feelings such as anger, anxiety, grief and embarrassment can become very intense. An opportunity to express them and talk about them in a secure place can help dissolve them, reduce the pain caused by them and make them easier to understand'. The fact-sheet went on to give guidelines on choosing a counsellor, and ways of helping a client to decide 'whether this was the counsellor for your needs'. It concluded that 'it is important to be clear about what you want and what the counsellor is offering'.

The problem was that Lotte had more feelings – mainly sadness – than she could handle, and had another place to express them (a women's group[8]). She did not know exactly what she wanted from counselling or what her needs were.

She realized later that what she had really wanted were reasons for her various problems, especially why she always felt so sad, and for the counsellor to help her work out what these reasons might be. Lotte explained: 'She did at first seem to understand me, or at least accept my version of things, also the difficulties I was experiencing in the group. So I got very attached to her, really dependent on her, and that was humiliat-ing and confusing because she wasn't a lesbian. I was older than she was, so it wasn't a mother thing.'

Lotte didn't want to tell the counsellor about the dependence in case she *didn't* understand this. She often said that they were equals, so Lotte felt that dependency was not OK. The counsellor said that the important thing was for Lotte to understand herself.

'I began to think: she is the only person who understands me, or some of me anyway, and that's only because she's been trained to work with screwed-up people. Therefore I am crazy, weird, and difficult for any ordinary person to understand, like the women in the group who didn't seem to understand me.

'I kept saying things to her like "I love coming here, I feel good with you, you're the only person who understands me". I was terrified of finishing, or that she might tell me my time was up, or whatever.

'I would have been able to stop therapy a lot sooner if she'd said something like – what's the matter with the people you know, and the women in your group, if none of them understand you? Are they all prejudiced against lesbians? Do they think you're peculiar, or that there's something wrong with you because you're not heterosexual? What's *their* problem?

'I sorted this out for myself eventually, and realized that the women in the group were covering up their prejudice against me – we hadn't got to talking about sexuality yet. One evening I asked them, and one of the women shared with us that she was afraid she might be a lesbian too because she was abused, and she had gone off sex with her husband.

'I asked the counsellor why she hadn't talked about things like this. Her answer was that this would have been judgemental, and wrong to interfere with the group process since she didn't know the women, and it wouldn't be counselling if she had worked things out for me, and it was more empowering that I worked them out for myself. I didn't believe her. I think she was happy to keep taking my money. I don't think prejudice entered her head. When I told her I had worked it out, she asked what I felt about the abuse issue and my sexuality. That was the end, for me.'

It is confusing, and often damaging, for lesbians to read about equality, self-definition, autonomy, and empowerment in a guide to therapy, and then to discover that the practitioner dismisses her sexual orientation as irrelevant – which is what Lotte believed had happened. She felt very let down, especially as she explained to the counsellor that she joined the women's group in the hope of meeting other lesbians who had problems similar to her own.

'I didn't actually *want* what she saw as equality', she said.

'It turned out that the idea was that I did all the work and she just listened and sort of summarized what I'd say. This was how I knew she'd understood me. At least I thought she did.

'She told me that she treated all clients as equals, and she felt this was good because I could think of it like "a group of two" and not too different from my group, but come to think of it, she never asked me what I thought "equality" meant.'

The political language of modern therapy's origins, as used in the codes of ethics, is now interpreted passively, with terminology such as supportive, receptive, non-judgemental, impartial, without prejudice, or non-discriminatory. This makes it difficult for a client to challenge a practitioner who is careful never to make comments that might be interpreted as prejudicial.

The 'apolitical' stance is further confused by the fact that this language was originally incorporated into modern therapies because what are seen as 'political' rights are basic needs.

Another illustration of the political nature of therapy (and the therapeutic value of political awareness) is that the understanding of where to begin to identify and demand individual or social rights is most memorably described by the Gay Liberation Movement slogan: Liberation is the realization of innocence.[9] The principle of 'client innocence' underpins the whole of modern therapy, in direct contradiction to establishment therapies' principles of holding a client responsible for her own problems or labelling them as 'neuroses' or 'psychopathology'.

It would, obviously, be very wrong for any practitioner to use a therapy session to promote *party* politics, but the role of oppression in creating individuals' problems – that is, political awareness – has been recognized long before therapy was even developed.

In reality, therapy practitioners do express their personal politics, even if they don't always verbalize them: in Lotte's case, the counsellor's views were demonstrated by omission.

Other views are more extreme, and oppressive to clients: as stated throughout this book, heterosexism is the route through which all other forms of prejudice are expressed.

'Heterosexism for me means when I feel patronized', an Irish lesbian explained. 'When I told my counsellor, an English straight woman, that I was very angry with her, it was a bit of a shock to me because she's usually very nice. She smiled her sweet smile – she's a beautiful woman – and said "It's good to have acknowledged that. I'm pleased you feel safe to express your anger here". Safe? I felt disarmed and about three years old. I couldn't even say why I was angry. It wasn't just that I'd "got in touch with my anger", it was because she'd said something quite insulting, and that's usually why I get angry with people. I suppose it was "progress" that I was able to "acknowledge" an insult from the great wise Earth Mother, but I could well have done without it. I lost my respect for her. When I told her in the end what it was, at an evaluation session, she smiled again, so sweetly, and said something like "Thank you for being so honest with me and I hope this awareness will help me grow".

'Whose therapy was it, anyway? I'd have liked it if she said "You're right, that was a very offensive thing to say. I'm sorry, it was my mistake. Is there a way I can make amends? For instance, do you often have people say things like that to you, and would it be helpful to practise some suitable answers, so they realize what it feels like?" Well, she didn't say that. I was very disappointed.'

Differences: diversity or divisiveness?

When a therapy client is more aware of differences than the practitioner, how can she evaluate these differences? How aware is she likely to be of the effects of these differences during the therapy? Changes in self-perception can have repercussions on the whole of a lesbian's life – quite apart from affecting the therapy itself. The degree to which these effects are the consequences of differences depends on how they are explored in the therapy. If the practitioner is unwilling even to acknowledge them, the outcome will be dependent on several factors, such as the lesbian's self-knowledge, self-esteem, awareness of rights, and understanding of therapy.

The more power-based the difference is perceived to be, the more disempowered the client can feel. Said one lesbian, 'The only difference which felt divisive to me was that *she* was the therapist'. The power (or perceived power) of a practitioner can affect the therapy for a long time. The important issues are how this power is used, and how the power differentials are discussed during the therapy.

Said an older lesbian: 'The first woman I saw was younger than me. This made me feel inferior.' Another lesbian explained that, in retrospect, she saw her problems as authority issues. 'I expected all therapists to be "all worked out" emotionally and that inhibited me – I was aware of holding back, and avoiding giving her any ammunition to criticize me.' Another said: 'I was baffled she wasn't forthcoming about personal information. Then I quickly became a "good psychodynamic client" and realized she wasn't supposed to!' A lesbian who worked long-term with an analytic psychotherapist said: 'She kept herself a mystery, which made me feel that she had all the power. This was positive in that I felt that she could "hold" me, and negative in that I felt relatively powerless without her.'

Psychoanalytic therapies are designed to create this power imbalance, but 'New Age' therapies have their power dynamics, too: 'I felt she was "wacky", more experienced in terms of her spiritual path – I liked that.' A lesbian counsellor said: 'There was a lot of spiritual competitiveness on my training, a lot of "holier than thou" stuff. My personal counsellor was tolerant of all this, but I would like to have explored why as a lesbian I felt less "spiritual" than they did. I joined this training because I developed healing abilities and was very nervous about the implications. I wanted it be grounded in proper training.

'Sexuality was never discussed on the course. I never got this issue – a huge issue – sorted out. So I don't do healing now. I didn't help that my supervisor was a man who thought he was the new Messiah. He wasn't celibate, but sexuality wasn't anything to do with his teachings. Incomprehensible. It's more important for me to be a lesbian and I know he didn't like that. I feel "spiritually abused" in this sense, and wasted. Why shouldn't a lesbian be a healer?'

Another lesbian said that she chose a male practitioner ' . . . to work out some difficult "father" issues and my relationships with men in general. He enabled me to come out as a lesbian. Acknowledging our differences was vital to my therapy. He was honest about his own "struggle" but encouraged my change and growth. I laid the ghosts, let go of the dead wood. I'm not sure that a woman practitioner would have worked for me.'

However, working with men can be difficult (and oppressive) when they are closed to issues around women's sexuality. One lesbian stated: 'Working with a heterosexual man, I got sick of needing to "educate" him about lesbian or gay issues – the experience of being in a minority, the siege mentality, and all that. Later, I worked with a woman. When I came out to her, she was *overly* enthusiastic. She came out herself two years later!'

One lesbian, now a psychotherapist, was not so fortunate. She said: 'I told her I would have preferred to work with a lesbian – there were none locally – and we looked at why, but I don't think she got it. Her differences – beliefs, values, heterosexuality – made her curious about me, but not very insightful. She often formulated things I said as problematic.'

Differences in sexuality can sometimes be an advantage. A lesbian therapy trainee explained: 'This was actually helpful. She was married, which caused me a lot of anguish, but I felt much safer about the boundaries and about her ability to deal with her own counter-transference. It also faced me with a childhood issue about my mother.

She was very skilled in enabling me to explore and consolidate my own lesbian identity.' Another lesbian who had a similar positive experience said 'we agreed to differ over our opinions of the "lesbian" label and this difference was important to me to establish my own identity'.

A Christian lesbian explained: 'The most important differences were sexual orientation and religious beliefs. I was very happy working with a straight agnostic person – my position was respected, and I felt more confident in exploring issues of sexuality and faith without fearing collusion – so I wouldn't have wanted to work with another Christian lesbian.'

However, compatibility can bring its particular advantages. For one lesbian: 'The most important thing for me in working with a lesbian counsellor was that she accepted my love for her, and did not judge it. This was so validating for me, as I had never had an experience like that. So many heterosexual woman think there is something wrong or unpleasant about lesbians loving them.'

There are times when differences become insurmountable obstacles. Class is a major issue, and the least dealt with in the therapy professions (which, after all, are only beginning to explore practitioner racism and have yet to discuss heterosexism). The practitioner *and* client 'norm' is still perceived as white and middle-class.[10]

One working-class lesbian said: 'This was a problem for me. Her middle-class experience sometimes irritated me – she didn't seem to understand the insecurity of growing up working-class, being bright enough to use the system but not to trust it, and being a lesbian in all that. I felt uncomfortable and defensive.'

Another lesbian explained: 'I could not relate to this middle-class man who used a lot of jargon, who did not know my background, or understand my language.'

One lesbian, herself a counsellor, said that the differences in class and life experience were more obvious to her now. 'I have a working-class background and middle-class opportunities (minus the money!), but with one counsellor I felt a barrier. I felt she was closed to possibility. I stopped working with her.'

A Black West African lesbian, a Christian, said; 'I don't like too many labels, but I felt my counsellor had not experienced anything that would give us common ground. Maybe that's a bit drastic – I felt she was unable to understand things I brought up, particularly in relation to sexuality and race. Then I joined a mixed group – basically, I was unable to function!'

This 'inability to function' can be a sense of difference so profound that a lesbian who feels completely isolated is in a position where therapy cannot take place. The more profoundly any difference is felt, the more power the practitioner is perceived to have, the less willing s/he is to discuss these differences, and the more in need of help a lesbian feels, the less likely she is to gain any benefit from her therapy. The therapy can actually intensify her crises and cause new problems. Even a relatively well-informed lesbian can be completely disempowered by a lack of acceptance of differences. It is a practitioner's responsibility, however unprejudiced they believe themselves to be, to provide an environment in which differences can be explored.

Help in a crisis: cushion-bashing or analysis?

If therapy is a last resort, when things have become too difficult to manage alone, a lesbian will probably arrive with a sense of urgency, and a mixture of hope and expectation that the counsellor is going to help. It is possible that she cannot take the time to make choices about practitioners, or has no choices. Would any client in this position be able to identify the nature of practitioner prejudice or abuse? A feeling of powerlessness, and a reliance on the counsellor's skills, often means that questions about rights are neither considered nor asked, and never will be unless the counsellor volunteers the information and sets aside time for evaluation (this latter is now an ethical requirement).

In addition to wanting support, help, or ideas for coping in a crisis (such as a death, an accident, loss of children in a custody case, redundancy, illness, or the break-up of a relationship), a lesbian may be wanting therapy because her basic needs are not being met elsewhere. Possibly, they never were, and so she has been unable to build up the personal resources necessary for taking a crisis as an isolated conflict or event. A comparatively small problem, or a natural phase such as the menopause, can feel like a life crisis, as if everything else that has happened to her all merges into one massive, unmanageable disaster (Young, 1995). In a crisis, she will have developed additional needs which can feel unfamiliar, or wrong, and, if she is able to think about this, may want therapy as an opportunity to be sure that she is never again left feeling so helpless. Coming out – at any age – can also feel like a crisis.

Part of therapy for any woman is to find out how to stop herself being, and feeling, victimized and powerless, now or in the future: this is what self-empowerment means. Life is never conflict-free. For a lesbian, every new conflict can reinforce or increase her awareness of the depth of heterosexism in society, in itself, often the cause of a crisis. Any or all of these factors on top of her presenting problem can result in the erosion of her personal resources, loss of self-esteem, and lack of confidence in her ability to identify and ask for appropriate assistance. Often, this becomes most apparent when she asks for help or support.

A lesbian has the right to expect that a practitioner would have some knowledge of prejudicial attitudes which affect a lesbian member of a minority population group which has experienced decades of marginalization. However, this is rarely the case.

She also has a right to expect that a therapy practitioner will take into account that any empowering moves she is planning may be limited by the community in which she lives, or resisted by people she knows.

The term 'social context' in the codes of ethics is meant to imply some understanding of different clients' situations. But it does not specify the compounding effects of oppressions – that is, the social contexts which *create* therapy clients.

At the time of writing, there is no requirement that training schools include workshops on anti-oppressive practice, although many do, sometimes because trainees insist on exploring the issues involved. In comparison, staff in statutory and voluntary sector health and social services are given frequent opportunities for training, for example on race equality, heterosexism awareness, sexual health issues (for people of all sexualities) or disability awareness. If they are members of UNISON (the former NALGO) and are lesbian or gay, they can attend their own annual conference. Self-employed therapy practitioners pay for their own training workshops and conferences. Some consider such trainings unnecessary. With so much else going on, and so many different client issues to be considered, the general feeling is 'Who's got the time to think about minority concerns?'

The experience of a counsellor who attended one of these workshops is included at the end of this chapter. She said: 'Everybody's sick of "oppression". Why does everything have to be political, as if we were all involved in a plot? I'm not a politician – I'm just trying to do my job. Why should I be seen as an oppressor? Some of us make considerable efforts to learn about the positions of people less privileged than we are.' The interview is included to acknowledge this effort, and to answer a question posed by a lesbian contributor: Can a heterosexual counsellor ever relate to a lesbian? One answer is that she can't truly, ever. What she can do is develop empathy, a quality that cannot be learned, although learning how to change prejudicial belief systems does enable blocks to empathy (and self-empathy) to be removed. This means, of course, self-awareness – another ethical requirement.

The examples which follow demonstrate the two most common types of prejudice reported by lesbians working with heterosexual practitioners. The first is heterosexism, and the second is the belief that the practitioner knows best. These attitudes are, of course, mutually reinforcing.

ALICE IN NIGHTMARELAND

Alice is an older lesbian, a single parent, and described herself as 'a mixture of working-class and middle-class'.

> My father was a self-made man. I went to university, one of the most feminist of all at that time. I got a good degree. I've always worked, when I worked, in professional jobs. None of this was of much help to me when my twelve-year relationship broke up. I had six sessions of Gestalt, which was very good – she let me go at my own pace, and just talk about my situation and my relationship. I talked to cushions, or to an imaginary Gertrud sitting in another chair. This released a lot of anxiety. Then something else happened, but the counsellor said she only worked to short-term contracts (six weeks) and I didn't know if I could deal with all this in that short time, so I had to find someone else. She wasn't anti-lesbian, but this felt like 'get your DMs off my cushion'.

What happened was that the male relative who had sexually abused Alice, when she was four years old, died suddenly. This could not have happened at a worse time.

> I wanted stability and security, to stay in one place, and feel grounded, with someone I trusted. I had just got a job, quite a good job, and I was organizing a women's event in the area, to get back into the swing of things, and to meet some new women. I knew what my needs were, and I understood what was happening – I was shattered, depressed, disbelieving. It was grief and rage and guilt because of the abuse – I knew what it was! I couldn't talk to Gertrud, the only person who I'd ever told about the abuse.
>
> I found another woman to work with, a heterosexual Freudian – there are no lesbian practitioners for fifty miles – but whatever I said about Gertrud she saw as something to do with my relationship with my mother. I wasn't up to arguing with her and I didn't *want* to be 'in control'. I had a lot of responsibility – the new job, the women's event, the children – and I had to stay calm.

I told her that the way we had split up was really crazy, Gertrud went crazy. The therapist told me that my mother was crazy, and that was why I got involved with Gertrud in the first place. I actually believed this. The key to everything! I went round telling all my friends. This therapist also said that being a lesbian was looking for a mother.

I desperately wanted to talk about being sexually abused, about Gertrud not being there for me, and each time I brought this up it was as if she didn't hear what I said. Once, she said 'all little girls are flirtatious at that age', and something about Oedipal issues. She had little girls of her own, so I thought she must be right. I have never had my sons' father with me.

I did love the man who had abused me, and he was the only person in my birth family who paid me any attention, and that was one of the problems. I was really shocked when he died. I argued with everyone and I had no support from my friends. I went through a big self-critical thing – I had always run away, so I couldn't run away from the therapist, I must sit it out, stay in one place, all that.

The whole therapy seemed to be for her – she wouldn't let me be a lesbian, she wouldn't let me be an abuse survivor. If I ever asked her about this, or got angry or something, she would say it was transference of my feelings about my mother. That was her big theory. She liked it when I talked about my feelings for her. I found out that she had a male supervisor, a psychoanalyst, and that freaked me out. But apparently it was OK for *me* to go crazy.

I left therapy, but I was so lonely and depressed that I went back to her, although it had to be on different terms. I said I wanted to go for a walk to talk it through. I felt more of an equal, but then she began to make overtures of friendship. She said we were very alike. That was the finish of it for me. All she needed to do was let me talk, listen to me, let me be myself, give me feedback, and leave me to work things out in my own way. I'm glad to say that I have now made things up with my mother.

I feel insulted that the therapist treated me like a 'case'. I was completely disempowered and lost touch with my sense of what was right for me. The whole thing was a nightmare.

JANE: THE INVISIBLE ANALYST AND THE REAL, LIVE, LESBIAN

Jane, a white working-class lesbian in her mid-thirties, came out as a lesbian as a result of a relationship with a woman at work. It went badly wrong, and she got very distraught. Her manager took her to a counselling agency nearby. She was referred to a centre for psychoanalysis.

I didn't know what that was, but I met a nice, warm, woman for an assessment. She said she would telephone me with a name and a number. I was very surprised that it was a man. He was the only one who would accept low-rate fees and who could see me in my only free time. I suppose he was a trainee.

I can't believe this, but I sat there for over two years with no contact whatsoever between us. It was quite amazing. I cried a lot and talked, by that I mean a monologue. He was completely distant from me. What I wanted was for him to be a real human being, to have some human contact. I saw him once in the street. I'm sure he saw me, but when I asked if he lived near there he refused to talk about it.

I would have liked some feedback, some guidance, but there were only what I know now are called interventions – about the death of my mother, several years ago, when I was very young. He hung on to that.

My sexuality wasn't an issue for me, as I was dealing with this outside therapy. I was finding other lesbians and coming out in that sense. I talked to some lesbians who were in therapy and they seemed to be getting something that I wasn't getting. I didn't even have 'transference'. I didn't care when he went on holiday. I didn't have any feelings for him. I didn't think about him between sessions. I felt so cut off from him I didn't even know if he was thinking or not. What was worse was that I also felt cut off from my own feelings, from myself.

I would have liked him to work *with* me, and pick up on things I said. I felt I wasn't interesting to him. Then I had another relationship – I suppose I was desperate for some human contact, and to feel 'real'. This ended suddenly and very badly. I felt dumped. I was devastated. I talked about nothing else but this. I knew nothing then about childhood issues affecting us as women. He never explained that my devastation might be re-experiencing feelings about my mother's death.

I ended up feeling stupid – that I had 'allowed' this to happen for more than two years.

I felt completely abandoned. He didn't take any responsibility. He should at least have asked me if I understood therapy, and what to expect.

Jane said the feeling that she was doing something 'wrong' stayed with her until she found out more about what therapy was supposed to be.

I think it is so important for lesbians who want therapy to have some information on what therapy is about, so that they can make a choice. I decided to find a lesbian counsellor. I would have felt OK working with any woman – but I definitely wanted a lesbian. This was also because I was still devastated about the ending of my relationship – the woman was also my best friend. I was more in touch with being a lesbian and I didn't want this to be made a 'therapy issue'. I just wanted better therapy. From the moment this woman talked to me on the phone I felt 'listened to'. She gave me the first useful feedback I'd had from anyone in all this time.

I asked her a lot about herself – she answered and didn't question why it was important for me to know. I felt respected. She trusted me, that I was asking for a good reason.

In the first session, she asked about my early years, the years before my mother died. This was the first time I'd thought that this period might be important and relevant to my life. Her approach completely changed my self-perspective. She's a real, whole, person, and that's the way she enabled me to feel about myself. This is the only way I could begin to approach these painful childhood issues. I never feel I have to take care of her feelings, but I am allowed to express care for her – my caring isn't dismissed.

Both of the damaging experiences described here are of psychoanalysis, the school best known for its principle of remoteness and neutrality on the part of the practitioner, and the most oppressive for lesbians and gay men. What is particularly relevant to this chapter is that any therapy which is clearly inappropriate for the client's needs at the time – and inflexible, even though these needs obviously change – can have a serious effect on every other aspect of her life.

Practitioners often talk or write of clients becoming dependent on them and of 'repeating patterns' of childhood behaviour in therapy, but both these examples demonstrate the power of practitioner counter-transference *outside* the therapy sessions, and the lack of awareness of the impact of this type of therapy on the client's life.

'Everybody's sick of oppression'

The counsellor who made this statement was feeling irritated. She had just come home from a training workshop on heterosexism, which she had left early. She settled down to read a newsletter, from a humanistic association that she had recently joined, and saw the notice inviting contributions to this book. She phoned, initially, to ask if her views would be included, and what the comment about 'sexual politics' meant.[11] On discovering that this meant anti-oppressive therapy, she stated that all counselling was anti-oppressive or, at least, non-oppressive.

She is white, middle-class, heterosexual, divorced with two teenage children, and lives in a rural area of northern England. She has five years' experience as a self-employed counsellor, following several years as a volunteer at a community centre.

'Any counsellor picking up a book on anti-oppressive therapy will probably think, Oh, no – what I am doing wrong NOW?' she said. She treats all her clients equally, is non-judgemental, and dedicated to the empowerment of individuals, according to their own definitions and realistic self-defined targets.

She applies the same principles to herself. She works hard on gaps in her theoretical knowledge. She reads several books about new methods of counselling. Her work is monitored by a peer co-supervision group and, when she can afford to, she goes to training or conferences. She has no Black clients, but, to prepare for this possibility, she had previously attended a workshop on racism awareness. She had not thought that being lesbian or gay had much to do with this, but the subject came up. She felt out of her depth.

During the workshop she had commented that at times her professional life these days feels similar to that of her clients. She must be constantly aware that she might at any moment do something wrong. She is encouraged by her colleagues to remind herself that she is a vulnerable human being, and to take responsibility for dealing with her own problems in her own time and at her own expense. She must know when to give up, for if she makes a serious mistake, she can damage a client and the therapy. Or the client will not come back, or might make a complaint. If it sticks, she is at risk of losing her chance of accreditation and possibly her livelihood: she has the children to care for. She feels she has to 'know everything'.

Much of her energy goes into keeping the balance between the necessary self-reliance, confidence, and self-validation, and anxiety. In the workshop, she referred to this as 'counsellor burnout'. Someone asked her if she was feeling oppressed. This is when she decided to leave.

In this particular group the counsellor was, unusually, in the minority – most were lesbians, gay men, and women uncertain about their sexuality, who wanted to develop their skills in challenging heterosexism and sexual harassment in the workplace. Most of them were much younger than she is. No one had shown any hostility towards her. She had mostly listened, as heterosexual people were asked not to 'come out'. She sat there and began to feel 'attacked, humiliated, and inadequate' and 'resented being identified as an oppressor of lesbians and gay men'.

In the interview she explained: 'I often felt overwhelmed by the task required of me as a counsellor – to have to think before I speak.'

It seemed appropriate to point out that her personal feelings were very similar to those of a member of an oppressed minority community – the rage and the walk-out as well as all the disempowering feelings such as guilt, irritation at being silenced, isolation, being in the minority, and a sense of inadequacy. She agreed, adding that at some level she of course knew this.

'Guilt and anger will get me nowhere', she said. 'What I'm actually experiencing is empathy.' Part of her resentment at the suggestion she was 'oppressed' was that she had a very strong idea of what an oppressed person was like – poor, despondent, living a chaotic life, being in a 'dysfunctional' family, or with children taken into care.

She concluded by saying that she would contact the workshop facilitator to explain, though she would not discuss her own feelings. 'It's very difficult', she added, 'to believe that you're doing OK, and that as a person you are OK, and to always feel that you're wrong and have to apologize to everybody for not being what they expect you to be.'

Most lesbians undoubtedly would agree.

NOTES

1. Codes of Ethics and Practice for Counsellors, British Association for Counselling, 1993. These codes are regularly updated, and additional or amended clauses are published in the association's quarterly, *Counselling*, or announced at Annual General Meetings. The Standards and Ethics sub-committee is 'interested in hearing of ethical difficulties as this helps to inform discussion regarding good practice'. There are separate codes for supervisors, trainers, etc.
2. The UK Council for Psychotherapy, unlike the BAC, is an 'umbrella' organization representing several Sections of related therapies, most of them also registering several different schools or training institutes. The UKCP codes apply to all, but each institute is expected to use them only as a basis. Policy is continuing to be developed. This association was founded in 1990, and the BAC in 1977.
3. The Royal National Institute for the Blind (RNIB) can give information on books available in Braille and/or cassette tape.

4. The issue of *Counselling* dated November 1994 (vol. 5, no. 4) contained several articles of relevance to this chapter. e.g. 'Counselling and psychotherapy: is there a difference?' (pp. 284–6); an article about emergency service workers which began: 'How does an ambulance driver cope when he (*sic*) arrives . . . ' (287); and two about psychodynamic theory and counter-transference (including 'eroticized counter-transference') (299). The term 'psychopathology' as related to clients occurred several times. The only article which I consider explored these topics with real integrity was written by a gay counsellor, Fergus Cairns. (See discussion, Chapter 1.)

5. Andrew Samuels is a frequent conference speaker and author on the subjects of politics and therapy, as well as a training psychoanalyst (Jungian) and humanist. The contents of his book *The Political Psyche* (1993), as listed in the Routledge catalogue, included: 'a special feature is an international survey into what analysts and psychotherapists do when their patients/clients bring *overtly political material into the clinical setting*'. (My italics.)

6. The fight for legal rights of access for disabled people was a major political issue of 1994. The Government first turned down the proposed legislation and was re-considering the issues as this book went to press.

7. One of several Information sheets published by the British Association for Counselling, most of them undated. They are 'not considered policy' and are 'subject to continuous amendment'. They are sold at around 25p each. The BAC also published a book which outlined the difference between counselling and psychotherapy, *Is It For Me?* (1989). Information Sheet 10 (JI/SC/88) states 'Fortunately, the distinction between counselling and psychotherapy is not a matter which need greatly concern anyone seeking help.[!] Most practitioners, of either activity, before any commitment on either side is made, will want to be sure that the help they can offer is appropriate for the individual concerned. If a [practitioner] is not prepared to discuss then it would be wise for the prospective client to seek help from someone else' (and presumably, not to be expected to pay for the assessment session?).

8. All details which could identify contributors have been changed except for those which would distort the meaning of the experience described. 'Lotte's' group was for women survivors of the mental health system. She was recovering from hospitalization following chemical dependency and did not want 'specialist' therapy. She had also experienced negative discrimination in an NHS psychiatric hospital.

9. The 1970 US Gay Liberation slogan opened Part 2 of *Sappho Was A Right-On Woman* (Abbott and Love, 1972).

10. Class oppression has always been central to any radical political movement. It is a frequent topic of debate in women's – Black or white – communities. It is also an important issue among lesbians. The first article I was aware of

which raised class issues for therapy practitioners was by Fran Mosely, in the November 1994 issue of *Self and Society* magazine, published by the Association for Humanistic Psychotherapy In Britain.

11. The notice requesting contributions from lesbians in therapy (by interview or questionnaire) stated that this book would be published as part of Cassell's new Sexual Politics list.

Part Two

Part Two

5 anti-oppressive principles in practice

The casework examples which follow integrate themes from lesbian life with the experience of therapy, and develop the practice issues discussed in the preceding chapters.

The subjects which the featured clients introduce in these first sessions were suggested by lesbian contributors to this book. While the interactions between clients and counsellors are written fictionally they are based on the perceptions of contributors, in particular on retrospective assessments of their own therapy by lesbians now in training or practice, including volunteer counsellors. The conventional dialogue format is used as a literary device and to provide more information than might be usual in a first session. The inclusion of sub-textual thoughts and feelings by clients and counsellors is both to add dimension to their personalities and to offer explanations for the nature of their interchanges, reasons for the counsellors' comments or interventions, and, in many instances, misunderstandings. Where the counsellors are 'composites' the motives for their responses are based on informed guesswork or their explanations to contributors who were either offered them or felt confident enough to ask.

The purpose of the casework examples is to provide a realistic demonstration of therapy as well as of the types of issues a lesbian client might discuss. While these cannot be taken as representative they are typical, as the contributors' personal circumstances and social experiences, and their feelings about discussing these with a stranger, are echoed in many lesbian writings.

Most of the featured clients are white, and of British or Irish descent. One is Black (African-British) and one is of German-Jewish origin. This is representative of the racial and ethnic origin of the lesbians who responded to the survey. One lesbian is newly disabled. Identifying details such as location, employment, relationship or parental status have been changed although an effort has been made to keep life situations or personal circumstances relevant to the dilemmas discussed.

The focus is, primarily, on *lesbian* issues and social prejudices (which are universal because of the similarities between different forms of oppression). There is not enough space here to deal adequately with complex issues or health-threatening problems, or with in-depth therapy. The intention is that the anti-oppressive approach can be used in different settings. The fact of being a lesbian in these examples can be related to the types of oppressions any woman might experience, and incorporated into understanding of the more serious problems. Many of these are extremes of responses to external stresses and severe forms of oppression, or demonstrations of the ways that different individuals try to adapt to external difficulties and obstacles to their personal development. The first example details this concept.

The order of the casework is meant to demonstrate the continual and dual nature of the 'coming out' process, that is, the disorientation often experienced by lesbians who are closeted and must maintain a 'heterosexual' identity or, at least, try to remain aware of and pre-empt potentially discriminatory situations. The structure of the casework section is explained below. The counsellors are all women, most of them heterosexual – the typical experience. As so many lesbian practitioners reported difficulties with non-lesbian support workers, the supervisor also is a heterosexual woman.

Each example ends (somewhat idealistically) on a positive or at least hopeful note. Where possible, references or further reading is provided or listed in the Bibliography or Resources section.

Trainees, in particular, may prefer to make their own interpretations or assessments before reading the Summary. Practitioner competence in terms of their approach to issues of equality, power imbalances, differences between themselves and clients, and recognition of prejudicial views, can be assessed also according to the NVQ/SVQ standards.[1]

Therapy as coming out

The examples reflect different transitional phases in a lesbian's coming out process, and relate this in the casework to the obstacles she encounters both in society and in therapy. These phases, though they are not meant to be taken as rigid, might include:

- Doubting the validity of lesbian identity as a consequence of hetero-sexism.
- Coming out to an important, or authoritative person, who is expected, or claims, to be supportive.
- Building a partnership or a lesbian 'family'.
- Joining, or forming, a supportive social group and creating a communal lesbian identity, and, often, confronting new manifestations of social prejudice with lesbian (or gay) communities.
- Exploring the nature of sexual relationships.
- Finding an identity, separate from a group, partnership or community as a lesbian, a woman, and a whole person.

Again for practical reasons, there is no couple featured here, but partnership issues are covered in most of the examples.

'Finding a lesbian identity' might include:

- Being involved in a lesbian – or, more usually, a lesbian and gay – community support project. There are very few lesbian-only resources, which is why so many lesbians work in women's or gay support centres.
- Being involved in sexual politics and lesbian community work, including, for example, a lesbian history or arts project.
- Becoming a 'professional lesbian' (such as a counsellor!).
- Personal spirituality – the meaning and purpose of being a lesbian.

For many lesbians, the ability to live, work or study without harassment, prejudice, stereotyping or the continual need to 'prove' herself, requires a good alliance with one or more heterosexual people who will respect her capabilities, and be supportive and enabling to her as a woman, without resorting to invisibilizing her sexual identity, her important relationships or her (necessary) political stance or activities. This is represented in the example of Natalie, who is a counsellor in supervision – with a heterosexual practitioner.

Each of these fairly typical 'phases', or transitions (which can be concurrent), can result in the need to negotiate the same types of obstacles, since the more open a lesbian is about her sexuality, the more aware she is of heterosexist prejudice. In the casework, these 'coming out' transitions are related to the therapy experience as follows:

1. (Chapter 6) Lil is using therapy as a resource to save her relationships. She is co-parent to a young child, and is aware that she is bringing work problems home, although she does not identify these as 'oppression' or 'heterosexism'.

2. How can a counsellor enable a lesbian client to come out to her? Therapy can rarely be effective, except in a serious health or practical crisis, without the client's lesbian perspective being understood. The examples here are Mara, a young lesbian, and Bella, an older lesbian mother.

3. Katie is a member of a close-knit lesbian social group. She has chosen to work with a lesbian counsellor because she wants some guidance from an impartial lesbian about her increasing sense of detachment from the group and her need to expand her world.

4. Donna, an African-British lesbian, is working in a housing project for people who are HIV positive or living with AIDS. She is the only Black worker, the only woman, and the only lesbian. She is exhausted from the assumptions that she is the representative of all these sectors of the population, and from the prejudice she is experiencing from her co-workers.

5. Devorah is a Jewish lesbian who has just started counselling training and is required to have personal therapy as a part of the course. The Diploma will enable her to make a good career move, and she would prefer therapy to be a 'professional arrangement'.

6. The final example, supervision, explores the way that similar 'lesbian problems' seem to occur at the same time. This is a phenomenon that Jungians describe as synchronicity, especially when the counsellor's problems echo, or possibly reinforce, those of her clients. The theme of a lesbian's search for an empowering and supportive authority figure is illustrated by the counsellor's crisis of autonomy, due to her increasing disability.

The anti-oppressive approach

This approach combines feminist work in the past 25 years in socio-political and multi-disciplinary therapy fields, with new writings by Black women and lesbian and gay researchers in psychology and its therapeutic applications. A report on non-statutory therapy has provided further valuable insight, in comparing these new professions with the mental health service users' community support services (Wood, 1994).

However, the anti-oppressive approach goes back much further than is realized: to psychoanalysis, especially the work of Anna Freud, whose studies of children and adolescents provide innumerable insights into adults' responses to stress (Peters, 1979:140–2) and invite a consideration of coming out as a 'second adolescence'. Incorporating the philosophy of Montessori education, and the humanistic culture of 1920s Vienna, she described as normal – rather than as 'neurotic' – the defensive strategies of a child's ego (sense of self) in her remarkable book published in 1936, as an 80th birthday present for her father (Sayers, 1991:161). Among the strategies Anna Freud identified, during the rapid increase of anti-Semitism, are: 'altruistic surrender', identifying with the aggressor, denial, fantasizing the opposite occurrence, 'controlling' violence in fantasy, displacing aggression onto fear of others, isolation, and turning against the self.

The association between these defensive strategies, and the more recent reports of children's ways of coping with, or trying to make sense of, abuse are striking. They raise serious questions about the function of British psychoanalysis in its founding years and its purpose in separating off Anna Freud's researches from the body of psychoanalytic therapy (see 'The London Anti-Anna Freud Symposium' in Peters, 1979:94–7).

Feminist writings on battered women's experiences of seduction and entrapment, and of their efforts to placate, avoid, or control abusive male partners (Browne, 1987) reveal almost identical strategies, although most adults of course have options available to, and inconceivable by, children. These studies provide as much evidence as anyone would need of the direct relationship between political oppression, expectations of gender and social role behaviour, targeted violence and sexual abuses. In addition, they provide evidence of how the broader concept of oppression permits (and encourages) specific and planned behaviours which create an environment that allows abuses to take place without objection from the victim or exposure of the perpetrator (Hansen and Harway, 1993:chs 3, 8 and 16).

Feminist therapy writings (Burstow, 1993) and lesbian and gay therapeutic and psychology studies – over 6,000 professional papers published in the USA and Canada – provide further correlation between oppression and mental health problems.

New lesbian and gay writings (e.g. Greene and Herek, 1994) are becoming available in the UK in a series sponsored by the Society for the Psychological Study of Lesbian and Gay Issues (Division 44 of the American Psychological Association). As stated earlier, the British Psychological Society has twice turned down applications for a lesbian study group and, at the end of 1994, turned down a proposal for a lesbian and gay group. Apart from texts in press (Davies and Neal, 1996) and recent papers in some British professional journals, these North American writings are the sole resources, along with a virtual warehouse of lesbian therapy books. However, they need to be studied within the British social and historical context.

A brief summary of these and other studies (referenced where relevant in the text) is that all individual 'problems' can be redefined as efforts to overcome oppressive external forces, and as symptoms of conflict and distress.

The most self-harmful of these symptoms – total denial of self-worth and the desire to exercise some control over the environment – is anorexia. This is surely evidence that the most basic of human needs is autonomy – more important, in these cases, than life. There is also a relationship between the oppression of women's sexuality and anorexia.

Body manipulation can create psychological and emotional trauma and almost total loss of self-perception. North American prima ballerina Gelsey Kirkland (1986) explained the connection between the rigid discipline of classic dance and the consequent oppression of normal sexual development in young girls. The impossible double-bind described by Kirkland – physical perfection, grace, and expression, all for show, and the overriding of normal sexual desires and creative autonomy – provides profound insight to the anorexic experience.

The function of oppression, throughout Western history, has always been the same – to deprive entire population groups of their autonomy, their cultural inheritance and identity, their human rights and, of course, their lives. For women, this is experienced also as the damaging oppression of sexuality.

The development of therapy, a century ago, was the consequence of the entirely new concept of individuality – a post-Darwin phenomenon – and of human rights. Post-Marxist psychoanalytic studies (Reich, 1970) resulted in the identification of the source of all oppressions: the oppression of sexuality. Sigmund Freud's first psychoanalytic text exposed the effects of this on women's sexuality in particular (Freud and Breuer, 1895).

Most significant of all, in view of the present 'false memory' debate, was the storm of protest over Freud's revelations about incest and infant sexuality, and the subsequent reading of his 'Oedipus Complex' theory without his introductory comments. With no preamble, or any of his familiar explanations, notes, apologies or provisos, the following statement opens his discussion on barriers against incest in the third of his 1905 papers *Three Essays on the Theory of Sexuality* (Anna Freud edition, 1986:360).

> We see, therefore, that the parents' affection for their child may awaken his sexual instincts prematurely (i.e. before the somatic conditions of puberty are present) to such a degree that the mental excitation breaks through in an unmistakable fashion to the genital system.

In other words, the 'Oedipus Complex' is *caused* by the parents' sexualizing of an infant. If an entire therapy and personal development theory is built on validating the perception of life, and the establishment of lifelong patterns of behaviour, by the earliest imaginings of the infant psyche, then it must accept also this early sexualizing by parents or primary carers. It cannot promote one without the other. Of course, this is exactly what British psychoanalysis does, and, now, psychodynamic counselling.

The principle of the anti-oppressive approach is to always ask the next question. Not 'Is there such a thing as an Oedipus Complex?' but 'If so, where did it come from? And what does that mean in terms of the oppression of autonomous sexuality?'

The feminist understanding of sexist oppression, as applied, for example, to women experiencing bulimia (Dana and Lawrence, 1988) is extended in more recent writings on the relationship between sexual abuse and women's anorexia (Hall, 1989; McLelland, 1991). Modern therapy needs to reassess all approaches formed before the mid-1980s in the light of the knowledge that, for most women, 'infant fantasies' become irrelevant when their most direct experience of oppression is sexual abuse, or, at least, a sexually abusive social environment.

The anti-oppressive approach makes no assumptions which cannot be supported by extensive research, and the above are just a few examples of realistic contemporary approaches.

British writings on cultural oppressions, in particular Black women's oppression, and the relationship to mental health and physical health problems, are beginning to appear in accessible form (Wilson, 1993; Mason-John, 1995). Earlier studies expose the further oppression of Black, poor, and older women in mental health institutions (Barnes and Maple, 1992; MIND, 1993).

A statement here by Sheila Ernst, a founder member of Red Therapy (see Chapter 1) and co-author of *In Our Own Hands* (1981) can be related well to lesbian consciousness. Addressing psychoanalytic theories about 'individuation' in *'Can a daughter be a woman?'* (1987) she reminded practitioners of the need for 'a constant awareness of the way in which the external world may reinforce a woman's fear of change'.

This book asks all therapy practitioners to relate these pioneering feminist and other anti-oppressive writings to work with lesbian clients and colleagues. The 'external world' is heterosexism, and the next question is why heterosexism reinforces a *lesbian* woman's fear of change, and, more significantly, does its best to prevent her from developing any sense of her own individuality.

The practitioners' perspective

The casework examples suggest different approaches, which may not be appropriate for all lesbians – even if their circumstances appear to be identical to those of the clients described. These include:

- Enabling a woman to identify herself as a lesbian in the first session.
- Identifying specifically *lesbian* issues.
- Exploring historical (social and individual) factors which result in internalized oppressions.
- Identifying present or potential social marginalization and personally-targeted prejudices and oppressions.
- Relating health and personal difficulties to specific and repeated elements of oppression.
- Enabling the lesbian client to develop her own therapy 'methods' – especially important, as the reality of lesbian life is the need to learn, quickly, how to be independent, self-reliant, and resourceful.
- Relating the characteristics of her expressions of distress to her personal optimum solutions, as opposed to her 'coping' strategies.
- Identifying more affirmative and empowering options.

In casework examples 2 and 3, two very different counsellors are faced with the same issue: how to understand the meaning of the clients' concerns from within their personal frameworks. One becomes aware that her client might be a lesbian, the other has not considered this possibility. Both of these examples demonstrate the need for practitioners to provide an environment in which any client feels able to discuss what may be the most meaningful aspect of her life – her sexual and emotional relationships.

For a lesbian, a relationship can be intensely important – even as an idea – especially if she is otherwise isolated from a lesbian group or community or if, without her partner (who may be her only friend) she will be completely on her own. Practitioners often make comments, with the best of intentions, such as 'Perhaps what you really need to do is make more friends'. A lesbian's answer to this might be 'Where?'

The common assumptions about lesbians' 'dependency' relationships (or, now, co-dependency) need to be reviewed in this light. A standard approach in the early days of US lesbian therapy was of 'merger', assumed to be definitive of the 'lesbian ideal'. One paper was titled 'Psychological merger in lesbian couples: a joint ego psychological and systems approach' (Burch, 1987). Another explained:

> While both women attempt to maintain an extraordinary level of emotional intimacy, societal prohibition ... creates a relationship ... of interpersonal distancing and disruption. This profoundly impacts the security of couple formation and may be an important factor in the intensity and prolongation of couple merger ... Merger occurs with characteristic frequency in lesbian couple relationships. (Pearlman, 1989)

The rest of the paper reads like Sexist Family Therapy Lesson One: clingy wives and neurotic possessiveness.

A more realistic (and updated) view is by Marny Hall, author of the 1985 USA 'consumer's guide' to lesbian and gay therapy, *The Lavender Couch* (and see McKenzie, 1992). Hall described, in a survey of established and working lesbian partnerships 'what amounted to a dependency taboo'. Most of the lesbians had had several relationships and some had been in heterosexual marriages. One said she was no longer 'willing to ride into the sunset with her beloved for whom she would sacrifice everything'; and another felt that 'four or five years would be fine'. The priority was financial independence, so work was considered extremely important. Ironically (and inevitably) it was work that interfered in the intimacy, including the sexual intimacy, of their relationships (Hall and Gregory, 1991).

An empirical North American view (Kurdek, 1994) is:

> [While] gender-related socialization is irrelevant to the relationship behaviour of lesbians and gay men ... same-gender relationships [which] develop without the support of social institutions ... and members from the family of origin afford an opportunity to examine how interpersonal dynamics play themselves out ... [including] information on how non-traditional attitudes regarding monogamy and fidelity affect relationship quality.

Other observations in this self-contradictory study were that women are 'socialized to value social relationships more than men'; and that the parameters by which people of all sexualities evaluate the quality of their relationships has been shown by comparative studies to be the same. This was an empirical study, so the concept of oppression was not introduced (see below).

One Jungian view is that lesbian love 'is not simply a sex-object choice ... nor an immature sexuality hopelessly fixated on the mother, nor a retreat from the challenge of a mature undifferentiated conscious life'. Yet, the writer adds, these caricatures each contain 'a seed of truth', and that to contain this paradox 'for ourselves, and our lesbian clients ... we must be initiated ... into the mysteries of the feminine, embodied and celebrated in the erotic love between women' (Carrington, 1993).

Kitzinger and Coyle (1995) report that lesbian (and gay) relationships are assessed in heterosexual, and sexual, terms, that consideration is rarely given to other forms of relationship, including relationships with non-lesbians, or to different sexual mores, and 'a concomitant neglect of the wider social context in which lesbian and gay relationships are embedded'.

In summary, a practitioner needs to keep an open mind, taking in the wider social and historical influences, both on a lesbian's relationships and on her individual well-being and confidence in her future. It is likely that when working from a lesbian framework, a sensitive practitioner will become aware of deep-seated internalized prejudices, in addition to her conscious assumptions, or stereotypical perceptions, of herself and her lesbian clients.

Identifying oppression

Practitioners unused to working in an actively anti-oppressive way, or whose principle is to be non-directive, may feel concerned about introducing the concept of oppression to clients, lesbian or non-lesbian. (Psychoanalysis, of course, has no concept of oppression.)

There are two opposing points of view. One is that the awareness of a powerful and entrenched social or political force which targets lesbians, or a minority of lesbians – the very young and the very old are particular cases in point – can induce feelings of helplessness and futility, and worsen negative self-perception (MacDonald and Rich, 1985). The alternative view is that the awareness that the abuse is not 'personal' can be very freeing – the victim neither caused it, deserved it, nor invited it. This suggests the likelihood of others in similar situations, opportunities for knowledge of how such things could happen, how to expose them, and how to work towards recovery from their effects, and most important, open discussion of the problem.

Practitioners' concerns about being 'directive' can be resolved by considering the issue from the perspective of the client. One lesbian counsellor, working in Scotland, who uses the Person-Centred approach (a non-directive approach which focuses solely on 'what the client brings') stated that she does give information that she feels would be helpful for clients.

She explained: 'I wouldn't withhold important information. I usually say "this isn't counselling" and that it is their choice whether or not to use it.'

The rigid separation of 'advice and guidance' from counselling is disempowering for many clients. It is an arbitrary separation. Debates will continue into the next millennium about whether 'professional counselling' is or is not a form of 'guidance'. There is a paid 'guide' there, contracted for an 'internal journey' and any comment, question or intervention (or silence) by a practitioner gives a message (sometimes the opposite message to what the practitioner intended). The way around this dilemma is to check with the client what would feel best for her.

In example 1, the therapy could not have progressed unless the counsellor was willing to identify the nature of the external problem and enable the lesbian to be aware of her legal rights. Withholding this information, and allowing weeks of therapy to pass before she realized what was going on, would have been exploitative and re-oppressive. In example 5, there are so many historical and present elements of oppression that the counsellor is unsure how to approach the issue, or whether to approach it at all.

My personal view, based on equalities training workshops, and other experiences, is that when oppression has been internalized to a self-harmful level, introducing socio-political concepts would merely be one more piece of difficult information that a client must try to absorb. It is more important that she first absorbs a more positive valuation of herself. The cue must be taken from her – usually, a lesbian's level of political awareness if made clear from her conversational topics or her language. That said, theoretical understanding of socio-political systems does not always result in a personal connection being made or, indeed, empathy with people in a similarly oppressive situation. Again, and as always, the solution is to keep an open mind and rely, as criteria, on the client's own needs and concerns.

For example, in Robyn's case, the identification of oppressive factors in her childhood proved a breakthrough in her long-term therapy, as there were parallels with her relationship with her partner, Rita.

Robyn described her childhood as 'ideal' – supportive parents who were encouraging and held her up as an example of a girl who would be able to get out of the restricted working-class environment and 'make good'.

She studied nursing, met Rita at the college, and they lived together for fourteen years 'stuck', Robyn said, 'in a battle'. Rita developed an addiction to alcohol, and was often verbally and emotionally abusive, and began to behave violently. Robyn spent all of her time trying to placate her and to keep the relationship going.

More than two years into her therapy, when the counsellor finally asked, Robyn said that she had known, since the age of seven or eight, that she was 'different', and that as a teenager she had opted out of 'all the usual socializing', although she was unaware of why. Instead, she joined the local non-denominational church, developing a strong attachment to the charismatic and evangelistic preacher.

It was extremely helpful for Robyn to understand the expectations her parents had of her – to be unlike other working-class girls (including her friends) and to 'make good', and to do this by the only route open to her, nursing, that is, caring for sick people. The oppression of her early sense of identity with no possible resource for finding out what 'different' meant and, later, the oppression of her developing sexuality by the preacher, led to the classic potent combination of sexist, heterosexist, and spiritual oppression.

This 'set me up for Rita's abusive and possessive attitudes and behaviour, and, again and again to take responsibility for her problems. It was the understanding of forces *outside* myself that enabled me to leave. First, I had to stop blaming myself for being the "wrong" person and the "wrong" kind of lesbian lover'.

NOTE

1. The NVQ/SVQ revisions to standards for equality-based practice (summarized in the Introduction) were published in March 1995, and the Competence Standards in October 1995. While it was not possible to annotate the casework examples, most of these explore the equalities principles, although few of the featured counsellors demonstrate them in practice.

6 bringing home oppression

When heterosexism is internalized by lesbians and gay men it becomes a negative self-image or self-prejudice. Homophobia is understood differently, for instance as a prejudice against, or fear of, the homosexual aspects of the self.

'Internalized heterosexism' is not a fixed state of mind or a measurable set of feelings, so it is a term with limitations. At least it *is* a term, more specific than, say 'shame', and the reverse of pathologizing psychoanalytic labels and demeaning social stereotypes. The advantage of this concept is the implication that if prejudice is *in*-ternalized, then it can be *ex*-ternalized.

Unlike a shock resulting from a single event, heterosexism is not simply internalized like a type of 'post-traumatic stress disorder' at the moment a lesbian comes out, although the reactions to her coming out certainly can be very traumatizing. The effects on her of hostile reactions will be complicated by her own feelings and beliefs, especially if she has been picking up socializing messages about homosexual 'perversion' since infancy.

As many lesbian and gay researchers have pointed out, negative views towards lesbians (or gay men) are expressions of political, social, racial, or cultural values (Shidlo, 1994). Therefore the people expressing these values may consider themselves justified, rather than acknowledging that they are prejudiced, and that their prejudice is sexualized self-validation as well as a denial of aspects of their own sexuality.

Whatever the intention, the lesbian's experience will be of heterosexist oppression, whether or not she names it as such. A high proportion of lesbians at some time in their lives have experienced guilt, shame, and other negative feelings or beliefs about themselves, based on perceptions of their sexual and emotional orientation, as a direct consequence of prejudice (Fein and Meuhring, 1981; Sophie, 1987; Neisen, 1993).

A negative self-image is not necessarily about sexuality alone, any more than heterosexism is solely about non-heterosexual orientation. However, because of the way it is targeted, it becomes associated solely with sexual identity and leads to a feeling of 'So *that's* what's wrong with me'.

Long before internalizing any conscious awareness of negativity about sexual *orientation*, a lesbian child will have developed a self-image based on whatever her immediate community, and the media, have reflected back to her. She may also have internalized prejudices and stereotypical assumptions – especially *gendered* assumptions and expectations – based on her race, ethnicity, class, religion, physical and educational ability, emotional expression, personality, size, perceived psychological health, and, most of all, her sexuality.

So, when she realizes that she is a lesbian (or believes that she might be) the self-censoring beliefs and feelings are already in place, balanced though they might be by other self-affirming qualities, usually the result of living in a loving and enabling environment, and personal advantages.

Anti-oppressive therapy does not aim to quantify or compare each type of oppression or self-prejudice, and instead explores the damage to identity which results from heterosexism. The focus is on the *ex*-ternalizing possibilities of self-negating feelings and beliefs. The approach is to revalue oppressed or buried qualities, and to confront the complex mixture of feelings which make up 'shame'.

Books on 'recovery', developed within the women's self-help movement, are useful references for clients and practitioners. They explore the specific experiences of *women's* socialized shame. This is seen as the root of all addictive (self-negating) behaviour, whether for a substance, a person, or an ideal.[1] 'Shame', therefore, is not solely a personalized set of feelings and beliefs. It is the consequence of oppression, and especially self-negating when a woman believes that she *deserves* to feel bad about herself.

How can a negative self-image be transformed? Taking the opposite of 'shame' to be truthful and non-judgemental self-valuation, the casework example which follows takes a knowledge of personal rights as a starting point in building self-esteem.

Lesbians have no specific legal rights, so a recognition of the anti-lesbian basis of gender discrimination – sexism – is a valid beginning.

As with any casework, it is important to enable a lesbian to identify the consequences of heterosexism (which need not be named as such) for example to her health, her relationships, or other important areas of her life. This helps to externalize the cause of her problems. This can be followed with a validation of the positive aspects of her lesbian self, and her potential abilities, in order to counteract past or present external prejudices.

This approach could include identifying whatever is (1) preventing her from being herself and/or coming out, and (2) pressurizing her to 'go back in'. It is important to consider, realistically, the *function* of the prejudice she experiences and to relate this to what is happening in her life. In other words, therapy works must effectively at the interface between a lesbian and her external world.

Unless the counsellor can *engage* with positive aspects of a lesbian woman the therapy cannot be actively lesbian-affirmative. If a counsellor's own prejudicial (and self-prejudicial) attitudes interfere with the 'therapeutic alliance', the therapy will be starting from a false premise and can reinforce what the lesbian experiences elsewhere. That is, it can be reoppressive.

Identifying a therapy focus

It is difficult for a lesbian to identify heterosexist expressions when they are indirect. If she has not been open about her sexual orientation she may be unable to identify what is happening as 'anti-lesbian'. A client may say, for example, 'I feel depressed because everyone I know thinks lesbians are crazy'. But if no one has said anything specific, she might think 'There must be some reason why I feel this way. Maybe it's me'.

This internalization can have repercussions on a lesbian's relationships, parenting responsibilities, or ability to earn a living, which is, of course, its intention. It can also affect her ability to work or study to her optimum level, to function well in new situations, to adjust to changes, and – in some cases – to continue her natural process of development.

Everything seems to *stop*.

Even a reasonably self-assured, adaptable, loving, and responsible lesbian can lose confidence in her ability to identify problems or to deal with new conflicts effectively, more so if she is a member of another socially marginalized population group and has no support as a lesbian within her own community.

Fear of discovery and isolation are among the factors which increase a lesbian's sense of disorientation and detachment – from her usually capable self, from her personal and sexual identity as a woman, and from the validation of her lesbian identity.

As a result, she can feel split into (at least) two people, neither of them able to function well, even if she has a loved and loving partner, absorbing work, lesbian friends, and a comfortable home. The sense of being 'split' can mean that her 'external' personality has invaded her sense of herself, and this disturbing feeling can be compounded by her fear of discovery. It is like living on the edge – on the interface between her reality and other people's realities (Abbott and Love, 1972). How she adapts to this depends upon her personal resources, and many lesbians are highly skilled at these manoeuvres.

The therapy approach will depend on the counsellor's ability to perceive such a situation from within the lesbian's individual framework and her particular social context and personal history.

Award-winning North American lesbian health psychologist Barbara Sang points out that this disorientation can be lifelong. It is not solely about youth, first coming out, inexperience, or a lack of coping or creative abilities. She reports, in a 1991 survey, that a high percentage of 'mid-life' lesbians were found to be hiding their sexual orientation from most – if not all – their family members, heterosexual friends, and co-workers. She states: 'This is certain to produce stresses, and make for distortion in the way they relate' (Sang, 1991).

Lil, a white working-class lesbian, explained how she began to experience this 'split'.

'One person is the Real Me – being at home, living, loving my partner and her daughter, dealing with ordinary household problems, the usual ups and downs, illness or money worries, arguments between us, hassles with friends, whatever.

'The other one is the Out There me – always on guard, waiting for changes in people's attitudes to me, hiding my home life, being careful when I buy magazines or books, and thousands of other things. Then there are all those questions – or digs – by people who assume that I am heterosexual or wonder if I'm not, or think that I'm available to play heterosexual power games. It's much worse if they know I'm a lesbian. What with everything else that's going on, it feels like the world and his brother are ganging up on us.'

What Lil is describing is oppression. It may not be as blatant or as violent as other forms of oppression, and is harder to identify. She added: 'It's easier to think "Did I imagine that?" and then forget about it.'

The 'out there' image, which a lesbian feels must be maintained, exerts a constant pressure. Gradually, it erodes self-confidence, dignity and honesty. Over a long period it becomes second nature to 'forget' about being a lesbian or, at least, about anything positive to do with being a lesbian. Internalized in this way, it can become part of a lesbian's character and belief system, and feel familiar, even 'right'. This was once defined as 'sane schizophrenia' (Abbott and Love, 1972). Many lesbians are, in fact, diagnosed as 'schizophrenic' and by other 'psychotic' labels by establishment therapy services (see Chapter 1).

The resultant conflict (as the real lesbian tries to come out again) sets up new stresses. These can complicate existing problems and affect the security of her life away from the oppressive or hostile external society. 'Bringing home oppression' does exactly what it is designed to do. It creates self-doubt and loss of awareness of personal resources, and can force conformity to the community's standards and behaviours. When these are lower than the lesbian's own personal standards, appearing to tolerate or collude with them compromises her integrity, stops her from complaining about unacceptable behaviour, and, often, leads to her belief that being a lesbian is 'the problem'.

LIL'S PERCEPTION OF THE PROBLEM

Lil is 29, and works in the customer service department of an office equipment leasing company. It is housed in a modern industrial estate outside the town, and supplies a large region with equipment and service back-up.

'That's where I met Bridget', Lil told the counsellor. 'She was working for the people that did the landscaping. Sometimes I'd share my lunch with her. That was before she had her baby.'

When Lil started therapy, she and Bridget had been living together in Bridget's flat for five years with Bridget's seven-year-old daughter Patsy ('a good, androgynous name').

At first, Lil was preoccupied with problems at work. She had started with the company as a secretary. Now, after two years in the customer service department – a better-paid job which enabled her to run a second-hand car – Lil was experiencing several problems. She said she could no longer cope with the 'sexy jokes, teasing and flirting by the men, and even some of the women, though we're mostly women in the office'.

'I really envy the way the other women deal with it', she said. 'They laugh it off, or give as good as they get. To me, it's embarrassing. I think they know this, because sometimes the men egg each other on to have a go at me. Even one or two of the women chat me up. I don't know where to put myself. I can't do anything about it. Maybe I should just forget the whole thing, go off somewhere, and get a job in some other town.'

Lil said she had lost her sense of humour. When she made any comments – like objecting to 'Page 3 girl' pin-ups or to sexist remarks – she was told she was a spoilsport or a pain, that feminism was out of date, and that the number of women in the office proved they had got their equal rights now.

'So I learned from the straight women – they must all be straight – how to talk back, with cracks or put-downs, and Bridget told me some good jokes, but I can't say them in a funny or natural way. The men pick this up, and instead of laughing they get angry or hostile and say I'm bitchy. I hate this part of myself, this fake person, getting wound up by their stupid, lager-lout mentality.

'I feel ignorant, too, because I never had sex with men and I don't get half of the jokes. So they think I'm frigid or old-fashioned or something. One of the service engineers is always sending me sexy seaside postcards with his expenses form. Things are really bad at home, too.'

Lil paused for breath. Instead of expressing anger or contempt, as the counsellor expected, she lowered her head. This change of mood gave the counsellor valuable information, but she decided not to comment, and to wait for Lil to say how work was affecting her home life.

Instead, Lil said, in a sad, quiet voice: 'I thought I had it all. I don't know what to do or where to go.' To make things worse, Lil's line manager had complained about her work and asked if she was feeling ill, or if there was trouble at home. Lil had agreed. She stopped talking again, and appeared also to have stopped breathing.

DETERMINING THE PURPOSE OF THERAPY

Lil is the counsellor's first lesbian client. After waiting for a few minutes to give her time to say more, or to recover from her obvious distress, the counsellor summarized what Lil had told her so far. She decided to delay discussions about practical concerns, so before asking how Lil felt about them working together she decided to depersonalize this question and find out what she hoped to gain from therapy – at least, from this first session.

Lil frowned, seeming unsure of how to reply. Even so, she did – in her response she gave a clear message about what she *didn't* want, which enabled the counsellor to get her answer. Lil said that she had come to therapy at the suggestion of Bridget, her partner. Most of her statements (and those in the following sessions) when they were not to do with work, began with 'Bridget says ... '. The counsellor decided on a non-directive approach which, for her, was unusual.

Everything 'Bridget said' sounded like a complaint, and was hurtful and demoralizing to Lil, who was aware of what was happening to her and felt unable to stop it. She and Bridget were fighting, instead of being, as they used to be, 'us against the world, with Patsy as a real gift'. Bridget said Lil smoked and drank too much, was irritable and put her down all the time, was hard and uncaring, less sexy, never really talked like they used to, and was always wanting to go to the lesbian disco (forty miles away) on the weekends when Patsy was with her father.

Bridget said that Lil was no longer the woman she'd met, sitting peacefully in the gardens. This was confusing to Lil, who felt exactly the same way about Bridget as she always had. But she agreed that she had lost interest in the women's or lesbian and gay books and magazines they used to read and talk about, and she was bored with the few lesbian friends they had. Bridget said (and Lil agreed) that she was also being impatient and snappy with Patsy.

Lil was very concerned about this, because she adored the little girl. She and Patsy had always been 'good mates', both of them united in their love of Bridget. Both of them enjoyed surprising her, but Bridget said recently that Lil had provided 'one surprise too many' when she had completely forgotten it was her turn to collect Patsy from the childminder.

There were other problems in the household. Bridget had recently started working part-time. This meant that they had *less* money than before. Patsy's father had always sent regular money, but under the new legislation the Child Support Agency had decided he should contribute much more, and Bridget's benefit had been reduced by this amount. While Bridget was fighting this decision together with Patsy's father (he and his new wife had two small sons), the part-time job had come up at a new garden centre, but fares, special clothing, and payments to a childminder ate into Bridget's pay. The hours also meant she had to give up most of her casual work, less frequent but better paid, building patios or barbecues.

'Bridget's a very capable, practical person', explained Lil. 'She's always managed money really well until now.' It did not help that Lil was spending extra money on cigarettes and drinks. Both of them were spending more on TV dinners and pre-packed meals (which, they dis-covered, Patsy preferred). Sometimes Lil would throw away her sandwich lunches and buy a meal in the staff canteen, not out of hunger, more out of a sort of resentment which she could not explain.

THE COUNSELLOR'S UNDERSTANDING OF THE ISSUES

While the counsellor listened to Lil, she was aware of so many different things going on that she was not sure where to start. It seemed to her that:

1. All the attention Lil was receiving seemed to be negative.

2. The 'personality split' which Lil described had led to her 'out there' self overwhelming her real self – her lesbian self.

3. The sexist jokes at work had worn her down so much that she had forgotten she had the right to complain.

4. Lil's feeling that 'the world and his brother' were ganging up on them was correct. The new child benefit rules caused financial crisis for many fathers and penalized all single mothers, including lesbian mothers, who were in receipt of state benefits. The counsellor (who was a supporter of women's rights though not an activist) saw this scheme as political. Single mothers – including those divorced, separated, or widowed, make up 18 per cent of households with dependent children (*General Household Survey, 1991*).

5. Lil was deeply hurt by Bridget's honest, though critical, comments, which reinforced her belief that she herself was 'the problem'. Clearly, she saw Bridget as beyond reproach, and perhaps Bridget believed this too, since it was she who suggested that Lil went to therapy. Possibly Lil took upon herself a lot of the responsibility for the partnership – it was Bridget's first lesbian relationship. The counsellor reminded herself to ask, at some stage, whether Bridget was already separated when they met, or whether she had left Patsy's father to live with Lil.

6. Lil was experiencing *loss* on several levels – her self-confidence at work, her 'good mate' little Patsy, and the familiar loving stability offered by the 'practical, capable' and previously stay-at-home Bridget.

7. Lil seemed to have lost touch with her inner political monitor, despite the fact that her conversation showed an understanding of her rights. She was envying the heterosexual women's abilities to 'cope' with the sexual teasing. This might also be causing her to doubt the validity of being a lesbian, or to believe that she was immature, or 'frigid'. Instead of perceiving these women as oppressed by sexism, colluding with it, and failing to support each other, she felt herself to be inadequate, ignorant

and immature. To her, 'real' women could cope with sexist men, flirt with women, and have a good laugh.

8. Having lost faith in her ability to deal with problems at work and at home, Lil was 'escaping' and effectively isolating herself further, drinking and smoking more, and wanting to dance at the lesbian disco as often as possible. She was 'bored' with lesbian friends, who might have been a source of support. The counsellor wondered if Lil felt they might disapprove of her present behaviour, especially if their 'family' unit might have been seen as an example of how a lesbian relationship could work. Did they know any other lesbian mothers?

9. Lil did not seem to have recognized that the changes for all three members of the household as a result of Bridget's new job were contributing to their problems.

10. Lil felt powerless, unable to do what she said she wanted to do – stop the sexist behaviour at work, get her relationship with Bridget back on course, and retrieve her position as Patsy's 'good mate'. Possibly what she described as resentment – throwing away her sandwiches and spending money on cooked lunches – might be about wondering if she could cope with work without the domestic stability that Bridget had previously provided. If so, she would almost certainly feel guilty if she wished that Bridget would go back to her classic 'wife and mother' role. However, this could also be about Lil's need to nourish herself or counteract her alcohol intake.

Counselling options

The counsellor decided to delay questions about whether Lil wanted therapy or merely agreed with Bridget, and to focus instead on the priorities as Lil saw them. She wanted to offer, without saying so, some positive attention to counteract all the negativity.

Not being a lesbian herself, she was thinking how courageous both Lil and Bridget were to set up a household, with a toddler, in a suburban district forty miles from any lesbian centres, and to have maintained Patsy's contact with her father – and, she presumed, kept up a reasonably good relationship with him themselves. She thought it would be unhelpful to express this admiration, since, by coming to therapy, Lil had made it clear that she did not feel able to tackle problems on her own. She wanted to share the responsibility. The counsellor considered that most indicative of the importance of this was the fact that Lil had found the money to pay the fee. She felt she should renegotiate this to her low-waged level.

The counsellor also wondered about Bridget's desire for a part-time job which made her financially worse off. She was concerned that this previously self-contained and mutually supportive couple had reached such a low point that therapy (at least, for Lil) seemed to be the only option.

She wondered if Lil had any supportive family, or friends of her own, nearby, and thought this unlikely. As Lil's tendency seemed to be to 'escape' from problems (and use what were, basically, 'pain-killers') or to distract herself from them, the counsellor wondered if she had, originally, 'escaped' from a hostile home environment. Did she see her life with Bridget as a sort of sanctuary, and Bridget therefore as a bit of a saint? If so, why would she consider leaving her? Did she believe that she did not 'deserve' her? Was therapy, then, also a 'sanctuary'? Did she feel she 'deserved' therapy, and if so, in what way? As a resource, or as having to 'pay' for being a problem?

The counsellor felt that Lil's best way of finding her own solutions would be by getting back in touch with her lesbian self. However, she recognized that Lil at present had some doubts about the validity of being a lesbian, although she had seemed to be comfortable telling the counsellor that she lived with a woman and her child. What was the basis of her experience, or re-experience, of internalized heterosexism? Was it that she perceived lesbian identity solely in terms of traditional 'family' relationships? If so, Lil could not, at this stage, be expected to develop renewed faith in this most important and valued aspect of herself.

The counsellor decided to focus on what Lil said she wanted: a better relationship with Bridget and with Patsy, and to improve the situation at work.

By concentrating on these priorities, the counsellor can provide the positive attention that she feels Lil wants, as well as validate her needs and her right to ask for help in situations which would be hard to cope with for many lesbians.

THE COUNSELLOR'S HOPES, SELF-DOUBTS AND RESPONSIBILITIES

In the longer term, assuming therapy continues, the counsellor hopes to enable Lil to get back in touch with her strengths – courage and responsibility – and to feel less stuck with her problems and less inclined to 'escape'.

She knows nothing about lesbian services in the area, and wonders if Lil does. She decides to research this herself, as isolation seems to be a major problem. She realizes that she feels bad for never thinking about the local situation for lesbians. She also worries that she might miss some important cues, and decides to make lesbian concerns a priority at her next supervision group meeting. As she has never noticed any books on counselling work with lesbians, she has a sudden thought that she is facing the only lesbian client in the world – and decides that this would be a good way of introducing the subject at her next supervision session.

The counsellor's intention is to validate this lesbian family and their lifestyle, demonstrate that she feels optimistic about it, and show that she sees as positive a lesbian's relationship with a little girl. She has a lot of questions she would like to ask about Patsy who, at age seven, would probably be developing interests and friends of her own outside the home, as well as forming relationships with her little half-brothers, and perhaps her father's wife. Although Patsy is not her client, she is concerned about the effects on the child of Lil's present problems and the consequences to her relationship with her mother, Bridget. Patsy is going through a transition, now that Bridget works different hours, although her own wider social and educational sphere might offset the domestic changes. She might even feel glad about them, since they give her more independence.

The counsellor thinks that the relationship priority is between Lil and Bridget (especially as Bridget thinks Lil is the problem). She wants to know if Lil really would like to leave.

Since the counsellor has observed that Lil believes the problems began at work, she feels it would be more effective to deal with this first, especially as she could think of several ways in which Lil could challenge the situation. If this strategy is successful, it could give Lil confidence in her ability to repair the rifts in her relationships, and enable her to plan for a different type of home life with a realistic expectation of challenges and change. The counsellor decides to avoid questions about Lil's life at age six or seven unless she raises this herself.

IMPROVING THE SITUATION AT WORK

Because of Lil's sense of failure and powerlessness, and her high valuation of practical abilities, the counsellor felt it would be useful to start by pointing out what Lil herself could do to improve things at work. Saying that she will come back to the home situation, she suggests they think about some strategies.

Lil is pleased that the counsellor recognizes her priorities. She says she usually enjoys her job – sorting out customers' problems and organizing the service engineers, all of them men, whose technical skills she admires. She finds the work interesting, as she picks up information about very different businesses and services. However, she thinks that the situation now would be the same wherever she worked, since she 'will always be a lesbian and have the same difficulties'.

Any change, then, will depend on her ability to recognize that what she has been experiencing is heterosexist prejudice and deliberate, motivated, sexual harassment. The definition of sexual harassment is 'unacceptable behaviour which is based on your sex'[2] (and 'sex' means 'gender'). If Lil could get back in touch with her political awareness – knowledge of her rights – instead of envying the other women's apparent ability to cope, she could see them as contributing to their own disempowerment – and hers.

The 'changing-room' atmosphere she described also meant that the men were dominating a space where women were in the *majority* – probably part of the reason for what was going on. Lil might also come to realize that as a lesbian she is in a unique position – she is more sensitive to, and therefore more highly aware of, the consequences to all women of unwanted sexual, or sexualized, attention and gendered put-downs.

Lil does not need to say that she is a lesbian (although many of her co-workers probably know) or to tackle the problem alone and risk hostility or being further scapegoated. She needs to find at least one other woman who finds the men's behaviour offensive and disruptive.

There is plenty of readily available information, such as leaflets from public libraries, Citizen's Advice Bureaux or Job Centres, about sexual harassment in the workplace[2] although they are not targeted at lesbians. Armed with this information, Lil could start complaining – perhaps to the individuals responsible and then to her manager – knowing she has the law on her side.

She was very unsure about starting what felt like a campaign, and did not want to complain. Alternative strategies were to distribute leaflets to the women by leaving them in the women's toilets, for example, to raise their awareness, or to ask for a video session or training workshop on equalities issues to be held by an external trainer. Lil did not like this idea either.

The counsellor asked if any of the complaints Lil received about the male service engineers were about flirtations with women customers. Lil replied that it had not occurred to her that men who harassed her might be doing the same to any other women they met. She said: 'I could kick myself.'

Then she had an idea. Since she sent out service quality assessment questionnaires with contract renewal forms, she thought it appropriate – and acceptable to the management – to suggest the addition of a non-specific question about service engineers' methods of personal presentation and contact with customers' staff.

The counsellor also worked out with Lil that next time her productivity was questioned by her line manager, instead of agreeing that she had headaches or backaches and problems at home, she would say that it was difficult to concentrate on the phone or on administration with all the giggles and chit-chat, and that perhaps he could sit in with her for a day.

Lil explained that the engineers would often moan or call her 'bossy boots' if she insisted on late afternoon visits, and that she had no authority over them. The counsellor suggested that she point this fact out immediately to her manager, who seemed to hold the attitude that Lil was responsible when things went wrong.

Because Lil was relieved to be able to talk to the counsellor about work-related problems – she had thought therapy was only about feelings or personal matters – she could then think about the loaded issue of authority and responsibility. As a result, she realized that she did have some power – legal back-up for her rights as a woman at work. She thought there was one woman she could ask to help with leaflet distribution. The counsellor, who realized that she was being very directive, decided to leave Lil to work out, in her own time, the fact that being a lesbian, far from being the cause of all these problems, was an asset if she felt willing to use it, both for herself and for the other women at work.

BETTER RELATIONSHIPS WITH BRIDGET AND PATSY

The counsellor told Lil that there seemed to be several things going on at home, and that it might be useful to identify them all. Lil knew that she was bringing work problems home – this was also something that 'Bridget says'. While the counsellor was waiting for the right opportunity to ask Lil whether she automatically agreed with everything Bridget said, she thought it would be more appropriate at this stage to take the focus off Bridget completely.

The counsellor checked with herself whether this was because she liked Lil, and was beginning to perceive Bridget as a bit sanctimonious and self-righteous. Since the counsellor did not know Bridget, her feeling of dislike towards her could be a reflection of Lil's own feelings – feelings that she did not, at this stage, feel justified in expressing. The counsellor also felt protective of Lil for reasons that she did not yet understand, especially as she also perceived Lil as courageous, hard-working, considerate, and naturally good with children (or, at least, with Patsy). She wondered if the loss of Patsy as a 'good mate' had caused the suppression of Lil's own spontaneity – she said she had lost her sense of humour.

Lil spoke with a strong regional accent, had the look of a countrywoman, and, occasionally, a far-away look in her eyes. The counsellor wondered if she still sat in the garden at work – which was where she had met Bridget – and whether she was a bit of a loner. This might be why she could usually relate well to the engineers; not just because of their skills, but because of their independence and the freedom of being out and about all day. It was on the tip of the counsellor's tongue to ask her what she dreamed about. But Lil had said she liked Bridget's 'practical, capable' qualities, and admired technical skills; and to introduce dreamwork or fantasy work with someone who was already showing a tendency to escape from her problems would be counter-productive at this stage. The counsellor believed that Lil herself had undeveloped technical skills, and so would gain more from a practical approach. This had, so far, seemed effective in tackling the work problems.

Talk and words also seemed to be something that Lil had had enough of. She spent all day in her head – on the phone arranging service visits with people she probably never met and filling out forms. She was worn down by cracks, jokes and silly flirtatious office chit-chat, and, on top of all this, Bridget's criticisms. She had lost interest in reading, at least, reading about women's issues. Had she ever read to Patsy? Had she stopped doing this? If so, how did she express her own voice now?

Because her only fun seemed to be dancing at a lesbian disco, the counsellor identified this as Lil choosing a positive way of dealing with the built-up tensions and aggression of the week. It was also far healthier than her other ways – drinking and smoking and throwing away her sandwich lunches, and buying canteen dinners instead – which only buried her feelings and created more problems. Dancing might also represent a need to be with lively lesbians in an uncommitted, irresponsible way. Perhaps this was the reason for Lil avoiding their friends, rather than the other way round.

The counsellor was cautious about making any more suggestions, or saying anything which Lil might experience as even faintly directive or critical. But Lil seemed to need a lot of encouragement.

She decided to resolve this by letting Lil dictate the way the therapy should continue, that is, giving her the authority without making her feel she was carrying the sole responsibility.

'What do you feel like doing, now, just at this moment?'

Lil looks bemused. What could the counsellor mean?

'I wouldn't mind a ciggie', she says eventually, 'but I know it's a non-smoking centre. I can't think. I'm a bit tired.'

'What's instead of a ciggie, usually?' the counsellor asks. Lil thinks for a moment. 'At work, I can't smoke in the office, and if I'm too busy to go out, I tidy my files or make lists or something. Or I might go and get coffee from the machine. Or I stretch and yawn or go to the toilet. It depends.'

The counsellor smiles. 'You're not at work now. What do you feel like doing? Do you want to go out for a smoke?'

Lil smiles and shakes her head. 'If you really want to know, I feel like curling up in a little ball on the floor.'

'OK. Go on, then.'

Lil looks at the counsellor as if she has just suggested Lil turn cart-wheels. The counsellor nods, smiling, and tosses her a cushion. Lil shrugs, takes it, but, rather than curling up on the floor, she tucks herself up on the small sofa she is sitting on, leaning her head against the cushion. She shuts her eyes and sighs deeply.

'Don't let me nod off', she mumbles. The counsellor, who has forgotten to ask Lil if she is getting enough sleep, takes her at her word. 'OK', she says. 'Now. What's the best thing you can imagine, a really good memory?'

'That's easy', Lil says, with a sleepy smile. 'When I got together with Bridget, we were in bed in her flat on Sunday morning. We had the whole day. Patsy was with her Dad. It was ages after we met, we'd finally got each other into bed, we'd stopped pretending we were just friends. We talked about what to do for the day, and laughed and . . . well, anyway, a bit later on I said I wished it was a year. We decided right then to live together.

'Anyway, we got out of bed – amazing – and got all Patsy's crayons, and Bridget found some old wallpaper. We sat in bed and drew out a plan of the flat, how I'd fit my things into it. Bridget got out again and drew in how she'd redecorate it – she even put in all the tiles she wanted to do in the kitchen. I did lists of stuff I'd need to bring from the room I had. We didn't talk much. It was the happiest day of my life, and it got better and better. Then she got us some tea and got back into bed and I put my pillow on her shoulder and lay on it . . . a bit like this, actually. Just like this.'

Lil stops talking, and the counsellor notices her expression change as she runs through some more memories and then gradually comes back to the present, looking deeply unhappy. She opens her eyes and sits upright, looking embarrassed, then suspicious. 'What was that supposed to be for?' she says.

The counsellor smiles. 'You said you were tired. I thought it might be a change for you to relax a little, let go of some of that tension you've been putting up with all this time. Also I wanted to find out a bit about you, what you like doing, the way you work things out.'

Lil is interested. 'Why?'

The counsellor replies 'It's your therapy, so it has to be done your way'. Lil looks surprised, and is suddenly wide awake. 'Oh', she says. 'But you're the counsellor. What do you mean?'

'You didn't see any obstacles, then? You just snuggled up together, made plans, drew pictures and lists of how you'd make a home together? You worked out, together, how you'd fit your things into Bridget's flat with her and little Patsy? Everything else presumably got worked out after-wards.'

'What everything?' Lil asks.

'What Patsy might think, whether it would affect their relationship with each other and with her father, how you would get on with Patsy, what anyone else in the block might think about you two living together, all that. Money, and so on.'

'Oh. That was easy. We loved each other. We didn't ever talk about all that. It was fine. It just worked out, like it was all meant to be.'

'So being a lesbian was the right thing for you? It could make everything else work?'

'Exactly. Exactly the right thing. Being a lesbian, and being with Bridget, that's what was right. It was always right.'

The counsellor notices again that Lil identifies herself with Bridget. She missed the question about lesbian energy and commitment making things work. She asks 'Is it still right?'

'For me, yes', Lil says immediately. 'For Bridget, I don't know. I think she still loves me. She's very pissed off with me, and I don't blame her. I'm pissed off with me too. She hasn't said for me to move out, just to sort myself out.'

'To sort your *Self Out* ... ' Lil does not respond.

During the next sessions, the counsellor decided to forget about verbal prompting, and to do what she had said she would do – let Lil direct her own therapy. She produced some large pieces of paper and a box of brightly coloured marker pens. Together, she and Lil, sitting on the floor, made a chart of all the different problems Lil was experiencing. These were separated into office, home, and problems that Lil saw as her own, including her many 'faults' according to herself and to Bridget. What 'Bridget said' was labelled with a big B. Lil quickly appreciated the fact that the counsellor was working *with* her, and not telling her what to do. She also wondered if the counsellor was a lesbian, as she seemed so supportive, but decided not to ask. She liked concentrating on herself.

It took longer for Lil to be able to write down the different questions affecting the relationship. Mainly this was because she could not see anything negative, or problem-causing, in anything Bridget was doing. It seemed to the counsellor that every time Lil felt angry about Bridget, she either talked about something sad or criticized herself.

To get around this, the counsellor explained that while what Bridget was doing was right for her and necessary for her and for Patsy, it must be having a practical effect on things at home, and on the amount of attention Lil was getting.

As long as she was not required to criticize Bridget, Lil was able to itemize, and put into boxes, the changes which had resulted. At home, she and Bridget added to this and made it into a sort of flow-chart, so that they could see how one thing had led to another. Lil felt good that Bridget was joining in the therapy, although they both wondered if this was 'real' therapy.

At a subsequent session, with Lil's agreement, the counsellor used the same type of activity – and Lil's imagination – to look at the effects of all the changes on Patsy. They also looked at what Patsy was bringing home from school, from the childminder's and from her father's home.

This gave Lil quite a shock. Although she and Bridget had often discussed when to tell Patsy about sex and about lesbians, Patsy had formed ideas of her own. As well as school-friends of her own age, there were her two small half-brothers.

Onto the chart went a lot of remarks that Patsy had made, or odd things she had asked Bridget about Lil. These included several questions about why they slept together and where their boyfriends were. This was a combination of Patsy's natural curiosity and several other people's. Patsy had always described Lil to people she knew, including her other family, as 'my best friend' and to school teachers and other adults who asked her as 'Mum's best friend'. She often asked Lil if she was going to have any babies of her own, and she seemed more worried than interested that Bridget might have another baby. She had started calling Lil her stepmother. Both

Bridget and Lil had explained carefully that it was not the same as Dad having a wife, whom Patsy could call 'stepmother' if she wanted.

An important factor was that Patsy's father had left soon after she was born. Now that she was older, he was proud of her and made a fuss of her, to the annoyance of her two half-brothers. The older boy made rude remarks about their own mother's possible production of a girl baby.

Patsy was told that a girl baby was the most yukky thing anyone could think of and that's why Dad had left her. Patsy, who was very attached to her father, believed this – it was, in any case, true. She had promised the boys that if ever Lil or Bridget had a girl baby, she would not bring it with her to her father's place. So at the age of seven Patsy was already learning about sexist attitudes and how to appease men and boys.

Lil was able to see that natural changes in Patsy, and the various problematic aspects in her life – including a momentary confusion about who her 'real' mother was – played a major part in her own relationship with Bridget. She was upset and annoyed with herself for not realizing this sooner. It was not just that she was being snappy with Patsy – Patsy was naturally paying her less attention, and playing more aggressive games that she had probably learned at school, from her half-brothers, or from television. She kept asking Bridget to rent particular videos, or to be allowed to stay up late to watch adult programmes. Lil had thought that this was all completely normal, and had left Bridget to deal with it, although they did talk about returning the video recorder to the hire shop. Lil loved movies, so the video stayed.

She understood that Bridget saw this as being childish, and avoiding her responsibilities as co-parent. She felt very hurt at Patsy's new interests and friends, but knew it was natural and there was nothing she could do about it. She had expressed this by arguing with Patsy as if she were an adult.

She decided, with Bridget, that she would take a more active and adult role in parenting, and try to counteract the various types of sexism and confusing changes that Patsy was experiencing. Other ideas Lil had were: the three of them going on wildlife-spotting walks; encouraging Patsy to make her own garden on the tiny balcony; buying a technically absorbing kit or game that she and Patsy could struggle over together; and going to the childminder's earlier to find out what the children did there – such as watching adult videos.

Lil wanted to meet the little boys and talk to their mother, though Bridget did not like this idea. Lil admitted to being angry about being denied a 'parenting' opportunity.

Soon afterwards, she stopped repeating what 'Bridget said'. She also realized she had been using the lesbian disco as another escape, and that what she needed was to become a part of a mutually supportive lesbian community and to make more friends locally. When she suggested this, Bridget said what *she* wanted was more time for herself, working alone in peaceful gardens, designing, and, eventually, to study landscaping. This shattered Lil's gradually increasing confidence in the future of their relationship, although Bridget could not understand why.

Much as the counsellor wanted to support Lil, she readily related to Bridget's wishes. She was a woman accustomed to spending most of the day on her own, finding casual, independent, and creative work that she genuinely enjoyed, and taking charge of practical arrangements at home.

She suggested that when Lil felt ready, they could talk about what happened when she first came out as a lesbian, and why 'escaping' seemed the best solution to whatever problems she had encountered. Home – and Bridget being a source of security, attention, and comfort – seemed more important to her, and there were probably issues for Lil to deal with about the loss of her childhood home when she came out. (She mentioned that she had lived in a 'room'.)

The counsellor felt it essential for Lil to focus on her own life, and validate her personal resources and abilities. It appeared she had decided what sort of lesbian she was through Bridget. Now it was important to decide what she wanted for herself, as a lesbian individual.

After some thought, Lil said: 'Yes ... I do want therapy just for me. I really must sort myself *out*.' The counsellor laughed. Lil looked shocked. Suddenly, she grinned. 'I just realized what I said.'

NOTES

1. For example, C. D. Kasl, *Women, Sex and Addiction*. London, Mandarin (paperback), 1990.
2. *Sexual Harassment in the Workplace: The Facts Employees Should Know*. Leaflet PL924. Department of Employment/Central Office of Information. Other Government leaflets are available for employers. More details, and valuable strategies, can be obtained from Women Against Sexual Harassment (WASH), 305 The Chandlery, 50 Westminster Bridge Road, London SE1 7QY; tel: 0171 721 7592. (See Resources for union lesbian and gay support in cases of sexual harassment at work.)

casework
examples

By the way ... I'm a lesbian
1: Medical manners and polar positions

At her GP's suggestion, Mara has booked to see the counsellor employed by the local health centre. She has been feeling run-down and depressed for weeks, has not been sleeping well, and now does not feel like eating. She found it hard to say what the problem was, and the GP, a sensitive young man, did not want to give anti-depressants to someone so young – she is 23.

Recently, he had prescribed antibiotics for a flu-type chest infection and had a good knowledge of her general health. He thought she might be lonely, and asked if she would like to 'have a talk with someone, in confidence'. Mara was not sure about counselling, but she liked the GP and realized he was trying to help. After thinking about it for a couple of weeks, she decided to give it a try. She made the appointment herself.

The counsellor looked at the GP's referral note for what seemed to be a long time. Mara watched her, feeling nervous. *What's she reading? What did the doctor say about me? What didn't he want to tell me? Did he tell her I'm a dyke? Does he know? This chair's saggy. I wish I could sit on the floor. What are all those books for? Do these windows open? Am I supposed to say something? What am I supposed to say?*

The GP's note said: 'Please see this patient. Let me know if you feel you need to see her medical records or have a meeting. I suggest six sessions, but do discuss extending if you feel it's necessary.'

The counsellor put the note on a desk behind her, and smiled at Mara.

'What seems to be the trouble?'

COUNSELLOR: So, Mara. Dr Williams suggested you might find counselling helpful? (*Mara nods.*) Can you say something about what's happening for you at the moment? Then we could talk about whether *you* think counselling's right for you.

Mara nods again, trying to sit still. She looks around the room. *How would I know? That's why I'm here. What goes on in here? Nothing much, by the look of it. Just a room with books. Not even cushions. Don't they all have cushions? Typical NHS. I'll just get it over with. She looks OK really.*

MARA: (*blurting it out*) I feel really bad. I've been ill. I'm splitting up. I mean we're splitting up. I don't know what to do.

The counsellor nods. *Splitting up. Does she mean she's splitting up with her partner? Or that she feels she's splitting up into bits? No. she said 'We'. Must mean her partner. She's fidgeting and looking around. That's understandable. She's never been here before and she doesn't know me. I wish the doctor had given me a clue. I must let her tell me in her own time.*

COUNSELLOR: This seems to be causing you a lot of anxiety.

MARA. *Here we go. Of course it's causing a lot of anxiety, otherwise why would I be here? I haven't said the right thing. Is there something wrong with anxiety?*
Yeah, well, that's my problem. Anxiety. And depression. The doctor thinks I've got depression, but he didn't want to give me a prescription.

COUNSELLOR: *Hm. She's batting it right back at me. OK. I feel a little combative today anyway. This room is freezing. Wait a minute, I'm responsible here.*
Not knowing what to do would make anyone feel anxious. What is it about splitting up that's making you anxious, particularly? Or depressed? Are they the same feelings or different feelings?

MARA (*sighs*) I don't know . . . you say anxious, he says depression. What it is, is splitting up. Is that anxiety or depression?
Maybe splitting up isn't really a 'problem'. Everybody splits up all the time. Maybe she only sees real nutters, head cases. So what does the doctor think's wrong with me, then?

COUNSELLOR: *We're here again. And she's batted it back to me again. I feel lousy today. It's so cold. Maybe I won't be able to work with this woman. Seems like splitting up is the issue.* OK. Could you tell me a bit more about that? I can't help if I don't know what splitting up means for you.

MARA: *This feels like a waste of time. I don't think I'm anxious. I'm pissed off. It's all right for her, she's got her stuff together or she wouldn't be a counsellor, would she?*

This is always happening. When I feel shitty and I hope someone will help me, they back off. Like the doctor. Passing me round. Community Care. I'm too much for people. They don't know what to do with me. She's just saying what I said to her. She can't deal with me. So I'm a monster, that's what Angie always says.

This kind of non-dialogue could continue throughout the session and for the next six sessions, with the counsellor being none the wiser, and Mara (if she came back) feeling less and less hopeful that the counsellor, or anyone else, could help her. She is splitting up with her partner *now*, at the weekend in fact.

Reopening communications

If the counsellor thinks that splitting up is causing Mara anxiety, she could start by concentrating on getting the session together, and establishing a good contact with Mara.

The most useful things for the counsellor to know, if possible, ahead of the session, are: Mara is a lesbian, she lives with Angie, her partner of eighteen months; Angie is moving out on Friday; Mara feels as if she's falling to bits, and has tried everything to make Angie stay. This includes pushing Angie around and threatening to smash her stuff, crying, not eating, staying up late, drinking beer and watching movies on TV, pleading with her, and telling her to go today, this minute.

Nothing has worked. Angie is weary but calm, and tries to keep the peace. She hasn't yet started packing, and she has been staying out a lot to avoid the continual arguments. She has also been flat-hunting, and has found a room in a shared lesbian house a few streets away. She hasn't told Mara this.

It would also be valuable for the counsellor to know that Mara has had health problems for months, and these have irritated Angie, who thinks she's making them up. Angie would have liked some attention herself. She does not really want to leave Mara, as she loves her very much. Both of them hate arguments, and both of them get upset. All they have done for the past six months is argue. There has been no sex. They are both broke and are stuck in Mara's tiny housing association flat with the TV and not much else. It is a quiet, lonely block. Most of the other residents are young people recently out of local authority care.

Angie has a job in a market, which she likes. Mara works part-time in a shop, which she hates. She thinks when Angie goes, she will give up work, go on benefits, and maybe have some friends round from the old days. The counsellor could have found all this out by asking some basic questions, at the same time as observing Mara closely. As she is a health centre counsellor, some routine health questions, and questions about her home environment, would not be thought unusual. She could have said that the GP's note hadn't told her anything. She assumed that the GP had explained that counselling was confidential, and nothing would appear on her medical records. It would have been good to check if Mara knew this.

Starting again from the beginning, it is obvious that Mara is shy or nervous, although she looks quite surly and resentful. Even so, she has a cheeky face. As she looks around the room, the counsellor feels that Mara does not like it much – which is fine, nor does she, and it *is* cold. She could say so. She notices that Mara looks at the window, door and bookshelves, and not at the counsellor. She shifts in the chair. Is it uncomfortable? The counsellor has never sat on it. She could ask about that.

Mara looks too small for the chair. She is thin. She is young (23 on the GP's referral note), white, with short dark hair. She wears jeans, a dark blue jumper, and black boots and a bum bag. She has three earrings in one ear which the counsellor is too far away to see in detail. When she handed over the GP's note, the counsellor saw that her fingernails are short, either cut or bitten down, she couldn't tell. Mara has a look about her, typical in this area, of years of under-nourishment, and a distant expression which the counsellor has noticed in so many young people who are unemployed, though she knows Mara has a job. (This affected the appointment time.) She looks tired, and does not seem to be breathing much. Her eyes are very dark and it is hard to detect any expression in them. The counsellor feels she is looking at a teenager, though she knows this isn't true. She wonders why Mara is not carrying a jacket, as it is late November, cold and very dark outside. She wonders if Mara is carrying a personal alarm or a torch, but she thinks that the bum bag isn't big enough.

Now she has this basic information, she can start by giving a few details about herself, confidentiality issues, and how the counselling works. She gives Mara the choice of filling in a basic health record sheet, or answering the questions. Mara opts for the second, so the counsellor does this as quickly as possible. Now she looks at Mara, giving her full attention.

COUNSELLOR: Do you live near here?

MARA: Yes.

COUNSELLOR: In a flat?

Mara: Yes. It's just on the estate.

Counsellor: On your own?

Mara pauses. I'm not supposed to have anyone living there. Better tell her.

Mara: No. But ... my ... the other person's going Friday.

Counsellor: Your flatmate?

Mara: Well, yeah. Not family or anyone.

Counsellor: Not family?

Mara's eyes fill with tears. The counsellor waits a little.

Counsellor: Almost family? A really good friend, anyway?

Mara stares at her boots.

Counsellor: Are you and your ... flatmate ... having a relationship?

Mara bites her lip. She looks flushed, unhappy and worried. Eventually she nods, and stares down at her boots again.

Counsellor: OK. I'll come back to this in a minute. You said you were depressed. I just want to check if this is the main reason, or if there's another reason for that. Are you eating OK? Sleeping? What's happening for you?

Mara: It's all the same thing, isn't it? How do you mean?

Counsellor: If you haven't been well, that can make you feel depressed. If you are on any medications or anything else ... ?

Mara: I don't do drugs, if that's what you mean. I had some antibiotics.

Counsellor: They can make you feel low. What do you eat, drink?

Mara: Vegetarian ... or trying to be.

Counsellor: Difficult, when it's so cold all the time. Drink?

Mara: *All this is going nowhere. What does anyone drink?* Beer, scotch if I can get it, vodka, whatever. Depends who's buying and where I am.

Counsellor: Where might that be?

Mara: In the pub it's beer; a club, maybe vodka or tequila.

Counsellor: At home?

Mara: Beer, mostly. Scotch if we ... if I ... if there's any money over.

Counsellor: We? You drink together? With your flatmate?

A long pause. Mara thinks she'd better get it over with.

Mara: That's right. We do. We did. It's my partner.

Counsellor: – Who is moving out on Friday?

MARA: Sorry. Yes. My ex.

COUNSELLOR: Ex now? Ex to be?

MARA: Ex.

COUNSELLOR: Is there anyone else for you or ...

MARA: (*startled*) Anyone *else*? I don't think so.

COUNSELLOR: It just didn't work out?

MARA: *Of course it didn't bloody work out.*
Well, what about the measles, then? And chicken pox, you didn't ask me about chicken pox. I had all those kid's things. I had the flu. I get sick if I drink too much beer. I get depressed. I get headaches if we fight. I don't sleep.

COUNSELLOR: (*wondering why it's so hard for Mara to talk about the one thing that is most obviously worrying her*) It seems to me that you don't want your partner, your ex, to go, and you're not able to think about anything else, and you also can't talk about it. OK. I'm going to make some assumptions here. If I'm wrong please stop me. Just so we can get down to the real problem. OK? (*Mara nods, looking nervous and grateful at the same time.*) I know that when it's difficult for people to talk about a relationship, it's sometimes because they think I'm going to disapprove, or get the wrong idea.

First of all, I'm a counsellor, I'm not here to disapprove of you. The doctors employ me to provide help or support that they can't offer. Second, everything you tell me is confidential. Nothing goes on your medical records. Third. I've done a lot of counselling work with families and couples – straight, gay, lesbian, and, though I'm white, I work with people from cultures very different from mine. By that I mean class as well as race. I don't always get it right. But if your partner – your ex I mean – is, for instance, a toyboy, or an older married man, or a woman, or an android from Mars, or, for that matter, a hermaphrodite crustacean, I'll cope. OK?

Mara stares at the counsellor in amazement. Hermaphrodite? What the hell is that? What sort of people does she work with? What a way to talk about people. Suddenly she notices the counsellor's mouth twitching. Her imagination is caught by the idea of Angie as a Martian. She grins.

MARA: Are you having me on?

COUNSELLOR: (*smiles*) I was kidding, of course. I don't work with animal clients. But I do see a lot of people who feel alienated. Also, as it happens . . . but never mind that.

MARA: You mean, people who *think* they are animals. My grandad was a bit like that. He was very fat. He pretended he was a Count or something. He was a refugee. From Poland, in the war. He said he was a polar bear, far away from home. He was a packer. He used to get drunk with the Polish sailors on the ships, and cry when he got home. He got fired. I can't remember why. He lived in the seamen's hostel.

The counsellor waits, wondering what sort of childhood Mara had, still wondering about the mysterious partner.

MARA: (*thinking she might as well tell her*) OK, I'm a dyke. I don't know why I didn't tell you. Sorry.

COUNSELLOR: Thanks. So your partner – ex – she's leaving? (*Mara nods*) Do you want to tell me her name?

MARA: Angie, Angie the Android. I like that.

COUNSELLOR: Oh? *Is* she a monster then?

MARA: (*she begins to cry*) No, it's me, I'm the monster. But that's demeaning to monsters. It's all down to me. She's going because she's pissed off with me. I'm a pain. I don't want her to go and I don't know what I'm going to do without her.

COUNSELLOR: You still love her?

MARA: (*looking horrified*) Oh, yeah, She knows that. I don't want her to go. I told her. She doesn't care. She doesn't believe me.

COUNSELLOR: And does she love you too?

MARA: (*looking surprised*) No. I mean she says . . . but we don't . . . She wouldn't go if she really loved me, would she?

COUNSELLOR: Maybe. It isn't always about love. That's what makes it so painful and confusing.

MARA: You're right there. It doesn't make any sense to me.

At this point the counsellor has to make some decisions. They are halfway through the session. Mara has finally said what the problem really is. Angie's leaving does not make any *sense* to her. She is experiencing it as a crisis. She feels helpless to stop her going. She believes it is her fault, and that she is the 'monster' who has driven away the woman she loves.

If Mara gives the impression of being a teenager, perhaps she *feels* like a teenager – confused, with no control over anything. She has probably come from a deprived background. She didn't think it particularly strange that her grandfather, a Polish refugee, was alienated, and said he was a deposed Count and a polar bear – she knew very well what 'alienated' meant. Maybe her grandfather had been described as an 'alien' when Mara was very young. Aliens, monsters – very typical contemporary language, and confusing for a child who was possibly very attached to her grandfather.

The difficulty she had in telling the counsellor that she was a lesbian could mean that she has met with a lot of disapproval from 'official' people, or expects to – or perhaps she doesn't tell people. Perhaps she feels more of a 'monster' than her 'alien' grandfather. But on the whole she doesn't like people disapproving of monsters, or putting them down. She had looked quite shocked at the counsellor's joke, and made the comment about 'being demeaning to monsters'. So she has some political awareness, but, it seems, no personal resources.

Her eyes look as if she shuts everyone out. Who has ever cared for her, and how? She doesn't know, even though she is a vegetarian, that poor health and the wrong food can affect her feelings. The counsellor wonders about the antibiotics. Did they cause thrush, on top of everything else? Mara said 'We don't ... ' Don't have sex? Would that be why? And she drinks beer, which could make something like thrush much worse. How much alcohol altogether, the counsellor wonders?

Mara has a good imagination and a lovely sense of humour. But her perception of love is a little simplistic: she doesn't believe Angie loves her, because if she did, she wouldn't leave. Maybe she has no family or friends who could support her. She really doesn't know what she will do without Angie. She has so little self-esteem that she isn't even angry about Angie going. But she has offered no specific reason for the break-up. Perhaps there isn't any particular reason, except that it isn't 'working'. Given more time, the counsellor would want to know.

1. If this is Mara's (or Angie's) first lesbian relationship.

2. Why Mara feels uncomfortable in this small, chilly space. Is her flat like this? Alienating? If so, perhaps the two of them never felt at home in the small flat. Perhaps they didn't know how to make it a home.

3. Why was she looking at the books? Curiosity? Or worry that the counsellor was going to 'look her up'? What was her previous experience of health or social service authorities? Was 'confusion' a problem in her family – certainly in her grandfather? Was it described as an illness? Mara didn't agree she was 'confused'. She preferred 'depressed' to confused, scared, helpless or angry.

COUNSELLOR: (*realizing that Mara is watching her with curiosity*) Are you wondering what I'm thinking?

MARA: Yes, I was.

COUNSELLOR: OK. I see it's really confusing that Angie wants to leave, that it doesn't make sense to you. I get the feeling that you're also scared of being left alone in that flat, that you think you won't be able to cope on your own, because here you are talking to me, instead of a friend. I wonder if you are really close to any other lesbians. It's good you told me you're a lesbian – sorry – dyke, because all of this makes a lot of sense to me.

(*Mara looks interested.*) I know a lot of lesbians talk about 'coming out' and that's what you just did, you 'came out' to me. But for you, being a lesbian without Angie maybe means being *shut* out of everything, just as it means you'll be shut back in your flat. Maybe it doesn't feel like a home, any more than this room feels like a counselling room.

So I should tell you that I'm heterosexual, which I forgot to tell you just now, so if we are going to work together, there might be times when I won't know exactly what you mean. I'll do my best and, anyway, my feeling is that your problem could affect anybody, losing someone you love – and I know about that – no good reason, no one to get angry with.

MARA: *Work? Does she think I need to come for a long time? Have therapy? She's supposed to be the one who knows what's going on here. I don't want to have to teach her about dykes. What do I know? So she doesn't like the room? So why doesn't she make it nicer? What does she mean 'if we are going to work together'? Who makes the decisions here?*

Mara experiences this as the counsellor's rejection of her. In her life, she has known doctors, social workers, people who were there when you had a big problem, and they made the decisions about what the problem was and what to do about it, if there was anything that could be done about it. Suddenly, she feels insecure. If this woman doesn't know what to do with her, then no one will. Then what?

COUNSELLOR: (*realizing immediately that she has made a mistake*) Sorry. That must have sounded awful. You don't want to hear about my problems. It's up to me to find out what the situation is for lesbians on their own. What would you like to do?

MARA: Look, you're the counsellor. I don't know what counselling is, really. People usually tell me what's wrong and what to do about it. I thought you'd be able to tell me what to do about stopping Angie going.

COUNSELLOR: Mara, I'll try and be honest with you. I'm not a social worker. (*Mara looks up quickly, and the counsellor realizes that she knows very well what a social worker is.*) I'm not here to give advice. I can't prevent Angie from leaving you. I'm not going to make decisions for you, as I don't know you at all. We *social worker is*.) I'm not here to give advice. I can't prevent Angie from leaving you. I'm not going to make decisions for you, as I don't know you at all. We just met.

What I can do is help you to make sense of the situation, and work out what's wrong, and help you see that it isn't all your fault – there are two of you in this relationship. We could talk about why Angie leaving feels like the end of the world, and if that's the only thing that's making you feel depressed and ill. Maybe you can ask her not to just disappear, but to keep in touch. Also we can work out strategies for you to deal with problems in the future. If other people have always made the decisions for you, it's no surprise that you now feel helpless.

Mara feels the counsellor's words bumping about and knocking against things inside her, things she didn't want to think about. What problems in the future? What can she see that Mara can't see? She feels even more helpless and scared. But at least this woman doesn't argue with her. She sounds tough, but nice, like she is on Mara's side, at least. But Mara didn't want to be in a lesbian 'situation'. Too many lesbians were in the same 'situation' as she was.

The counsellor wonders if she should be more directive. Mara seems to be so oppressed that she believes anyone in a position of authority will have all the answers, and stop bad things happening. Or is she *hoping* there is someone who isn't confused, who can explain what's happening, who can make sense of things? But she must know this isn't true, from her past experience.

The counsellor believes that if she maintains an illusion of having the answers it won't do Mara any harm, just for this very bad week.

> COUNSELLOR: OK. It's nearly time to stop. I'm wondering if you and Angie could find a different way of communicating with each other. What would you say to her, if she was here, in the room with us now?
>
> MARA: I'd say: What do I have to do to make you stay? I've said that, anyway, over and over.
>
> COUNSELLOR: Does she tell you?
>
> MARA: No. She just says, it's not about that, it's because we're not getting anywhere, that it's no good staying.
>
> COUNSELLOR: She wants things to happen, the relationship to grow?
>
> MARA: (*angry*) I said – she wants to go.
>
> COUNSELLOR: (*after a pause*) How about both?

MARA: Both? Both go?

COUNSELLOR: No, sorry. I mean, she goes – moves out, if she feels stuck. But is the relationship really finished? I mean, has she said 'goodbye' definitely?

MARA: 'Goodbye'? No, not yet. Maybe she will when she goes.

COUNSELLOR: Do you think she is as confused about this as you?

MARA: Yes. Yes, she is. She said she can't think straight – she needs space to think, time for herself.

COUNSELLOR: I understand. By the way, does she know you are seeing a counsellor?

MARA: Oh yes, she thought it was a good idea.

COUNSELLOR: Would you like her to come with you next time?

MARA: (*Next time? Who said anything about next time?*) Yes, I'd like it, but I don't think she'd come. She was pleased I had somewhere to go, get some help. She said she can't cope with me.

COUNSELLOR: Well, now you're coping with yourself. (*Mara looks surprised.*) Do you want to come back? You don't have to decide now. You can phone, or drop in and see the receptionist.

MARA: I don't know. I don't know what to do.

COUNSELLOR: You don't have to 'do' anything, you know. Except perhaps have a good hot meal and get some rest. No one can think when they're tired and depressed and upset. I saw you looking at the books. Do you read much?

MARA: (*embarrassed*) Sometimes. It's difficult, I'm dyslexic.

COUNSELLOR: Oh, I'm sorry, I should have asked you that. How many times have you wanted information, and haven't been able to get it, because you couldn't read it?

MARA: (*with a huge sigh*) All the bloody time.

COUNSELLOR: I suppose teachers and social workers and people thought you were stupid?

Mara doesn't want to remember all this. But Angie hurt her a lot when she said: 'Don't be stupid. Why can't you understand? You're like a big stupid kid all the time. I want a woman.'

MARA: I'm not stupid.

COUNSELLOR: (*smiling*) I know. I think maybe some new words would help this situation.

MARA: Such as?

COUNSELLOR: You probably know them all. Assertive. Negotiate. Alternatives. Self-esteem. Self-empowerment. Nurturing yourself. Your options. Imagination. Lesbian community?

MARA: Big words. Social worker talk. Except 'lesbian community'. What's *that*? None round here.

COUNSELLOR: I expect that's one of the problems. Would a party for Angie be a bad idea?

MARA: A divorce party? Angie the Android v. Mara the Monster.

COUNSELLOR: But no wrestling. You want to stay friends, don't you?

MARA: (*her eyes fill with tears again. Jokes are fine, but this is real*) She's the only friend I've got.

COUNSELLOR: Why don't you tell her that?

MARA: I will. I do. I mean, I really love her, you know.

COUNSELLOR: Well. See what she thinks about a party. I'll look forward to hearing about that next week.

MARA: You'll be here?

COUNSELLOR: I'll still be here. Oh, and make a monster.

MARA: (*who was up and almost out of the door*) You what?

COUNSELLOR: For Angie. A big, soft, cuddly, funny, lovable monster. For a present.

MARA: (*convinced now that the counsellor is a very weird person*) OK. Whatever you say. A monster. Right.

COUNSELLOR: A nice, *lesbian* monster. Not an alien. OK?

MARA: (*understanding*) I get it. OK. See you next week. And . . . thanks.

By the way . . . I'm a lesbian
2: Sexuality through the ages

Bella is trying to write the great lesbian novel, of course starring herself, about Bella the only lesbian parent in the country with a long-term stable partnership, an ageing but still able Mum who adores Bella's partner Nancy, and an aware, 14-year-old daughter who is teaching her younger sister about feminism, men, sex, society, and gay liberation.

Bella joined a women's writing group (unfortunately, all heterosexual women) as soon as Nancy's employer introduced flexi-time. Bella and Nancy could at last share parenting responsibilities, and Bella could have some time to herself.

Bella is 48, and Nancy 37. Nancy likes the children well enough but is content to leave the parenting to Bella, who is at home all day. She does not like Bella's Mum, whose liking for her puzzles her greatly as they have nothing in common. She thinks it might be because she is a quiet, reasonable, hard-working sort of person, while Bella, although a woman of few words, is assertive ('stubborn'), politically astute ('critical'), respectful of her daughters ('she spoils those girls'), and, sexually, definitely having a good time ('can't keep her hands to herself').

Bella takes no notice of her Mum's remarks unless she interferes with Bella's own parenting. However, the two girls are capable of responding appropriately, and with suitable civility. They are very attached to their grandmother, who visits often. She never gets the better of them and is unable to hide her admiration – of the younger girl, especially.

Bella wants to write a sexy novel, not a 'mothers-are-wonderful and lesbian-mothers-in-particular' sort of novel. Feeling a little out of touch with lesbian culture, she decides that the way to do the research is to leave Nancy in charge and explore the lesbian venues in the district. That is, a monthly social at a lesbian's home forty miles away, and a gay bar, predominantly men, held on Tuesday evenings in a tacky pub near the football ground.

She knows that while she and Nancy have always had a good sex life, domesticity makes things occasionally predictable. She could not say what might be more exciting (and Nancy asks her all the time). She believes there is probably nothing more she can learn about her body. She decides to keep an open mind.

Nancy shrugs, and believes this is just a stage Bella is going through – developing her new persona as a novelist. She knows how attached Bella is to her home and her family, and that she would not do anything to risk this stability, which is also a source of great pride to her, considering how isolated they are from other lesbian parents (and any other lesbians, for that matter). In addition, for all Bella's demonstrativeness and sexually upfront gestures, Nancy believes that, faced with an attractive and attracted lesbian, Bella would flee. Nancy remembers how long it took her to persuade Bella that she was indeed a lesbian, that six somewhat intoxicated former relationships with women, married or not, must be telling her *something*.

When Bella set off on her survey of lesbian life in the wild, rural west, she fell in love with a woman half her age. Nancy shrugged her shoulders, packed her bags, and moved in with a friend from work until it was all over.

Bella's 14-year-old daughter Esther (named after her father's mother) announced she was going to the family planning centre to start on the Pill; and 12-year-old Cynthia (named after Bella's mother) began to wear strange clothes and disappear at weekends.

Bella's mother had a mild stroke, gave up her flat, and moved into 'Nancy's room' which she knew perfectly well that Nancy never slept in. Bella's new lover, shocked at all this activity and feeling totally to blame, sold her motorbike, and rejoined her friends forty miles away. She could do nothing more than occasionally telephone to see how everything was. Everything was appalling.

Bella abandoned her novel, and, guilt-ridden, devoted herself to her mother's care. Nancy, sympathetic, often came to help but refused to be involved in anything resembling responsibility.

Bella had begun to drink again after three years of abstention. She pours her heart out to a woman volunteer counsellor at the alcohol and drug advisory centre in the nearby town.

The counsellor often supports women carers, and supplies Bella with information about carer support networks, benefits, respite care, day centres and various domiciliary services. Bella, who already had most of this information, expressed gratitude but did not propose to make use of any of it. She was convinced she was responsible for her mother's stroke, and for her daughters' sudden abandonment of their bright, untroubled, girlish ways. She could not bear to burden them with care responsibilities, and thought that the wisest thing was to let them continue their relationship with their grandmother on the same terms as before. It wasn't as if they saw any more of her, since they were hardly ever home.

Bella feels ashamed that she is unable to tell the counsellor that she is a lesbian. She simply says she is a single mother, who'd had a short affair, which she'd had to finish when her mother came to stay, and that she'd 'gone back on the bottle'.

She talks mostly about her drink problem – including her previous two years in an AA group at the same centre – and says she is very scared that her alcoholism had 'come back again'.

The counsellor asks her if she thinks this is because of all the changes lately, the shock of her mother's stroke, and the reorganization of the household and her domestic routine.

Bella says: 'It *was* a terrible shock. My father died of a stroke, seven years ago, and after that I . . . my marriage broke up. I moved here. I wanted the girls to live in the country – also, as far away from my husband as possible. I got divorced. I didn't want any custody problems.'

'Were there any?'

'Not really', Bella answers. 'He doesn't *want* the girls, but I didn't want him snooping around, checking me out, looking for reasons to make trouble. He's the resentful type. I was having a hard time as it was, drinking and hiding it from them, and from the neighbours – you know how it is.'

'I do', the counsellor says, warmly – herself a recovered alcoholic. She wants to know why Bella was worried about her husband snooping around, and is struck by the series of recent events which seem like history repeating itself.

'You must be finding it very hard', she says, 'that the same sort of things are happening all over again.'

Bella considers this. 'Yes, some of the things – except that Mum, thank heaven, didn't die. One thing goes wrong and general chaos ensues', she says.

'That's always the way when you lose someone – though as you say, your mother is getting better. She'll probably recover in time, if it was just a mild stroke, and if she is reasonably fit.'

'Yes', Bella says, 'I do try and work these things out. I prepared myself for the girls becoming women – though it has happened a bit suddenly. Maybe I shouldn't have joined the writing group just yet. I think Mum's stroke has affected them a lot more than her living with us, since she always came to stay whenever she felt like it. She's a different person to them now. I don't know why I've started drinking again. I hate myself. Mum doesn't know. She'd have another stroke.'

'Let's look at when you first began to drink. Can you remember?'

Bella remembers very well – she's been through this several times. Wishing she could have seen the same counsellor at the project, who knows everything about her, she now begins to filter out information which she does not think is relevant.

'I suppose like everyone it started gradually – I was a couple of years older than Nancy . . . What am I talking about, I mean Esther. I was 17 and I'd just failed my driving test. My clutch control was hopeless – I stalled the car three times and nearly hit a tree going backwards. I'd bought a bottle of whisky to give to my instructor, but I told him I would keep it till he managed to get me through the test. I drank the whole lot over the weekend, but it didn't have much effect.

'Then, the usual things: sex, men, more drink, dope, all that Sixties stuff, and then of course feminism. We were free! We could do what we liked with our bodies. No one told us everything was so addictive – you remember?'

The counsellor nods. 'And tranquillizers?' she asks.

Bella shakes her head. 'Funny, I never smoked – well, not tobacco I mean – and no one I knew took tranquillizers. Uppers more like. Heart-starters. I took a few of those, methedrine and poppers and so on. Amazing I'm still here, really.'

'We're both still here', the counsellor says, smiling and remembering her own youth – as much of it as she can, since most of it was blotted out by whatever anybody gave her.

'We are, aren't we?' says Bella, cheering up a little.

The counsellor prompts her. 'You were saying about how you began to get hooked on alcohol.'

'Oh yes', Bella says. 'Thanks. Well, I got married, I had two children, I never worked outside the house – I haven't a clue what I lived on before that – men I think, a bit of dealing, usual things. He hated me being a feminist, although he was supposed to be a Marxist – he was always doing union work, he was a steel worker then, plenty of money, but of course when it came to women's rights that was another story. I had an abortion, who didn't in those days? He hated that. Then it was Greenham. I'm trying to remember, it's all a bit of a haze. I didn't live there, just camped a few times. It got very heavy at one point. I managed to stay out of jail. Clubs and booze and sex was a treat after that. Of course it was . . . ' she tails off.

'Of course it was . . . ?'

Bella sighs, still struggling with her conscience. Being a lesbian hadn't gone down too well in her AA group, and she had stopped talking about it. She'd let the others think it was 'part of the disease'; and she's still unsure about the relationship between alcohol and sexuality. She feels content being a lesbian, and had lived for several, drink-free years, with no problems about her sexuality. Another part of her wonders, and wonders, . . . *why* had her marriage split up? She really cannot remember. W*as* it all those wonderful relationships with 'bisexual' women and 'political lesbians' who'd abandoned their men? (Though some went back to them.)

The counsellor watches her, recognizing the struggle between the addict and the independent, mature, and obviously caring parent and daughter. She decides to take a positive approach.

'When did you join AA?' she asks.

'I came here, for counselling, soon after I moved here. Then I joined AA, but I kept on drinking for, I don't know, a year or so, I was very lonely. It was for the girls really – they were big enough to start asking difficult questions, and we never had any money. I realized getting stoned wasn't the answer. The good times were over. This was reality. It was really bleak. I sat on a hill looking down at the river. It looked very peaceful, I wanted to float off. Then I heard some children's voices. I panicked. I'd left my two girls on their own in the house. I ran back. They were trying to make some food. They gave me such looks . . . I can't tell you . . . they both had such *old* faces. I'd lost my little girls. That did it, really.'

The counsellor waits to see if Bella will make any connection between the 'lost little girls' and the fact that these girls are now young women, apparently sexually aware young women, and by the sound of it, going through the normal stage of asserting their sexual independence – perhaps with a little extra edge, since their grandmother is now living with them. But Bella has stated that she had 'prepared herself' for this.

Something clicks in the counsellor's mind. She asks 'Just the two girls? Do you have another daughter?'

Bella looks surprised. 'No. Why?'

'You mentioned another name just now.'

'Did I?' Bella says, knowing perfectly well that she did. 'No. Just a mistake – they've always got friends in and out of the house.' She feels uncomfortable with this lie.

'You said you had an affair, just before your mother had a stroke?' Bella realizes that the counsellor thinks 'Nancy' is the person she had the affair with. *Now* what should she say? This is ridiculous, she thinks. What's the matter with me? Why can't I tell her the truth?

'No, that's not right.'

'You *didn't* have an affair?'

'Oh, yes, I did. Yes. It was an experiment really. No, that's not right. It was great. I was in love. It was wild. Flying along on the back of a motorbike. It wouldn't have lasted. Funny, though . . . ' she is struck by a realization.

'Yes?' the counsellor prompts.

'This is really strange. My heart's banging away here. What was so exciting about it . . . well, it was exactly like drinking. Does that make sense?'

'Very much so', the counsellor responds. 'Do you mean it was addictive?'

'Yes, that's it', Bella says, relieved. 'I was completely out of my head.

Stoned. At my age ... you know ... someone so young, good-looking, a great dancer, unemployed and not bothering to find work, just hanging out, screwing around ... '

'Drinking?'

'Oh, yes', Bella says grimly. 'Drinking all right. Just like I did. It was a bit sick, when you think about it. I mean, I was sick, not ... just me. There I was, hooked on someone who was boozing their life away and didn't seem to care. I sort of admired ... ' She stops, trying to work out how to explain without saying that her lover was a woman.

'The drinking? The hanging out?'

'All that', Bella answers. 'All that. I felt ... I felt ... '

'Sort of pulled back in?'

'Not really.' Bella tries to sort this out. '*Clean*', she says after a while. 'It was ... I wasn't really there, I was "researching my book". I wasn't really doing this. In the day, life was completely ordinary. I wasn't in love at all. Everything changed – in the house I mean. But I didn't miss ... It was only when we actually *met*. Everyone thought I was having a mid-life crisis. Is this making any sense?'

The counsellor nods. 'Most of it. So when your mother had the stroke, your relationship ended, and you started to drink again. And everything changed in the house.'

Bella looks at her. 'I'm dying for a drink', she mutters.

'Do you know why?'

Bella becomes distressed and shaky. She looks around the room, taking big gulps of air. She sniffs, now a little weepy. She moves around in the chair, clenching and unclenching her fists.

The counsellor says 'Get up and move around, if you want to. Open the window if you like. It's OK. Just go with it.'

Bella gets up and walks around the room, looking at everything – the walls, the pot plants, the carpet, her own chair, the door.

After a while, and when Bella appears to be calmer, the counsellor asks 'Do you know what you're looking for?'

Bella frowns, still wandering about the room, no longer looking any-where. 'Something ... something ... This is sh – sorry, this is hell.'

'Go on, it's shit.'

'OK. Shit. But not *good* shit. I wouldn't mind a hit, actually. No, what am I saying, of course I don't. But I *do* want a drink.'

'Is that what you're looking for?'

Bella stands still. She turns slowly, and comes back to her chair. As she sits down, she says: 'Maybe I *was* looking for a drink. But no. It was something else ... '

'Something you've lost. Whatever it was, it's obviously causing you a lot of anxiety.'

Bella nods, very shaken now. She looks worried, as if she's grappling with a huge problem. She clenches her fists and begins to pound her thighs, over and over. 'Lost. What have I lost? Lost is it. That feels right. But what?'

Noticing what she is doing, she stops, then glances around for something else to do with her hands. 'Maybe I should write a list. That used to work for me, after AA meetings. I'd write lists of what I wanted. You know, like the steps?'

The counsellor gives her some paper and a marker pen. Bella stares at it, unable to think of anything to put on her list. She writes 'Lost' at the top, and stares again, hopefully, forgetting she meant to write 'List'.

'It's blank', she says.

'Well – do anything. Put Number 1.' Bella does this. Then she draws a circle round it. Then she stares at it again. Then she draws another circle beside it, linked to it, and adds small crosses under each of them. That makes her feel better. To herself, she says: 'Well, I haven't lost this. I'm still a lesbian, at least. Am I, though? Of course I am. I think.' She sighs. She drops the pen, and it makes a mark in the middle of the piece of paper. Feeling self-conscious, she draws a dotted line between the figure "1" and the mark. Then she puts a circle around the mark. Thinking she had better try and do *something* constructive, she draws another circle and more dots.

She likes the look of the lesbian symbol, so she draws another one. This time the circles don't touch each other. More dotted lines. She thinks: 'I'm not completely a lesbian today. I'm drifting away from myself, a bit.' She holds the piece of paper away from her and looks at it hard, wondering if it means anything. She looks at the counsellor, despairingly.

'This isn't getting me anywhere.'

'What did you draw?' the counsellor asks.

'Draw? I thought I was supposed to be doing a list.'

'Maybe it is a list', the counsellor says, because she can't think of anything else to say, and doesn't like to ask Bella if she wants to show the drawing. Bella looks at her. List? She sighs again.

'You're a writer, you told me', the counsellor says, thinking that Bella might need a reminder that she is capable of creativity.

Bella smiles, 'I'm in a women's writing group. That doesn't make me a writer.'

'Everyone's a writer. Everyone's got a story to tell. It's just getting it out, getting it down on paper, that's the problem. Would it be easier for you to do that list in the group?'

Bella says 'I don't know. I never wrote things when I was in AA. Usually we listen – in the writing group I mean – we listen to each other's work, sometimes it's a poem or a beginning of a poem, sometimes it's just a few lines, or something copied out that one of the women liked. Nobody's written an actual story yet. I think maybe a novel was a bit ambitious. Obviously I can't string two words together, let alone tell a story. I can't even tell my own story today. I don't know what's wrong with me.'

'Well', the counsellor said, 'You don't know me at all. Groups are different. Maybe you don't want to tell me your story. Maybe you have your story on that piece of paper. It looked to me like you were "stringing" *something* together.'

'Was I?' Bella looks at the paper.

'Yes', the counsellor says. 'Weren't you doing dotted lines? I can't see it', she adds quickly, 'but I noticed you doing dots.'

Bella looks at the paper for a while. Is it supposed to mean something, she wonders? At least it isn't bottles.

She notices, pleased and relieved, that she doesn't want a drink now. The panic has passed.

'Do you want to tell me what you've drawn?' the counsellor asks, wishing she'd taken that Art Therapy course.

'Women', Bella says suddenly. 'Women. Female signs, you know? The dots connect them up.'

'Well, that makes sense. There's you, your two girls, and now there's your mother – four?'

'No', Bella says, feeling a bit sheepish. 'Actually, there's five, except one hasn't got her cross on the bottom.' She picks up the marker pen to add the cross. The counsellor moves quickly. 'What?' Bella says.

'Wait a second', the counsellor says, 'before you change it. Who is woman number 5? The one without her cross? Is it Mum?'

'I don't know that this is supposed to be us', Bella says doubtfully.

'Who, then?'

Bella thinks for a while, closing her eyes and wondering if it's time to tell the counsellor the truth. She glances at her as if trying to anticipate her reaction. The counsellor smiles. 'It's your piece of paper. One of them must be you. Number 1 maybe?'

'OK', Bella says. 'I'll go with that. Why not? Number 1 is me.' The counsellor waits. Bella looks at all the other circles and marks and dotted lines. This is bloody hopeless, she thinks. I'm obviously the one who's lost her cross. The others are Nancy and ...

'I know what it is', she says, feeling a bit tearful.

What has happened, as Bella quickly realizes, is that she has begun to doubt her own sexuality. Being in a group with heterosexual women and wanting to write a sexy lesbian novel; the tension there used to be between Nancy and Mum (denied by Mum, who probably thought that 'nice Nancy' was a good influence on Bella); Mum's closer attachment to Bella's younger daughter – more obviously a 'little girl' than the assertive, feminist, Esther (not named after her!); and Bella's own efforts to give up her mothering, domestic role and share parenting responsibilities with Nancy.

The message Bella's Mum has been giving her is clear – being an independent, assertive, explicitly sexual and expressive individual is not OK for a mother of growing girls, nor is being openly lesbian and demonstrating her affection for Nancy – now was the time to start setting sexual limits for the girls. Mum's frequent visits had meant that she often witnessed Esther's teatime lectures about feminism and gay liberation.

Bella says nothing of this, and instead explains to the counsellor that passing her driving test would have meant a lot to her: more freedom, less fuss about catching the last bus home and phoning up if she missed it, no need for Mum to collect her and grumble, and most of all (she giggled) 'somewhere to snog'.

She suddenly remembered that her sexual dreams were full of wild adventures, and phallic symbols such as motorbikes. She had also forgotten until now that the driving instructor was 'too tactile for comfort' and that he had let her down, 'chatting me up instead of teaching me to drive properly'. She was looking forward to 'getting out of his clutches'.

'So the bottle, then ... ' The counsellor is beginning to understand.

Bella smiles. 'A phallic symbol? I wonder. It was more like giving his sexuality back to him – drowning it out, you know, too much booze and he wouldn't ... ' She stops.

After a pause, the counsellor says: 'But *you* drank it.'

'Yes', Bella says, looking stunned. 'I drank it. Drowning out my *own* sexuality?'

'And just now, you were desperate for a drink? But the drawing helped.'

Bella nods vigorously, and looks at it again. 'So that's what it is. A list of my *own* sexuality. Oh.'

'Yes?'

Bella looks at the counsellor. 'I wrote "lost" on it.'

'Well', the counsellor smiles, 'That figures, doesn't it? So the drawing is ...'

'The different aspects of my sexuality', Bella says quickly. 'Look. Mother, daughter, carer – not sexual, that one – lover, separated, lovers, together. No, that's too many.'

'Can't you have as many as you want?'

'One would do.'

'OK', the counsellor says. 'Which one?'

'Adult', states Bella firmly. 'Adult woman.' She begins to cry.

'What is it?' the counsellor asks.

Bella sniffs. 'I've been really stupid', she says. 'This just about sums me up. I couldn't tell you this. I bet you knew I wasn't telling you something. I'm a lesbian.'

'I see', the counsellor says, surprised. 'Yes, I do understand why you couldn't tell me. Did you know about that before you got married, when you were 17 for example?'

Bella is also surprised, and very pleased at this response.

'I think I did', she says, 'but I did want kids. And all those dreams muddled me up, all those *male* things, you know.'

'Maybe they weren't really about men.'

Bella frowns. 'No? What, then?'

'You told me – all the things you wanted. Independence. Sexual freedom. Power?'

Bella doesn't like the word 'power'. She feels very uncomfortable at the idea of it. 'I've spent my life fighting power', she says, worried.

'Your *own* power? Or the idea of disempowering yourself, or others? What was your alcoholism about?'

Bella remembers the AA group very clearly. 'Step One', she says, 'Alcohol having power over me.'

'Is that why you said before, that you hated yourself? Your power? Or wanting power? And that's why you felt "clean" with your lover?'

Bella begins to cry again. 'It's so confusing', she sobs. 'I don't *want* power – it's exciting, but it's too disruptive. Look at me – I'm taking care of Mum because for once I*'ve* got power over her. It's awful.'

'You're being very hard on yourself', the counsellor says gently. 'This must be very difficult for you, because I believe you really do care about your mother. You can't think of her as sexually disempowering of you.'

Bella felt a jolt throughout her body, and wished the counsellor hadn't said that. 'I feel really bad', she said slowly, 'about the abortion. The girls don't know. Mum knows, but only because my husband – ex-husband – went and told her.' She bites her lip.

The counsellor doesn't know what to say. She is a Christian and opposed to abortion, though not to sex or to birth control – condoms – which, at present, she thinks of as sexual health. She sits there, staring at Bella, and feeling confused and guilty. Bella senses a coldness between them, a sharp contrast to the counsellor's previous expressions of warmth and understanding.

The counsellor struggles for something appropriate to say, and notices that Bella looks at the clock and begins to fold up her drawing. She coughs.

'Bella, do you want to come back next week?'

Bella feels uncomfortable. 'I think . . . Can I let you know? I'm not sure. I want . . . I want . . . '

'Bella, if you want a *drink* . . . ' the counsellor says, feeling alarmed.

'No, no. I mean I do. But no. I think what I want is Nancy.'

'Your . . . lover?'

'Partner. She left when . . . I want her back.'

'I wish you luck with that. I hope it works out for you. You know the door here is always open.'

Bella is flooded with love for Nancy and warmth and gratitude for this woman. 'I didn't mean to sound . . . you've been really helpful. I don't know what I'd have done . . . '

The counsellor holds her hand up. 'Thank you. But could I say just one more thing?' Bella looks anxious.

'Nothing heavy', the counsellor says, hastily. 'Just that, well, you're not responsible for my feelings, or my issues, or for anyone else's, OK? Could I suggest that you get some help with caring for your mother? I know you *feel* responsible for her, but you also said you were afraid of the alcoholism coming back. Maybe you need some space between you?'

Bella gazes at her for a long time, not hearing the counsellor, and feeling alternate cold and warmth shooting through her body. Oh, no, not the menopause on top of everything else, she thinks.

'Good God', she says suddenly. The counsellor tries not to flinch. 'Bloody hell. Yes, I think I *will* come back next week. In fact I think I'll buy my own motorbike. Now that'll stop me boozing, won't it?'

3: Identifying lesbian issues

This example explores reasons why a lesbian might choose to work with another lesbian in therapy, and how similarities and differences can be approached by the practitioner. As with the other casework examples, this is not meant to be representative of a single session. Its purpose is to establish why Katie, the client, has prioritized a lesbian perspective, and how she is enabled by the counsellor to focus on her various conflicts by reconnecting with her own identity as a lesbian woman.

The counsellor feels it is completely normal for a lesbian to want to work with her in preference to a heterosexual practitioner. However, she keeps an open mind and starts by trying to establish Katie's perception of herself and the other lesbians she knows, before exploring why she wants therapy – she might decide she does not want therapy after all. The counsellor takes her lead at all times from what Katie tells her – and what she doesn't say. She knows that Katie's lesbian identity is important, because, as a counsellor, she is hard to find; she does not socialize locally, and is registered as a lesbian with only one service, a lesbian and gay helpline in the next county. She is aware that in this sense she has more power than a heterosexual counsellor would have, if she is the only lesbian practitioner in the district. This means that if things go wrong, Katie's priority gives her far less choice than a heterosexual client would have.

This is a familiar situation for the counsellor, and she has had to learn some psychological and emotional juggling skills to maintain the balance of equality which she feels is essential, to lesbian-affirmative work in particular. She is aware that she needs to be extra sensitive. For example, she has had experiences in which women who have internalized prejudice about themselves as lesbians begin to doubt the counsellor's capabilities.

She values herself as a lesbian and a counsellor, and takes herself very seriously. Life has been difficult for her as a single lesbian mother – both her children are independent adults. Her son recently married, and she is enjoying her freedom. She respects herself for her own achievements in the face of considerable family hostility. She would not do or say anything that is diminishing of herself or her skills, nor collude with negative or prejudicial perceptions of her (from any client or colleague). When she is criticized or, alternatively, assumed to be a 'sister' with someone whose political views she would not support, she is aware of resorting to middle-class detachment behaviour. She has often heard herself being patronizing. This is something she is working on in supervision – without much help. Her supervisor, a heterosexual woman, is more determinedly middle-class than she is.

Her first task is to consider what might contribute to power imbalances between herself and Katie. They are both white women, and there the similarity ends. Katie is younger, at 26 by almost twenty years, and working-class, of Irish and British parents who live in this northern town. The counsellor is from the south. She has experienced some hostility from her new working-class in-laws and is unsure if this is about her lesbian sexuality or her southern, middle-class manner and speech. She has experienced mistrust from working-class lesbians who dislike any form of elitism and 'professional lesbians', and anyone who sets herself up to be a 'wise woman' or 'earth mother'. The counsellor (who doesn't consider herself remotely 'motherly') understands this and can empathize, to a degree, from her experience of being with middle-class heterosexual mothers who feel that she has 'let the side down'.

Even so, she finds herself wondering why Katie doesn't bother about her appearance – she's fat, and is wearing a tight T-shirt and leggings with an outsize man's shirt, and dirty trainers. Her hair is thick and curly and needs a wash. Her face is pale and blotchy. The counsellor wonders if she should ask about eating difficulties – then she stops herself, realizing she is being judgemental. For all she knows, Katie's childhood diet might have been fish and chips. Her complexion suggests that she drinks a lot. The counsellor thinks she may have nowhere else to go except a pub.

One of the clues she picks up about Katie's prioritizing of lesbian issues is that she did not ask about the type of therapy – only if the counsellor was a lesbian. So the first thing she does is to explain the way she works. She hands Katie a pack she gives to all clients – a set of her institute's ethical codes and complaints procedures, a copy of her certificate, and a short explanation of her approach and practice style.

Katie is surprised and thanks her, but does not look at the pack. She has never had therapy before, and gives the impression that she does not really want therapy at all. The counsellor, who has now noticed that Katie wears corrective spectacles, asks if Katie would like anything explained. Katie shakes her head.

> KATIE: I'm not really sure about therapy – I only wanted to talk to another lesbian – someone I'm not going to meet in the pub or anywhere.
>
> COUNSELLOR: OK. Let's just talk. We probably have different ideas about being a lesbian. Do you want to start with that?

KATIE: Different ideas? What do you think – I mean, do you mind if I ask you what –

COUNSELLOR: What being a lesbian means to me?

KATIE: Is that OK? I don't know the rules here.

COUNSELLOR: We should talk about that – it's your rules, and of course it's fine to ask me. The problem is that I came out a long time ago, and the way that I think about myself has changed so much that it's been a part of my life – always changing my ideas of what being a lesbian was, and always expecting to change again. Not so much now – it's other people's ideas about me that are unpredictable. I don't know if that's helpful.

KATIE: (nods) I can relate to that in a way. There's a lot of things changing for me too. I feel a bit bored with my friends – that sounds bad, but, well, that's why I'm here. So I guess it's OK?

COUNSELLOR: It's OK. This is where you say all the things you don't want your friends to know about. That's what you want – to talk to someone you're not going to meet in the pub.

KATIE: (smiling) So what would happen if you went to the pub?

COUNSELLOR: It's up to you. What would you want me to do?

KATIE: I don't think you'd come to this pub.

COUNSELLOR: We'll work that out later. Now, you said on the phone that you'd just finished a relationship. Let's continue that conversation and then you can tell me why you're here.

KATIE: (feeling put down) I forgot. This is therapy. OK. Problems. I have a few problems, but my relationship wasn't one of them. It felt all right to finish it. She's fine about it too.

Katie stops talking, feeling that she was coming across as angry. 'I'm here by choice', she thinks. 'So why don't I just say what's going on?' She tells the counsellor that she's thinking about being a separatist. Lately she has begun to hate men. The men at work are a pain – one older man was giving her a hard time. This was her third lesbian relationship and she now has an ideal partner in mind, though she can't imagine where she might meet this woman.

She feels good about being a lesbian and has a circle of friends, some of them each other's ex-lovers. Now she feels a bit stifled by them, wondering if they just hang out together because there isn't anyone else or anywhere else to go. When they go to the pub, all of them look around to see if anyone new has come in. They know all the local dykes.

Katie says that she would like to do more political work, and then she says she'd like to work in a befriending project for homeless young women – she heard that they were advertising for volunteers and wondered if they had a lesbian worker. 'When I came out, at 17 like that song, there was nobody.' She likes films, music, crafts, and cooking, going on women's demos and Pride marches – but she hasn't made it to London yet. That's for the future.

She also wants to change her job – she works at the Benefits Agency – and a month ago she went to the local college to see the women's careers adviser. She had been thinking about learning aromatherapy, but there were no courses available, and the adviser had other ideas.

The college is now a university, and is developing a gender studies department. Katie, who had a good education, would qualify for a foundation course for a women's studies degree. This is something she would love to do, but the grant is too low.

The counsellor acknowledges this information, then asks Katie what would be important personally about doing this course, if she could.

Katie says that it was just an idea, but part of her 'political plan'. She is worried about her own racism. On a training day at work she realized how differently she related to the Black women – most of them of Caribbean origin – and Asian women – from India and Pakistan. They had never spoken about their feelings until the training day. She felt ashamed of what they said about everyone assuming they were all the same as each other.

She talked to her lesbian friends about it – all of them white – and the conversation moved to oppression and imperialist capitalism, and somehow led to SM. Most of her friends are both intrigued and repelled by it. Politically, they agree, they are definitely opposed to it, but personally, some of them want to understand it. One said she thought SM dykes were probably making it up, 'just being tough like when we were punks. It's the same thing'. Katie agreed, and they all forgot about it and ordered another round of drinks.

She became very quiet, and, eventually, the counsellor asks her what is happening. Katie is more subdued than when she arrived. The counsellor looks at her more intently, and realizes that under her huge cloud of hair she is a nice-looking woman and has a peaceful face. As soon as she notices that, the counsellor sees Katie the woman, instead of an untidy, overweight, and slightly slobby client.

Katie explains that all her friends are in couples, which seems to make political conversations very short. One of the women has always been very interested in her, even when she was with her partner, and is now paying her a lot of attention.

Then Katie says she has bad PMT these days, which she has never had before, and it is making her depressed. She drinks too much beer, more than usual since she has been on her own. 'Just to be social', she explains. 'I feel OK on my own. The woman I want isn't there. But I feel left out of it, and at the same time I feel I can't do without them. I like them all in a way. But – I dunno.'

The counsellor feels that Katie has a clear idea about her interests and what she wants to do in the future. She is self-aware and self-responsible, and able to make use of available resources. What is her problem? Katie suddenly gives a big sigh, and says: 'There is something I want to talk about. It's not about being a lesbian – I don't *think* it is.'

The counsellor asks if she would first like some feedback, as there are several things going on for Katie and the counsellor wants to check that she has understood. Katie is surprised, but she is feeling shaky and glad to have a break.

The counsellor has been thinking about what Katie has said, and sums up in her own mind:

1. Katie would like to be a separatist – she wants to focus her energies on lesbian women only. She has probably reached her limit of heterosexism at work and one of the older men is giving her a 'hard time'. The counsellor wonders if this is anything new, or if it's the first time Katie has experienced this as harassment. Political awareness is one thing. *Feeling* the effects of oppression is another. The racism awareness workshop will have brought up some new issues for Katie, but at present she is aware only of guilt about her own different treatment of the Black women and the Asian women.

2. She has just ended a relationship, apparently by choice. She has also ended a *phase*, and now has an ideal woman in mind. Perhaps she wants a deeper relationship – a real partnership instead of another affair with a friend of a friend, who might also be a friend of a friend's ex-lover. She is feeling closed in by her social life – this is not her idea of lesbian empowerment, and this may be why she wants to do more political work, or support young lesbians, giving them what she didn't have when she first came out.

3. She is also feeling objectified or harassed by one of her friends.

Sexually harassed? Is this putting the group friendships at risk? Is she suddenly feeling alone?

4. She is trying to get information about her future options.

The counsellor decides to feed back the main points of what Katie has told her, trying to focus on the lesbian issues and relating them to what Katie said herself about changes.

That is, she tries to put her own perceptions into Katie's personal framework instead of using political language or concepts. She feels this is correct. Katie is well educated, knowledgeable about lesbian political issues and able to at least raise them with her friends, and she is interested in doing a women's studies degree or learning body therapy. The counsellor wants to know what this really means to Katie, who seems to be good at discovering what is on offer locally – London, she said, was for the future. The counsellor realizes that Katie's work means that this sort of information is readily available, so she tries not to read too much into Katie's research capabilities.

The counsellor assumes that 'PMT' and 'depression' are connected with what Katie has yet to say, and she further assumes that this is about sex or sexuality issues. Why would she mention SM, unless it was to make a point that 'everyone forgot about it' and 'ordered another round of drinks'? The counsellor feels that what Katie most wants to do is *understand*. She also wants to validate Katie's own strengths – if she is worried about sexuality issues, she will need to feel strong in herself to be able to confront them.

> COUNSELLOR: There are several ways of responding to you, Katie. First of all, you are talking to me as another lesbian. So I'll start with lesbian issues. I'm wondering if your interest in working with younger women is because you want to get back in touch with what it meant to you to be a lesbian when you were 17. You've had three relationships, you know what you want, and your lesbian friends are ... well, I get the impression that they are a little less than your perception of the ideal lesbian. You said you were bored, and I'm wondering if you are also feeling disillusioned. After all, you are growing and changing, so your needs are changing too. You want to know more, do something different. You feel 'closed in' on the pub scene – everyone knows everyone.
>
> I think the next thing would be to talk about this man at work, and the woman who is interested in you. You said you feel OK alone, and you're feeling pressurized. How's that so far?

Katie is pleased that the counsellor has been really listening – that's the problem with her friends. They all know each other so well that they have stopped listening to each other. Katie realizes she does this too – she'd forgotten people were always changing. This connects with her guilt about assuming all Black or Asian women would feel the same way about life, and be a single group like her lesbian friends.

KATIE: That sounds about right to me. I don't fancy being 17 again, though – I don't think that's it. That was a bad time.

COUNSELLOR: Do you want to talk about it?

KATIE: No, I'd like to forget it . . . but there's something about it. It's a bit like what's happening now. Do you know what I mean?

COUNSELLOR: What's happening on the outside? Or how you feel about yourself as a lesbian?

Katie thinks about this for a minute or two.

KATIE: Outside. Yeah – definitely. I think I've always been the same as a lesbian. I was OK – I was in *lurve*, I mean in sex. It was my first sexual relationship. I never looked back.

COUNSELLOR: Is she still around?

KATIE: (*frowning*) No. Her parents, my Dad – he's a real bastard – they split us up. She went to college, university I mean. I don't know how she is. I took off. I lived in a hostel. I got a job.

COUNSELLOR: University where?

KATIE: (*after a pause*) London.

They look at each other in silence.

COUNSELLOR: Your father – are you still in touch with him?

After a long time, Katie, looking very upset, and trying not to cry, blurts it out.

KATIE: I think he might have abused me.

COUNSELLOR: Oh, Katie. It must be really painful to have to think about that.

KATIE: (*pulling herself together*) Painful? No. I hate him. It makes sense to me. He's always drunk. He'll drop dead one of these days. The sooner the better.

COUNSELLOR: How much can you remember ... I mean, what do you remember? You said 'I *think* he might have abused me'. You must have a good reason for thinking that.

KATIE: Just ideas. This man at work I told you about, he's nothing like my father, he's really nice usually. But when he comes on to me, I feel really disgusted, and that's how I felt around my Dad all the time.

COUNSELLOR: So thinking about this as abuse ... helps you feel right about hating your Dad?

KATIE: That's right. It *is* abuse, when men do that.

COUNSELLOR: Do what?

KATIE: Oh, you know, touch you, and put their arm round your shoulders and pretend they're leaning on the chair. And when you go out for anything they're always just passing, and they get you in the corridor and breathe all over you. He does it to all the young women there. He says I'm cuddly, chunky, all that crap.

COUNSELLOR: Does anyone complain?

KATIE: We all do. That's why he's giving us a bad time. He won't talk to us now. He gives me all the hard cases. It's OK, I know what to do next. He reminded me. Dad did that, too. He'd ignore me, then he'd think of something really nasty.

COUNSELLOR: Tell me.

KATIE: Real dirty tricks, messing things up for me, problems with Mum, money, stuff for school ...

COUNSELLOR: What did *you* do?

KATIE: I was good at school. That was my best thing. He knew that, so he tried to screw it up for me. One of the teachers was really nice. That helped. I locked myself in my room and did my homework, and listened to tapes and stuff. I got an old telly from my aunty, so I got into stuff they weren't doing at school. I never watched rubbish – he was doing that downstairs. Drinking.

COUNSELLOR: Was reading difficult for you? I mean, how is your eyesight?

KATIE: (*surprised*) Em. Yes. It was. National Health glasses weren't that good when I was a kid. I knew how to read through. I bought these myself, they're good, they cost a lot. I had to, so that I could get a better job.

COUNSELLOR: You're very resourceful.

KATIE: We all are, at home. Have to take care of myself.

COUNSELLOR: How did you take care of yourself as a child?

KATIE: Stuffed my face. I was in a gang when I was about 14. I was all right.

COUNSELLOR: Except you think your father might have abused you.

KATIE: Yeah. That's the problem.

COUNSELLOR: Go on.

KATIE: Well – you know. I said, I've always felt the same, as a lesbian, I mean. Well, everyone I know feels like I do about their fathers. We were talking about that too, that night when we were ...

COUNSELLOR: Talking about SM? and oppression?

KATIE: That's right. Someone said SM was because of sexual abuse. Someone else said 'We're all screwed up, if you put it like that'. *That's* when someone said 'Let's forget this, it's too heavy', and we all had another drink.

COUNSELLOR: But *you* didn't forget about it. You came here.

KATIE: Look – I know it's nothing to do with it. But SM – what I mean is, my father, he was really abusive in a lot of ways, he was violent too, to Mum and us. She doesn't mind him drinking now, he just goes to sleep, and he doesn't do it now 'cos he knows we'd all have him.

COUNSELLOR: (*thinking hard about where to go from here*) I get the impression that what you want to do is be on your own, find out what choices you have, be yourself; not be part of a family, or a gang or a group, or even part of a couple. This man at work, this woman you know; remembering how abusive your father was ... It all sounds very *invasive* to me – as if no one will leave you in peace to work things out for yourself. Just to be a lesbian, your own kind of lesbian *and* a woman. This thing of everyone having to cope, all in it together – home, your friends – sounds like the same thing to me. I get the feeling you're really ready to move on from all that.

Katie nods, over and over, looking a bit stunned.

KATIE: That's right, that's right. It's all connected. I do want to go. I'm not sure where or how or what I'd do, but ...

COUNSELLOR: It's a lot to lose?

KATIE: It's a lot to lose, yeah.

COUNSELLOR: Have you *ever* been on your own?

KATIE: Well, no. Never. Except ... when I was in my room, with my tapes and the telly, finding out about everything. I wanted to be in it. So where am I? Signing people on. There's nothing for them, not the kids. I've got to find something else.

COUNSELLOR: But your family?

KATIE: Yeah. That'd be difficult, being away from them. The kids too – one of my sister's got two little boys, my older brother's got three, two girls and a boy. There's more on the way.

COUNSELLOR: Are you the youngest?

KATIE: No – my sister's the youngest. It's really hard for her. She's depressed too. I remember when she came home from school, about a year ago, I was round there. She'd had her first sex education lesson – I mean, at 16, a bit late.

COUNSELLOR: And it was all about AIDS and condoms?

KATIE: That's right. It's hard, isn't it?

COUNSELLOR: It is. It's terrible. So, she's 17?

KATIE: (grinning) All right, all right, I get it. Typical therapy.

COUNSELLOR: It was you that said everything was connected.

KATIE: I did. I don't know how. What were we talking about?

COUNSELLOR: Quite a lot. You. Your sexual identity. Your need for independence. Thinking that your father might have abused you sexually as well as in every other way he could. Hating him. Being a lesbian, being your own woman.

KATIE: Woman?

COUNSELLOR: (puzzled) Yes, woman, of course ... What is it?

Katie goes very quiet, blinking and looking around the room. She moves her head from side to side slowly, as if she's looking around inside her mind.

KATIE: This is really funny. Really funny. Can I say ... it'll sound really strange ... but I never thought of myself before as a woman. I mean I do, I'm into women's politics, all that. But I've always been just Katie, just a kid. Then I was a lesbian, when I was 17 – that's what, ten years. Everyone round me has always been the same as me, sort of. Family, we're all a unit – the gang. That was great. These dykes I know, I've known them for years ... about five years I think ...

COUNSELLOR: So, because nobody has ever treated you as a woman, an independent adult woman ... your father ...

KATIE: That's right. I was just a brat. The Blob. I was always fat. So's he, he's a real slob too. No, no one's every treated me like a woman ... I get it. That's what's wrong with everyone.

COUNSELLOR: (lost) What's wrong with who?

KATIE: Us, me. My friends. We're all like a bunch of 15-year-olds. Like we're not really allowed to have sex, so we all go down the pub and booze up and smoke and ...

COUNSELLOR: Have sex a lot.

KATIE: Yeah. Something wrong with you if you're not having it.

COUNSELLOR: And you don't want it any more.

KATIE: No. None of it. Them. Sex. All that 'we're gonna change the world' stuff. What are we doing about it? Nothing.

COUNSELLOR: So do it.

KATIE: What? Do what?

COUNSELLOR: Change *your* world, for a start. You obviously want to. You've said it several times. Move on, go, get a new job, learn something new, be on your own. What would you do if you met this ideal woman, how would you and she change the world?

KATIE: That's my dream (*she closes her eyes and thinks, a smile on her face*). She's a strong woman. She doesn't take any crap from anybody. She knows a lot. She wants to help people. She's smart. She's got a lot of energy. She's a super-dyke. GSOH. About 30 – a mature woman. She gets things done. We'd do things together. I don't know what things. I don't know what there is we *can* do. We're only dykes. Who's gonna listen to us?

COUNSELLOR: Super-dyke and you can do a lot of things with all that energy. So, what does she look like?

KATIE: What does she *look* like? What's that got to do with it?

COUNSELLOR: You never imagine what your Dream Dyke looks like?

KATIE: No. I don't. I don't go much on looks. What does a super-dyke look like, then? (*She peers at the counsellor. Is she one?*)

COUNSELLOR: (*laughing*) Don't look at me – I'm the wrong generation. You've got to make your own life, fight along with women about the same issues. Make other people realize what they are doing. Don't you really know what your ideal woman looks like?

KATIE: Go on. Tell me.

COUNSELLOR: Well, first of all, from the inside, she is strong enough as a woman to face up to her father, who he really is, what he's really like, tell him, if she thinks she should, so that she can *leave* him. He's dominated her life for long enough.

KATIE: (*looking a little pale*) Right, right. Go on.

COUNSELLOR: Otherwise – well, I think she looks a lot like you.

4. Equal opportunities
... or multiple tokenism?

Racism is as old as history. It is from Black lesbian writings of recent years that we have learned so much about sources of, and the nature of prejudice, to whom it is directed and why, how and why stereotypes are created and their purposes, and, most important, the recognition of the interlinked chains which keep differently targeted oppressive systems together.

There have been Black people in the British Isles for over 500 years, and there have always been Black lesbians everywhere, whether or not they defined themselves by this European term, or as separate from their own communities. They have been active in every human rights campaign, yet the first collective statement of their history and experiences was published only in 1993 (Mason-John and Khambatta). This work, and earlier writings in women's or lesbian publications, reveals that for British Black lesbians, real liberation and equality remains an ideal.

The Black civil rights campaigns preceded postwar feminism by several years. But in the British women's and gay liberation movements of the 1970s, legal rights and freedom of sexual expression were prioritized over race equality. Racism was not a 'feminist issue' in the 1970s; so Black lesbians have been organizing, networking, demonstrating and challenging stereotypes for over twenty years, with little support, and considerable hostility from groups with different interests or needs. Lesbian issues were low on everyone's priority lists.

One of the Black lesbians talking in *Making Black Waves* states: 'Black women ... had a really tough time. I remember going to a women's meeting in 1978 and suggesting that we could create some international links, and the women laughed, they laughed at me' (Mason-John and Khambatta, 1993:11).

Black lesbian women, a minority within several other minorities, were required to 'break their identities into acceptable fragments'. They brought racism awareness to white, middle-class feminism, and lesbian groups. They brought women's issues into Black rights and anti-racist and anti-fascist groups. With Black gay men, they brought lesbian and gay rights into Black communities, dealing with the complex social issues and political oppressions in all these arenas. They worked to make rights groups accept the connections between the different forms of social marginalization.

A new anthology of essays on social and cultural issues, including mental health, was published in 1995 (Mason-John), and the lesbian perspective is slowly being included in writings on Black women's health (Wilson, 1993), or reports of reoppression within the psychiatric system. Montsho (1995) exposes the racism, heterosexism and ready prescriptions of mood-altering drugs in the NHS psychiatric system.

Many of these gains were lost in the closure of lesbian and gay units following the implementation of Clause 28, and at the time of writing there is only one funded Black Lesbian and Gay organization (in London), and its funding was reduced at the beginning of 1994. National groups are either privately organized or use space in majority white lesbian, gay or women's centres (see Mason-John and Khambatta, 1993). Some Black women's centres, transcultural counselling projects, and lesbian and gay centres which offer formal counselling, are addressing Black lesbians' issues (at least in London), but it is difficult to find counselling or therapy resources which are sensitive to Black lesbians' needs – in particular, the fact that 'counselling' is a white European concept and was structured with no awareness of Black women's traditions (including spiritual traditions) and their heritage of self-organization.

Definitions of 'Black' are individual and vary according to country of descent, race and ethnic origin of parent(s) and, often, by external definitions. Where racism is endemic, and where everyone who isn't pure white is treated differently, identifying as Black is a political statement. 'Black' can include descent from African, Asian (from the Middle East through to China and the Pacific/Melanesian) nations, Latin America, and Atlantic and Indian Ocean islands (Mason-John and Khambatta, 1993:9).

Through centuries of colonialism, the assumption and enforcement of white superiority created racisms within racisms. These complicated the existing cultural or religious differentiations and resulted in (purposeful) stratified divisiveness, internalized and still in evidence now. As one Black lesbian wrote, 'suspicion and distrust of each other has created these tiny factions . . . jealousies, insecurities and paranoia, *all the things that are results of being oppressed*' (my italics; Mason-John in Mason-John and Khambatta, 1993:53). The visible evidence of racial class and status under colonialism was, of course, skin colour; another issue among women is the multiracial and multi-ethnicity of being Black.

As an Asian-British lesbian contributor explained: 'At home, I was called "chi-chi" or "half-caste". Here, I spent my schooldays passing for white and my young adulthood passing for straight – we're a very religious community. That's what internalized racism is about – the "bad" bit must stay out of sight, but white people see it … it's about visibility – no one can "see" that I'm a lesbian, either.'

When is a stigma not a stigma?

Donna, an African-British lesbian in her mid-thirties, works in a project which provides short-term accommodation for people who are HIV-positive. There is an associated supportive long-term project for people with AIDS-related illnesses. Donna is one of three paid workers, and there are five volunteer staff. She is the only Black worker, the only woman, and the only lesbian in her office. All the staff, except one, are gay men.

This reflects the profile of the present service users, which was one of the reasons that Donna was appointed (although she is not HIV-positive) to network with health organizations, Black groups and women's groups. Donna wanted the job because the pay was good, and she supports the aims of the project. The job makes her feel 'worth something'.

Her previous job was administrative work in the local authority information department. She has four years' experience as a volunteer in different community groups, including lesbian, gay and ex-drug users' support projects. Two of her friends are HIV-positive.

Problems emerged at work when Donna raised the issue of the way that residents were moved to the long-stay project. She felt that a 'goodbye' ritual to acknowledge the significance of this transfer would be more respectful than the present 'checking-out' system. The gay men felt that any ritual should be a 'welcome' at the sister project, where there already was a sensitive resettlement schedule. The transitory nature of the accommodation offered – shared rooms and a hostel system – meant that people often left as soon as they could find a better place to live.

Donna pointed out that the options should at least be available, especially if they were changing the user profile to include people who might have different needs from those of white gay men, and possibly less strong community support. Sex workers, she pointed out, had no community at all. One man said that AIDS crossed all boundaries and made other considerations secondary.

'Why am I here then?' Donna asked, angrily. One of the more sensitive men, Harold, said: 'Because we acknowledge that AIDS isn't solely a white gay men's disease – it hasn't been for years. People who stay here can be put in touch with lots of other organizations. I feel my role is as a communications worker, sort of channelling people through. And I think that's the nature of your job, too, Donna – only you bring them in.'

'Sounds like a sort of battery system', she said, annoyed, 'Chickens in, eggs out.' There was total silence. Then one of the men gave an explosive laugh and quickly clapped his hand over his mouth. The others looked either embarrassed or angry. The non-gay man looked around, puzzled, and then stared at Donna.

'What did I say?' she asked.

'Oh, come on, Donna', said George, an older gay man, and the one she liked the least. '*Chickens*? Gimme a break, you're not that green. Oops, sorry, no offence meant.'

Harold said 'I think that's enough. Donna, didn't you know that ... ?' Donna nodded, realizing what she'd said.

'Sorry, I didn't mean any offence either', George added. 'I think you should give her lessons on the old Polari, Hal, or we are going to have one *serious* communications breakdown.'

Donna said: 'I think that should be two-way, George. I'm not green, I'm Black, I'm a lesbian, and I've never been to London, so you can't expect me to know all your backslang or whatever it is. I'm here to work with women and Black people of all sexualities, so I don't want to have to spend more time learning about gay men's culture. I think I know enough to watch my mouth if I'm working with gay clients. OK? It just slipped out. Oh no, I suppose that was the wrong thing to say, too. Can we go on with the meeting?'

A quiet, but peeved, voice at the other end of the table said 'I thought I was the Chair today'. After that a clear divide appeared in the project.

Half of the men were cool towards her. Sometimes she heard them chatting to each other about their nightlife, and found a lot of what they said offensive. She tried to be non-judgemental, but felt she should pay attention, in case it was deliberate. The others, including, surprisingly, George, were, as she told her counsellor, 'Excruciatingly nice, and completely patronizing'.

Donna's supervisor, a white lesbian who worked at the long-stay project, had asked if she wanted more support. Donna, who was about to ask that herself, agreed. The supervisor said: 'Everyone who works here is entitled to six counselling sessions if they encounter a really difficult client or feel under stress or demoralized. It's in your contract.'

'Great. Thank you', said Donna, who already knew that. She could not find a Black lesbian counsellor in the district. Having had more than one response on the lines of 'A *Black* lesbian? *Counsellor?* Is that what you said?', she made an appointment with a white, younger lesbian woman, who was herself HIV-positive and working at a substance abuse project, counselling addicts and recruiting workers for 'street' services.

When Donna arrived she said: 'Welcome, Donna. Please sit down. First of all, would you like some tea or something? And then we can spend five minutes while I apologize for not being Black and you tell me how you feel about us working together.'

Donna, a bit startled, said: 'Er, yes, tea, thank you. I have to say, this may be new for you but it's nothing new for me. So I guess I'll cope. I mean you're a dyke, that's the main thing.' The counsellor swallowed hard, made the tea, and said something like ' ... open my mouth and put my foot in it'.

'It's OK', Donna said. 'Really it is.'

The counsellor smiled. 'Thanks. I'm a bit blunt. I'm working with people who have no boundaries at all, and they are usually chaotic and out of it. So I state my boundaries from the first minute.'

'Please don't change anything for me', Donna said.

'I expect you just want me to listen?'

Donna said: 'No ... I really need another woman in my field.'

'So, is it a work problem?'

'No, I mean as a lesbian. Work is good, and I'm busying myself and justifying my existence, or should I say my wages. The problem is the men, the gay men. They're all white, and some of it's getting a bit silly, but that's OK – I mean, I have to accept that they are probably dying or believe that they are. I'm not HIV-positive by the way, though I thought I must be ... well, no big deal for you, I suppose, I shared works – needles, spoons, everything. Years ago. I'm really very lucky.'

The counsellor nodded. 'Did you go first?'

Donna thought about this. 'Well, yes, come to think of it, I did. It was always me sharing *my* works, all my stuff, too, clothes as well. It got expensive. So it was either dealing or ... and I thought, enough.'

'Good. Anyway, you said you didn't want drug counselling. So how can I help? Are you comfortable here?'

Donna nodded. 'It's fine. A little noisy.'

'No one will be able to hear you, then. And the notice on the door is respected.' The counsellor waited.

Donna explained what had been happening at the project since that difficult meeting, and how her outreach work so far – over six months, now

– hadn't brought in any new applicants from the communities she worked with.

The project manager had told her that was the way it went – no one at all, then a flood. 'We should be glad, in one way, if nobody comes and we have empty beds. It might mean that there are plenty of services, or that people's families are taking care of them, or they haven't heard of us. Well, keep pushing the boat out. I was thinking maybe women don't want to come into a project which is practically all gay men. How do you feel about some preparation for the big day?'

Donna asked what he meant. He explained: 'I mean, we have to confront all these issues, or we won't be able to relate to the service users when they do arrive. Which they will. I thought maybe some awareness sessions – I was thinking of race equality and maybe a women's issues day.'

Donna said that she could facilitate a race equality session, with the help of a male Black worker from the sister project. She asked her lesbian supervisor to help with the women's issues day, but the supervisor thought this was inappropriate. She was interested in holding a workshop, but felt that if they facilitated this together it would interfere with their supervision relationship, and her position as supervisor for the two other paid workers.

The race equality day went ahead, and, as Donna told the counsellor, 'Everyone behaved immaculately, but I got a bit fed up with their self-forgiveness routine. Like, they were all brought up here, and they never socialized with Black people, and this was what they had learned, along with homophobia.

'I couldn't get them to accept this was part of the same system. The women's issues day never happened, so I got a pile of leaflets and passed them around. But the dynamics changed. At least they were able to raise the subject, but silly old George – I mean this *is* generational – said he couldn't understand why I was getting my knickers in a twist about sexual harassment in a *gay* centre. "Frankly, my dear ... " (he always talks like a 1940s movie star) "no one here would have the balls." I didn't answer.'

The counsellor said: 'I need to ask this. I'm wondering why they haven't gone through all this before. They are support workers for people with AIDS? Didn't basic equal opps training cover all this?'

Donna said: 'They are housing workers, really. Their training was good, yes, but the focus was on health issues, bereavement, managing change, and living with stigma – all the essential things. I can't criticize them for focusing on their own needs in that way. It's just that I'm sick of being Blackwoman/Spokeswoman. I have to *work* there, I'm not like a trainer who can come in and go out. We all agreed not to take group material out of the room that day. But what they said is now in my head. It does affect the way we all relate to each other now. Maybe it was a bad idea.'

'What's bad about it?'

'I can't trust them. It's made me more different than I am already. I know they are trying hard, but it's so patronizing, sort of making a point of *not* being racist or sexist – and they're hopeless at that, though not as bad as George – and they keep *asking* me things. It's a farce.'

'What are your feelings about all this?'

Donna sighed. 'You mean why do I want counselling? Like I said, to have a lesbian woman in my field – not a supervisor who goes on about boundaries. She's right, I suppose, but my feeling is, who cares? Let the men know that women – lesbians – support each other and can rework the boundaries if necessary. I have lost some respect for her now, like she doesn't want to push it? She's in a good position and maybe that's as far as she wants to go, not to make too many waves.'

'She has to be impartial?' the counsellor asked.

Donna nodded. 'But I'm talking about work again. For me, it's already hard to be a Black lesbian around here, In the past I've had some of that "exotic" shit dumped on me. I had a stand-up row with a white leather dyke in a bar. Everyone listened, including all the straight people downstairs, choking on their beer, probably.

'The manager said to keep it down, or that bar was *shut*, as of now. I shut it. I mean I shut up.'

'It's an upstairs bar?' The counsellor named the pub.

'Yes', Donna said. 'All the lesbians I know are able-bodied. There's not many other places. Where do you go?'

'I don't have much time to go anywhere, but, for the record, my partner and I and our friends usually go into the city. I like to keep work and play completely separate.'

Donna nodded. Then she said: 'Everyone at work is – I don't know – sort of *careful* with me, some because they are scared I'll call them racist or sexist, which they are, or because they don't want to offend me. They make a point of asking me questions, or telling me what they've read in the paper, or things that come through the door.'

'Not good?'

'No', Donna said. 'I get the same information. I can read, I had a good education. My job is outreach, right? So I have to know what's there to reach out to and why. I do that every day. Either way, it cancels me out. I'm the big bad wolf, or wise Black Mama, or a fragile victim, or stupid and uninformed and incapable of reading my own mail. You know, ESN?'

'That is really disempowering, like you're having to deal with all their issues. I'm sorry to have to ask, but what's ESN?'

'Oh. Uh, well, my grandmother told me that in the 1950s when there was a lot of immigration from Commonwealth countries, all the black children were put into ESN schools, without even being tested. Black equals Educationally Sub-Normal.'

The counsellor was silent for a moment, blinking with embarrassment. 'I'm ... I'm sorry', she muttered. 'I had no idea.'

'How could you know? I want to say – about the men at work – they are not all bad news. Hal's OK, I think, and actually the straight guy is fine. Everyone is really nice to him, they all tease him and pretend to flirt with him. He swears he's never been to the park or the local toilets – that's something that *really* gets to me, cottaging and cruising for young boys – and they give him packets of condoms at the weekends to "distribute round the local lads". He's very good-natured about it, a nice man. He's got no idea how he got ze virus.'

'Ze Virus?'

'Sorry', Donna said. 'George again. It's infectious – oh, shit. I keep doing that. It's a song from a show he saw in London. The lead singer's a transvestite, or maybe transsexual, I can't remember. They did a Piaf-type song about "Ze Virus". All in the best possible taste, of course.'

'Of course', the counsellor said. 'Donna, I picked up something like envy just then. Would you feel better if they were easy with you, like they are with this heterosexual man? All this chat . . . do they ever ask you anything, you know, *personal*?'

'Thank you. Thank you. That's exactly it. I'm sure they've got hearts of gold and they are good with the residents, but I'm not a *person*. I think, what am I doing wrong? I always got on OK with people at the council. You had to.'

'Ah', the counsellor said. 'So that's why you're here. "What am I doing wrong? It must be me." Yes?'

Donna gave a big sigh. 'Yes. Maybe I shouldn't have done the race equality workshop.'

The counsellor said: 'It wasn't your idea, you told me. Can you remember why you agreed to do it?' Donna thought about this for a while. It felt like some kind of validation of her. The reason she was offered the post (or she was told) was because of her voluntary experience, including training other volunteers, and her information work and local contacts. 'It is since that day that things have got strange', she said. 'But they might have been strange anyway.'

'Did you experience this kind of thing at the other places you worked? People avoiding you like that?'

Donna remembered it very well. 'I blanked it out. Before I knew I was a lesbian – that's about eight years ago – I didn't want to think about anything much. Racism, of course, but you might know – do you? – at that time, everyone was bending over backwards to be nice to Black people. It was an asset. Jobs, grants for arts projects . . . a good time.'

'What did you get out of it?'

'Nothing', Donna said. 'I didn't go for any of it. Well, I did. A computer training course, but I would have gone for that anyway. It wasn't just for Black women. Typing, at the council, wasn't exactly my scene either! Anyway, then I came out. And so life began, and here I am.'

Donna observed herself closely during the next week. She was in a constant state of tension, and felt irritated a lot and occasionally angry for no particular reason. She was aware of talking non-stop – giving the men information before they could assume she didn't have it. She felt depressed and tired.

In the next session, she told the counsellor that sometimes she felt she had enormous power. She could cry 'Racist!' and control the whole room if she wanted to. No one would dare to disagree, but she felt completely disempowered as a woman, and invisible as a lesbian. She was included in 'lesbian and gay' conversations, and sometimes the men forgot to say 'lesbian' or tacked it on after 'gay', which made her very angry.

She also felt that she was being unreasonable, as some of them were obviously trying to make her feel at home, and usually the atmosphere was friendly and supportive. They all shared concerns about AIDS issues, and no one had mentioned her HIV-negative status. It was possible that the management committee members who interviewed her hadn't mentioned it to the project co-ordinator. On the other hand, perhaps they had, and Donna wondered if this was behind some of the resentment she occasionally picked up, especially if a resident had to move on, or someone they knew was hospitalized or died. She decided she was being 'paranoid'.

The counsellor suggested that before Donna gave herself any more negative labels, she could define her personal assets. She explained that, in her view, the work people did was more about channelling talents than being 'well educated'. Donna named, among her capabilities, getting and passing on information, long experience of resolving personal difficulties, computer and administrative skills, and sensitivity to prejudicial attitudes or behaviour.

She said that what was making her depressed and anxious was being the subject of so much attention, but feeling like an 'object' instead of a person. It wasn't the type of attention that she wanted. There was no acknowledgement of her individual needs or her emotional issues around AIDS, being excluded from the friendship and support of the men, and being a worker with a new remit, in an area where she was solely responsible and wrongly assumed to be the expert.

The counsellor asked Donna to define what she would like to do to change these complicated power dynamics. 'Just to be allowed to do my job, be trusted to do it right, and capable of learning, and to be treated like a whole person, to be myself', she answered immediately.

'How might that happen?' the counsellor asked.

Donna went over what she had just said about herself. She couldn't see that she had any options. She still wanted to focus on what she was doing 'wrong'. 'I'm not perfect', she said. 'Why shouldn't I be paranoid if I want to be?'

The counsellor laughed. 'OK. Be as paranoid as you want, but can I suggest you look at what *they* are doing wrong, too?'

Donna said: 'They are dodging around me, doing their thing their way and not trying to come to where I am. So really they are distancing themselves from me and making their own group more solid. Some of them try to wind me up. Some of them are at least now aware of the issues and trying to learn. But they want *me* to teach them. I'm no expert. I want to be a part of the project.'

The counsellor said: 'You want to be part of a community?'

'That's right', Donna said, feeling very upset and lost. 'So many deaths . . . I want to support gay men, but also share our experiences, learn from each other. We *must* do this.'

'OK. I want to sum up here', the counsellor said. 'I've heard words like "learning" and "teaching" and "sharing" and "giving information" quite a lot, and wanting your own space with people you can choose to be in it. I've heard that they want to work with you, but they don't seem to know how. You are one woman in, what, eight or nine men? To them you represent three minority groups. So where does that leave you?'

Donna tried to visualize her position in relation to the men, but she couldn't get a clear picture. She was on her own, and that didn't feel too bad.

'What have you been doing here, today?' the counsellor asked, breaking the silence.

Donna shook herself into the present. Was it time to stop?

'Talking?' she said, facetiously.

'And so ... ' the counsellor prompted.

Donna appeared to be looking inside herself. 'OK', she said, eventually. 'That's what I need to do? Talk?'

'Talk you can do. It's about making them listen.'

'I don't have the authority', Donna said.

'You have the *law*', said the counsellor.

'Oh, yes. So *that's* what I have to teach them.'

'Teach? or train?'

Donna said: 'Thank you. Train. People who *want* to know.'

5: Personal meaning in alien languages

Acting the scapegoat

Devorah is 34, a trainee on a post-graduate diploma counselling course. Her degree is in European languages, and she says she does not see what this has to do with counselling.

Trainees on this course are required to have personal therapy for a minimum of two years, in addition to supervision for any counselling work they do. The letter from the training director emphasized to the counsellor that this is *personal* therapy, rather than coursework supervision, which is provided by the training centre.

When the counsellor says 'Tell me something about yourself', Devorah describes her job. She is an information worker for a charity. Her project is raising funds for rural education in India ('not a popular cause', she adds, wryly). She is researching the effects of poor healthcare for mothers on the freedom of their children to take up educational opportunities ('cashing in on the in-thing'[1]). She then describes where she lives – a flat in a nearby suburb.

The counsellor asks: 'And how are things for you, personally?'

Devorah talks about some difficulties she is experiencing in her training group. All of the men and women in her class are white. She finds this odd, in contrast to where she lives and works. 'It's a multicultural and international staff', she says, 'and there's regular training on intercultural relations.'

'What made you choose this training?' the counsellor asks.

'My boss recommended it. It's inexpensive, it's near home, it's "recognized", it's academic, and it's quick!'

'Quick?'

'Yes – it isn't one of those modular courses. I just want to get my certificate, so I can do more interesting work.'

This would be 'reception and debriefing' for returning field volunteers, some of them only 18 or 19 years old. They go for teaching or work experience, or to see the world, or because they want to help, or to learn about other cultures. Some want to go straight back, others feel disorientated, some are outraged at the conditions, some are in love, others exhausted and ill. The last thing they want to do is write reports. Some of them feel very attached to their 'adopted' culture and the children they worked with.

'Did *you* work abroad?' asks the counsellor, wishing she'd taken the chance when she'd had it. Living near the docks all her life, she used to watch the ships and wonder if she would ever go anywhere. Instead, she joined CND and got married (twice).

Devorah shook her head. 'My older brother lived two years on a kibbutz. I wasn't fit. That's why I'm doing the training. You either have to be a former volunteer or an accredited counsellor. There's in-house training too. Everything keeps changing, of course.'

'Do you want to tell me about being "not fit"?'

'No, no, I'm fine now', Devorah smiles. 'It was the usual thing. Parents freaking out – Jewish Princess turns dyke, shock horror – off to the local shrink. You know the sort of thing.'

'I don't', the counsellor says, only then finding out that Devorah is a lesbian. 'It sounds appalling.'

'It was a long time ago. But I've got a psychiatric record as unstable, like it was a nervous breakdown, which is what my mother still says. If I get upset or angry, she says "Shouldn't you get some more of those pills?" I never took the pills.'

'They sent you to a psychiatrist? Not a rabbi?'

Devorah looks at her blankly. 'We're not *religious* Jewish, not Orthodox. Hardly anyone is these days.'

'Sorry. I was being presumptuous', the counsellor says. (And you were stereotyping, she tells herself, firmly. She covers up her mistake by being super-professional.)

'I think we've reached the point where we should talk about whether we are going to be working together', she says.

'Fine with me', Devorah says cheerfully, apparently unfazed by the counsellor's bloomer. 'The main thing is you're on the college list, you're experienced, you're accredited, and you look human to me!' (They both laugh.) 'It's a working arrangement, after all.'

'Is it?' The counsellor looks at the letter again. 'It says here "personal therapy". I'm supposed to write and confirm that you've had it.'

'And that I'm now emotionally and psychologically fit and stable and back together again.'

'What? I'm to *assess* you?'

'Isn't that what it means?'

'I should hope it doesn't', says the counsellor, indignant. 'I only need say you understand the therapeutic process and the therapeutic relationship, that you are open to self-exploration, and that sort of thing. It's very unlikely I should have to say that much.'

'So I can be unstable, and still be a counsellor?'

'It doesn't *say* that, exactly.'

'It would be nice. Everyone thinks I'm crazy anyway. Someone scattered bits of hair all over my desk once. Also someone left me a wig. But they're nice to me now. They call me Dotty Devi. Better than Dolly Levi, anyway.'

Realizing that Devorah has got to the main point, the counsellor concentrates. She feels that they have established a reasonably good rapport, although she wonders if she should know who Dolly Levi is, and the significance of the wig. She noticed that Devorah assumed that they will work together, and feels 'hired', but decides to leave discussions about mutual commitment until later.

'Who thinks you're crazy?' she asks.

Devorah explains that her co-trainers are 'a bit stiff and analytic' and want to focus on 'problem-solving' and 'skills' instead of their own experiences. Two of them are psychology graduates, and talk about working with 'neurotics' or the 'worried well', and want to know about 'phobias'. 'Except homophobia', Devorah mutters, and goes on quickly saying that even in small groups, they 'describe' their feelings instead of expressing them. Some are 'uptight about the course, as if it was a university'.

'They don't want people to think they are losing their self-control?' the counsellor asks.

'I think they want to appear clever, or mature. Which some of them are. They like debating theories – object-relations theory at the moment. It gets quite dramatic sometimes.'

'What do you make of these theories? What was it that you said about phobias?'

'Actually I think it's an advantage for a counsellor to be a bit crazy.' (She suddenly looks intently at the counsellor, who assumes a bland expression and tries to appear as sane as possible.) 'My family are all over the place, and who can blame them?'

'What do they think about you doing counselling?'

Devorah's eyes light up. 'I'm flavour of the month again. "So at last", says my Grandpa, "you join the community again." '

'Do you?'

'Not that one. A lesbian community, maybe. Or a women's community would be good. Pity there are no women-only courses around here.'

'Isn't there a Jewish lesbian women's community?'

Devorah looks confused. 'That isn't all the same thing. I've met some radical Jewish women, activists and feminists. I don't know any Jewish lesbians. It's very un-Jewish, you know. My grandparents are religious, my older brother does all the right things. All the women have to sit and watch the men praying. I don't fit into any of that.'

'Or into your course, you say.'

Devorah shrugs. 'I'm the independent type. They don't like me. They don't like being challenged, or personal arguments. They say I'm intolerant – sometimes I crack up, um, laugh, I mean.' Again she fixes the counsellor with an intense stare. The counsellor suddenly experiences an urge to appear wild and unruly, and is unable to stop herself from laughing aloud.

'What did I say?' asks Devorah, a bit shocked.

'I've just remembered who Dolly Levi[2] is. Now, I'd like to give you some feedback.'

The counsellor's understanding of the issues

1. Devorah is used to people thinking she's crazy. She does not fit in anywhere, although she must be well thought of at work, even if she is often teased. Maybe she's thought of as a 'good sport', laughing at herself before anyone else can. She feels it's OK to be different, as this is independence. She seems very work-oriented. Everything is clear cut – career planned, therapy mapped out, an efficient-sounding course. The counsellor wonders if the prized certificate, as well as being a

passport to what sounds like a fascinating job, would also mean to Devorah that she is no longer 'crazy'.

2. Devorah seems to have no faith in anyone but herself. She looks extremely tired, her clothes are crumpled, and her hair is untidy, although otherwise all there – no sign of any clumps torn out. She feels prevented from expressing herself and her needs in the training group, and instead is drawing attention to herself by challenging people, arguing, and appearing intolerant. So she is not making any friends there, and is possibly jeopardizing her certificate. (The letter said also '. . . and can demonstrate a potential for empathy, an understanding of herself, an appropriate level of self-acceptance, and valuation of those of her personal qualities which can be applied to her counselling work'. She wonders if Devorah read the letter.)

3. The counsellor suspects that in an all-white group, and a (so far) theoretical training, Devorah is experiencing personal disorientation. If her frustration at being unable to express her *self* has become argument or confrontation, the people concerned are possibly stereotyping her behaviour as 'culturally inappropriate' for a professional counsellor – indicated by terms like 'intolerant' and 'challenging'. It sounds as if the 'intolerance' is two-way. Perhaps she has been identified also as a 'problem' or even 'neurotic'. Do they know she's a lesbian?

4. Devorah is separate as a lesbian from her family (everyone? the counsellor wonders), from Jewish feminists, from her religious and cultural traditions, and from her co-trainees. She must be feeling frustrated and isolated. Perhaps she was describing herself when she talked of the young volunteers returning from India.

5. The counsellor wants to follow up the grandfather's question 'So at last you join the community?' She wonders if this was an ironic reference to the founder of psychoanalysis, or a comment on the strong tradition of community-building among Jewish people. She knows that there is a Jewish family welfare organization, and had thought this was why she had never had a Jewish client before. She realizes how much she does not know, how often she assumes that people take care of their own. She decides this is something she should check out.[3]

COUNSELLING OPTIONS

Since Devorah has made it clear that she expects to be treated as a 'professional' in a 'working relationship', the counsellor decides to go along with this at first, establishing Devorah's perception of personal therapy, the counsellor's approach and methods, and professional responsibility. She wants to validate Devorah's strong need to appear self-sufficient. If the only other option is to be 'crazy', it will be important to find an alternative to what the counsellor perceives as a mixture of defensiveness, a need to be 'heard', and to express her vulnerabilities and doubts. The counsellor cannot think of any way that Devorah could do this without being open about herself and her feelings, which is what she wants to do. How can she protect herself from the hostility she is encountering?

The counsellor wonders why she wants to change her job. Perhaps that's a bit 'crazy' too, especially fundraising for an 'unpopular cause'. Thinking of her own children, one of whom doesn't bother to go to school if he doesn't feel like it, she feels saddened. She believes that Devorah is as strong as she makes out – perhaps she has had to learn to be – and that, channelled appropriately, this would be one of her best qualities for herself, and as a supportive counsellor.

She suddenly feels cold, and wonders if that's how Devorah feels, or how she perceives people. She seems dismissive of her relatives, and perhaps she also misses being the 'Princess'. Is that what she meant by being 'flavour of the month'? The counsellor knows that she must prioritize Devorah's *personal* needs, and establish a personal, rather than a 'working' alliance, perhaps by explaining why this is essential. She dislikes the idea of intellectualizing this.

The counsellor believes that what Devorah means by 'sane' is being in charge of her life and able to help herself and other people adjust to external change, loss, and transitions. Perhaps she feels 'useless', especially if her work isn't effective.

She would like to enable Devorah to develop a stronger sense of herself – to bring together the 'separated' aspects of her identity, and, if she doesn't want to reattach to her own cultural roots, to establish her own. She also thinks that a little admiration – perhaps ironic – would be a good idea; but the kind that doesn't come with any expectations of fitting in to some 'ideal client' or 'ideal counsellor' mould.

She wants to check out if Devorah experiences her co-trainees' attitudes to her as anti-Semitic or ethnicist. She thinks there may be some academic point-scoring going on.

Her conclusion is that what she should offer Devorah is what she would offer any client – her natural approach to *all* people. This is also the way she expects to be treated herself, and points this out if it doesn't happen, though rarely, these days, in a confrontative way.

She finds it extraordinary that she has been added to an 'approved' list without her knowledge. She assumed that the magic words 'accredited' and 'psychodynamic' against her directory entry are the cause, although she no longer works in a psychodynamic way. She struggles with her conscience for a while, thinking of a stream of trainees coming her way, feels bad, then decides she deserves to be on anyone's 'recommended' list.

AGREEING A THERAPY FOCUS

The counsellor summarizes her thoughts (except the last one) to Devorah. She gives brief, factual observations, avoiding any suggestion that Devorah is a 'problem'.

She explains the ambiguity of the situation – that while Devorah does not seem to be getting any personal support or affirmative attention, she came to therapy only because it was a training requirement.

Devorah approves of the counsellor's calm, factual informative approach. This is how she expects a counsellor to be – unperturbed. She feels understood. She realizes she must answer the question. Thinking 'what have I got to lose?' she says: 'To be honest, no, I wouldn't have thought of *therapy* – let me tell you about the shrink sometime – I was thinking more of counselling. But sitting here feels better than what's happening on the training. I guess they know how we feel after all, or maybe they think we're crazy, that's why they insist we have therapy.'

She frowns. 'I've just worked out why I'm here today. It's the same as anywhere else. I'm always the one in the wrong on the course. I wanted to do something right. I really want to get the certificate, but I feel like giving it all up right now – *enough*.' She makes a slicing movement with her left hand, away from her body. Giving a deep sigh, she sits back in the chair, biting her lip. Eventually, she looks at the counsellor, half-expectant, half-apprehensive.

'This is where you dump whatever you've had enough of', the counsellor says.

'That's easy, is it?' Devorah laughs sardonically and looks hurt.

'No', the counsellor says, sympathizing for a moment with Devorah's co-trainees. 'It's the hardest thing of all. How are you going to stand up straight and be assertive without all that junk on your head to balance? What's going to replace it?'

The logistics of this makes Devorah blink. She wriggles her head and shoulders, shakes her left arm, and flops forward in the chair.

'What are you doing?' the counsellor asks, now feeling irritated.

'Beginner's Gestalt', says a muffled voice.

'Is it working?'

Silence. The counsellor realizes her mistake. 'All right. Devorah, I get the message. No therapy jargon. OK?'

Devorah sits up, a little shame-faced. 'Well – it *was* a bit corny. I had to do all that in the hospital.' (The counsellor raises her eyebrows.) 'I wasn't *that* crazy. A year of out-patients psychiatry, then six months of group re-rehab-irritation. We watched a lot of movies.'

The counsellor waits. Devorah clears her throat. The counsellor raises her eyebrows again. Devorah wriggles around and pulls faces.

Finally she says: 'I *was* crazy.' She sits up straight. As if describing a movie, she says: 'This is thirteen years ago. My parents came round to see why I hadn't turned up at my second cousin Joe's Barmitzvah – Grandpa and Grandma were very upset, they said. They'd all gone on ahead and I was supposed to meet them there. I was in bed. With a woman. First time. My father did the Great Laurence Olivier Grieving Thing.[4] My mother – well, I never thought she was capable – such *language*. Anyway, I ripped my father's beautiful Barmitzvah coat for him – his best bespoke – he can be very Orthodox when it suits him. I never saw the woman again. I didn't even see her go. She was just ... gone. My father was shocked, and my mother was yelling at me "Put something on, put something on" – I mean, I just jumped out of bed – talk about coming out. Anyway, I went for her as well and my father grabbed me and I kicked him. It hurt. I've never been like that before or since. Except in the therapy group.' She laughs.

'You let them in?'

'They have a key', Devorah says, stunned by this response. 'It's my father's property. You don't think he'd let me live in my own place, do you?'

The counsellor realizes she has allowed herself to be entertained by Devorah's jokey manner, and missed important cues. There are more major issues here than she feels capable of dealing with. She first needs Devorah's agreement on the next step.

She states this, pointing out that is the story of her first sexual relationship with a woman. It changed, permanently, Devorah's relation-ship with her family, and her prized position as family jewel. Worst of all, it gave her a psychiatric record which labelled her 'unfit', and stopped her from taking the opportunity to find out what Jewish people were doing to build their own nation. Devorah hadn't minded too much about this – she was just beginning to meet more lesbians, very secretly. But she decides to skip this, and to tell the counsellor about her family.

'I like my grandparents best. They're more – this might sound funny – more *Jewish* – my father's just a businessman. They have a flat in the block as well. They're, I dunno, sort of feeble and pale and wrinkled and skinny, and sad and funny, and critical, but not bossy like Mum. They use all those Jewish joke expressions and they hate it when I copy them. I tease Grandpa, I say he learned to talk like that from American movies.

'Grandma's got a Mittel-European accent, she was a refugee. They married here. They never hug me, but I feel – sort of – hugged, sort of cute, and told off, all at the same time.

'When my father finally broke it to them why I was really in hospital, he and Grandma apparently looked at each other and shrugged, and he said "Goyim, the other one?" My father stormed out. My grandpa is actually very religious but what he doesn't see he doesn't see. They've never said the "L" word. Nor have I, to them. I went as far as "gay Goyim" once, and all I got was a cold stare. Then I got a big bowl of soup or something.

'Grandma plays Mahler on her old stereo. Grandpa plays Black American funky jazz on the CD Dad got them – wholesale – for their anniversary – 50 or 60, I forget – but Grandma won't touch it. "Gadgets!" she says. "Vedder Report – vot a name for an orrcheshtra." I love her to bits.'

The counsellor absorbs all this information, staggered at Devorah's facile irreverence for her grandparents, whom she obviously loves.[5] Devorah wonders why she cannot talk about anything seriously today. She feels awful. She tries to cheer herself up by imagining what Grandma would say if she knew Devorah was in therapy again. She decides to tell them straight away.

The counsellor points out, as tactfully as she can, that the session is almost over. She is surprised that Devorah is chuckling to herself. Feeling put out, she repeats what she said, trying to get the session back onto a professional footing. She wonders what's funny about saying that it's almost time to stop.

'This is where I do the feedback and we decide about session times and boundaries and so on.' (Devorah recovers her composure and pays attention.) 'I'll give you a pack with my Code of Ethics and your complaints procedure, and so on. That tells you your rights as a client. OK?'

'The Client is Always Right. I have those. We were given them on the course.'

'Fine. Now, first. I'm wondering if you've told anyone in your group about any of this.' (Devorah shakes her head.) 'They might be more tolerant and less critical of you if they knew about your NHS group, for one thing.' (Devorah frowns.) 'You can't be the only person in the whole class who has had some sort of therapy, surely?' (Devorah brightens up a little.) 'Two. You haven't mentioned anything about other lesbian relationships, although I'm assuming from something you said that you do know other lesbians.' (Devorah nods.) 'If the time that your parents found you was your first lesbian – or your first *sexual* – relationship, and you never saw the woman again, what's that left you with?' (Devorah's face closes completely.) 'Three, you are Jewish, and I get the impression that you know several ways of being Jewish, you don't seem to relate to any of them, and the only way you're experiencing this at present is by being class scapegoat. Four. How do you take care of yourself? Do you pay your *self* enough attention? Do you cook? What music do you like? Do you live alone?'

Devorah raises her left hand, looking grey in the face.

'Enough?' says the counsellor.

'You're a tough lady, aren't you?'

'Mm-hmm', says the counsellor with a smile, 'although you should know by now that in counsellor-speak that means empowering, informative, and supportive.'

'*Supportive*?' Devorah echoes.

'Wrong?'

'It sounds like . . . you sound like you're *angry* with me. Angry, I know. Supportive, that's Grandma.' She frowns, wondering if she should have said that. After all, she'd be angry if someone she was trying to help was sending her up. She'd forgotten how humiliated she felt in the hospital therapy group. She never has to see this woman again, so maybe that is why she is being so flippant, doing exactly what her father hates her to do. She suddenly realizes what annoys her about one of the men in her group, who says things like 'as my Scouse Uncle Danny might say . . . '. She feels embarrassed. What *must* the counsellor be thinking of her?

The counsellor, meanwhile, is taking several deep breaths. To Devorah's great surprise, she says 'I'm very sorry. I *am* angry. Not *with* you, *for* you. Perhaps you need to work with someone more analytical. I should tell you I'm a feminist – ex-feminist, I should say – peace activist. I have six kids, two of mine and four of his. It's like group therapy in our house half the time. My youngest, my son, is disabled. He's got . . . well, you don't need to know about that.

'My husband's Irish, from Belfast, he's a teacher. One of his friends from the school is a lesbian, a white woman. She lives near us, with a Black woman – an African-British woman – with two children. One of them is at school with my husband's older daughter, who lectures us all on racism.

'I was wondering about your training group and why the tutor or facilitator doesn't support you. Are you the only lesbian, and do they know that?'

Devorah, now looking flushed, decides this must be the famous counter-transference in action. She is overwhelmed. She cannot remember the last time anyone got angry on her behalf, except in a training group at work when a woman defended her from a colleague who suggested she shouldn't make judgements about places she'd never been to. 'Devorah is empathic', the woman, a Bengali who ran one of the sponsored projects, said coolly. 'She imagines the situation and she has good information. She is speaking, I think, for the children.' The man apologized, and Devorah hadn't said another word for the entire day.

'It's OK', she says finally, in a small voice. 'It's all information. I can deal with that. It's my job, right? I was thinking of you before as *one* person. A professional. Like my boss. Calm. In charge. I don't know much about her home life. Now I can think of you as someone with a big family, a member of the human race. That feels better. I'd like to learn how you manage with your family. I don't know if that's . . . you said about boundaries. I do live alone. I hate it. I haven't had an affair for nearly a year, since my arm . . . I can't cook at the moment, I usually get take-away, or I go out with friends or people from work. Not so much now, with the course and everything. Anyway, I'm here to learn . . . '

The counsellor interrupts her. 'Devorah – you learn *that* on your course. Here, this is therapy, this is for you, Devorah the person. It's you who will be doing this work, if you decide to do it, and you who is doing the course. Not some remote professional. You'll be working with young people – strong, adventurous, big kids with guts. They'll need all your warmth and encouragement. Isn't this how you want to be? To be your *self*? Is this something you can *learn*?'

'Hah!' Devorah says, trying hard not to cry. 'I get it. *Experiential* therapy.' The counsellor smiles. Devorah, suddenly noticing the time, looks around for her jacket.

She picks it up, and says: 'It's a pity you're not a Jewish . . . well, then you'd be perfect.'

'A Jewish . . . Princess?'

Devorah laughs aloud. 'No. I don't know what it is about you that makes me so outrageous. I wanted to say "Jewish lesbian".'

'Oh! No, I'm neither. Nor am I perfect, by the way. We need to talk about how you feel working with a heterosexual, Gentile, married, older woman.'

'Am I going to be a problem for you? I should have asked you that, shouldn't I?' She looks worried again.

'The problems', says the counsellor firmly, 'are out there. They seem to have stuck to you. As I said, this is the place to dump them, before they squash you.'

As if on cue, Devorah staggers a little. The counsellor thinks she is acting, until she struggles to get her coat on.

'Are you OK?' asks the counsellor, helping her. (Devorah nods weakly.) 'And, do you want to tell me about your arm?'

'Thank you. Yes. It's RSI – Information Technology Operator Seizure. That's another reason I want to change my job. It'll go. I have physio – the office insurance covers it. I'm mostly doing phone work now – fund-raising.'

The counsellor apologizes. 'I just assumed you were left-handed', she says.

'Sadly, no. I'm not exactly lover of the year at the moment. Can't even shake hands.' The counsellor solemnly shakes her left hand.

As she shows Devorah out, she says: 'Something I meant to ask you. Is this the first time you've been in a class, or a group, with just white people?'

'Well, I'm white, for that matter, but, yes, it is, outside family things and weddings, and so on. I hadn't thought of that – school, university, work, even gay clubs – yes.'

'And is anyone else on the course gay? Or lesbian?'

'I don't think so. They haven't said. Why?'

'Perhaps that would be a good place to start. Just to point that out. And how you feel about it.'

'I'll think about that. There will be training, next year I think.'

'You want to wait till next year to talk about it?'

Devorah smiled and said ironically: 'Could we talk about this another time? I think I need a big bowl of Grandma's hot soup.'

NOTES

1. 1995 was Oxfam International Year of Women.
2. Dolly Levi was a matchmaker, a character played by Barbra Streisand in the musical film *Hello Dolly*.
3. A part of the Jewish ethos is a strong sense of community, and an

encouragement for Jews to perceive themselves as a global population with history, continuity and tradition. Jewish activists have a high awareness of the constant revivals of European anti-Semitic attacks: half the Jewish population of the world was destroyed in Hitler's Holocaust. There are different religious traditions, of course, and, in the context of this book, the European tradition of humanistic psychoanalysis, best expressed by Sigmund Freud. Also see his extraordinary challenge of Moses, the acknowledged founder of Jewish monotheistic religion (Freud, S., 1938). See Bettelheim (1992) for discussion on World War II ghetto Jews, and modern American Jewish ethics and community ideals. There are several Jewish welfare organizations in the UK, offering a complete range of social services, including services for disabled people, respite care, child care, advocacy, counselling, etc. These are listed in telephone directories under 'Jewish Care'.

One of the Jewish lesbians contributing to this book asked me to emphasize that she had received from heterosexual staff at a Jewish welfare service the same high quality of counselling and support in a difficult custody case as would be offered to any other Jewish family. She was unable to find support from lesbian counsellors, who felt unqualified to work with children.

4. Laurence Olivier played a stereotypical Jewish father in a dismal remake of *The Jazz Singer*. When his (married) son has an affair with a Gentile girl, Olivier rips his coat melodramatically and rushes out of the house, declaring his son dead. This action is, in fact, part of the traditional ritual acknowledgement of death.

5. See Burstow, B., 'Jewish women', in *Radical Feminist Therapy*. London, Sage, 1992. Bonnie Burstow, also a Jewish activist, and women-identified woman, offers these suggestions to counsellors (p. 87). 'If you find yourself strangely irritated by a Jewish client, you may be reacting negatively to valued Jewish or working-class Jewish characteristics ... chances are you are perceiving and judging according to dominant norms ... do not assume that she is avoiding feeling if she intellectualizes ... we typically both intellectualize and feel.' Burstow also gives several examples of internalized anti-Semitic oppression, including clients making statements about disliking Jewish traits and stereotypes.

FURTHER READING

Beck (1982)
Christmas (1990).
Kaye-Kantrowicz and Klepfisz (1986), pp. 29, 30.
Kramer (1976). (Includes the often-quoted traditional wisdom: 'if you live

with children you bring sin on them because you give them a chance to fight with their parents'.)
Smith (1991).
Solomon (1989). (This book was dedicated to Myrtle Solomon (1921–87).)
Trigangles (1986).

6: What if I haven't got chakras?

Natalie is a lesbian counsellor in supervision with a heterosexual psycho-therapist, Daphne. One of the reasons why she chose her, apart from liking her and respecting her abilities, was because she worked in the only private therapy centre in the district which was wheelchair accessible. Natalie's spine was damaged in an accident when she was four years old. She told Daphne about it when they first met, and about the operations she'd had over the years, and how being a counsellor, and having her own therapy, had helped her to acknowledge that her degree of disability was increasing.

Natalie had not been out for very long and would have preferred to work with a lesbian supervisor, someone more holistic in her approach, but on the whole the arrangement worked well. Daphne was very knowledgeable and experienced with complex and health-threatening problems. This balanced out her blank spots in terms of lesbian issues. Still, as Natalie often commented, Daphne was learning.

One bonus was that working with her had encouraged Natalie to apply for professional accreditation, which came through a few months ago. She said that this made her feel 'useful' and validated as a counsellor. She did not identify herself as disabled, and felt a little ashamed that she wasn't involved in campaigning.

She had, a little half-heartedly, joined the management committee of the community centre where she'd done her voluntary practice, and was trying to start a lesbian group there. She was thinking of giving this up, as she was tired of being a spokeswoman for both disability *and* lesbian issues. She wanted some time for herself, as her work was demanding and she was often in pain. She lived alone now, so, for personal support, she told Daphne, she had joined a local women's group. That's all she would say about it.

Daphne, who described herself as a 'retired feminist', was active in the campaign for the rights of access, and was the chair of a local voluntary group who provided support for carers of disabled children.

In this session – the first one after a holiday break – Natalie is feeling stuck with three of her lesbian clients. She hopes that Daphne will be able to support her in enabling them to find their own ways through their particular difficulties.

Natalie always keeps clients' names confidential. But to avoid confusion – all those 'she's – they are Vita (who is in a stormy relationship with Vi), Sylvia (who is severely depressed following the death of her long-term lover, Valentine), and Jill (who has just announced that she is sick of lesbians).

Usually, Daphne asks for formal notes in advance and for one case to be prioritized, with additional time made for any urgent concerns relating to other work. Natalie explains that everything has become so complicated and confusing that her summary notes had to be abandoned. She feels she has lost touch with her own intuitive abilities. What she would like to do is simply *talk*, and therefore apply more energy to what has become a rigid situation.

Daphne is a little annoyed, but trusts Natalie's instincts. It just means she will have to work a bit harder without the help of the neatly-typed notes, which had the added advantage of separating one client from another. She settles down for what she is sure will be a very long 90 minutes.

Natalie, who is very much in awe of Daphne, feels relieved that her suggestion has been accepted. She explains the situations as follows.

Vita has been in therapy for six weeks, most of the time complaining about her lover, Vi. She told Natalie that she is always expected to be in charge, organizing everything, and giving Vi her full attention. When Vita 'goes on strike', Vi falls to pieces, becoming a 'trembling jelly' and gazing at Vita forlornly, with huge moist eyes. Vita said she usually sighs, resigns herself to the situation, and copes with whatever is going on. Then, miraculously, Vi perks up and becomes her usual lovely, appealing and sexually abandoned self.

Natalie has never been quite sure what Vita wants from therapy (or from her) as she talks around the subject, saying 'Well ... I'd like Vi to be stronger, to take more responsibility for herself', or 'I want Vi to look after me for a change'. The mystery was solved in this week's session. Vita explained, in an offhand way, that the real problem was sex.

They had both become hooked on SM sex games, which were now dominating their lives. Natalie had asked if Vita felt like giving more details, or whether it had been difficult enough for her to finally bring up the subject of SM. Vita looked a little surprised, saying 'Not particularly – after all, that's why I wanted to talk to another lesbian'. Natalie was taken aback and a bit offended, since her knowledge of SM came only from books, all of them about heterosexual activities. She was of course aware of the lesbian feminist view, and she saw the issue in terms of the exploitation of lesbian and gay sexual experimentation by the porn industry, but assumed she had got this wrong as usual.

Vita willingly gave more details – in fact, she talked non-stop, and Natalie was fascinated. Vita said she was doing all the 'work' and all the 'giving'. She said she practically 'melted' – she was so turned on by Vi's willing submissiveness and her longing to be dominated, tied up, and spanked, 'et cetera', that she was getting 'a bit hooked on it'.

The trouble was, Vi wouldn't make love to her any more in the way that Vita liked, and wanted only to 'give as good as she got', which, said Vita with a wry smile, 'hurt'. Natalie tried so hard not to scrunch her face up that her ears wiggled when Vita said *what* hurt, and she was sure she had gone red in the face. But Vita took no notice, and was anyway looking sad and pensive.

What had happened – why Vita finally wanted to talk about it – was that Vi had told two of their Black lesbian friends, and invited them to stay after the meal and watch. Vita, horrified that Vi should even mention it to anyone else, felt deeply ashamed when she saw the shocked expressions on her friends' faces. They had immediately walked out, leaving their food uneaten, and were obviously upset. Vita hadn't been in contact with them since.

At this point, Daphne interrupted Natalie. 'There seem to be several different issues going on here. Could you pause here for now and say what you mean by being "stuck" with this particular client?' Natalie was a bit flustered but soon recovered. She said: 'I'd like to talk about the other two women, then find out if there is any link between them.'

Sylvia, whose doctor had referred her to psychiatric care for her 'breakdown', had discharged herself and thrown away the anti-depressants. 'I want to feel everything, but I don't want to meet anyone.' She had to move to a small flat found for her by the psychiatric social worker.

Their house had been in Valentine's name, and since she'd never made a will – they both assumed that Sylvia would die first – Valentine's children now owned it, along with most of Valentine's parents' furniture. The son wanted to modernize and sell it, and promised Sylvia a reasonable settlement. She'd had to sell most of their joint possessions to pay the deposit on the flat and the first quarter's rent.

She couldn't face looking for a job, and now had a medical record which said 'reactive depression', although her benefits were slow in coming through. Natalie was not charging her for the counselling and knew that Sylvia's pride would prompt her to pay something as soon as she had some spare cash. Natalie would deal with this when the time came.

In their last session, Sylvia announced that she hated everyone – Valentine, the children (who had children of their own), all her lesbian friends who had enjoyed their company but never came to visit. She had not let these friends come to the psychiatric hospital, and they seemed to be put off by her constant depression. Natalie was very concerned that Sylvia was now suicidal, but she did not agree and refused to go back to the doctor. 'Valentine used to drink like a fish', Sylvia explained. 'When she gave up, we both swore off pills or anything addictive for ever. I'm blowed if I'm going to start taking drugs at my age. They just want to shut me up, that's all it is.'

Jill said that she had had enough of lesbians and politics. The meetings she went to, where she used to feel so empowered and supported, were now making her feel helpless and insecure.

'Everyone's so angry all the time', she said. 'It's not the "victim" thing, it's not that at all. It's just that whatever we do, something new comes up – it's been one long battle. First it was the lesbian teacher who got scapegoated by the media, then the local women's refuge funding was cut, then the False Memory thing. You know all the rest of it, it's non-stop.

'Now it's personal – one of the women is having a dreadful battle for custody of her two kids and her husband's being a real pig. Another woman's being harassed by a man in her block, he's completely lesbo-phobic and she's very scared of him.

'We'd all agreed to separatism, and now one of the women who set up the group has decided she's bisexual. She works with a lot of gay men and she's got into gay politics – age of consent and all that – and now we're getting into arguments about queer rights and gender nonconformism. Last week we all agreed to turn up in butch drag, as a statement.

'She was really angry, and she said she felt mocked. There was a big argument. We all went out and got drunk, we've never done that before.

Then I went home and hit Lena, for the first time in my life. I don't know where to turn now.'

Jill had originally come to therapy because she wanted reasons for everything that happened – why were men so sexist? Why was everything such a battle? Where did all this prejudice come from? She spent most sessions asking these types of questions in an anguished voice, frequently crying, and saying she couldn't tell her political sisters about therapy as they disapproved of it.

She felt very lonely and did not know how she would ever make it up with Lena, who was now threatening to leave. Lena was taunting Jill, saying things like 'What would your goody-goody separatist lot make of that, eh? Battering dykes?' Jill said she felt like hitting her again.

Natalie paused for breath and Daphne stared at her blankly. Neither of them knew what to say. Daphne felt she should say *something*, since she was, after all, the supervisor, and being paid (quite well) for this job. She said: 'I'm very glad, as an initial comment, that you have already got your accreditation. I can't imagine what the BAC would make of all that.'

'I expect they'd want me to convert it into Transactional Analysis – except that I've forgotten all that now.' Natalie was glad of the chance to lighten things up – that was Daphne's strength. Whatever the situation, she put things into proportion in a way Natalie found strange but it somehow worked. 'Anyway', she continued, 'it doesn't apply.'

'T.A.?' Daphne asked. 'Right', said Natalie. 'These are all lesbian issues. I've just realized this. There's nothing in the textbooks to cover any of it.'

'It's good you've made that connection', Daphne said, 'But I was thinking of Sylvia. I mean, it's a fairly classic ageist situation, isn't it? Death of a long-term partner, children tucking the bereaved spouse into an oldies home while they collect the cash, stubborn refusal to accept being old and weak.'

Natalie thought deeply. 'Yes, that's true, and of course I've always worked with her grief. She got my name through the local bereavement service – amazing – I didn't know they bothered about lesbian issues. Things must be improving.

'No, you see, the whole point is that she's lost Valentine, her lesbian lover, who was a lot younger. Maybe she had a vague idea she'd get cared for in her old age. By the way, she's only 58. I don't know how I gave the impression she was old and weak. She's not. She's healthy and tough and stubborn. The problem is that she's cut herself off from her lesbian friends

– she's a very proud person – or they've abandoned her, or a bit of both. That's terrible.' Daphne still couldn't think of this as a specifically *lesbian* issue, and waited to be enlightened.

Natalie continued: 'I do *feel* for Jill – I remember when I was a gay young feminist, if you know what I mean, in my consciousness-raising group. Women just out of psych care, or who finally left their husbands, used to come along. They didn't know anything about feminism, they just wanted to be in a women's group. We were a bit discouraging at first, then they started to talk about sexual abuse.

'I don't think any of us said another word for the whole time of the group – we let these women talk and talk – it was great that they *could* talk. One of them had a disabled sister, cerebral palsy I think, and the father had raped her too. She was an extremely bright girl, and she *stopped* talking.

'We couldn't believe what we were hearing. I think that's when I decided to study counselling. I worked for a bit at a community centre as a volunteer. It felt OK. Here I am.'

Daphne, who felt her job was to keep Natalie's attention on her clients' concerns, asked: 'I understand you empathize with Jill's feelings of helplessness and anger. But I imagine you wouldn't go home and take out your anger on your partner. What was it that made Jill suddenly change character, drop all her principles, and attack her friend? And Vita and Vi . . . they sound familiar somehow. I assume that's not really their names?'

Natalie grinned. She certainly wasn't going to help out here – sometimes she felt mischievous when Daphne demonstrated her ignorance about lesbian history. Daphne realized she had said the wrong thing (she was aware that she often did) and said: 'Anyway, what does SM mean to you? When I interrupted you there you looked annoyed, or confused perhaps. What was that about?'

Natalie tried to remember. Yes, she *had* been a bit annoyed. She had wanted to talk more about SM and get it off her chest, but had been about to say something else which seemed more important. What was it? She asked Daphne.

'You said something about some friends of theirs who'd got upset and left. And what's her name . . . Vita . . . had been embarrassed that Vi had told them about it.'

'Thanks', Natalie said, 'Of course, that's it. Vita was *ashamed* that Vi told them, not embarrassed. And they were Black lesbians. That's why they were so offended. Why did you interrupt me, anyway?'

Daphne said: 'I felt you were moving away from your client's issue, which I thought you were saying was the way that the games were dominating the relationship, and Vita said she was feeling sexually . . . frustrated? Not getting the attention she needed?'

Natalie suddenly felt angry and put down. 'Don't you understand? They were *Black* lesbians. You know? SM? Slavery? Sometimes I feel I have to educate you about women's politics.'

Daphne raised her eyebrows. 'Do you? You should have said. I am aware of Black women's history, and of all the other arguments against SM. It isn't only about slavery. Anyway, as we have agreed, I am here to enable you to concentrate on your clients' issues, not yours. You're not Black. Why are you so angry?'

Natalie decided not to say anything. Daphne was right in one way. And the reason Natalie had broken her usual supervision system – no notes, just talking – must mean that there were personal issues going on for her which related to each of her client's dilemmas. But this wasn't supposed to be therapy. On the other hand . . . She said: 'If an issue of mine is interfering with my clients, isn't that what supervision is for?'

'Of course', Daphne said, 'By all means share your own issues. But please direct your anger at the cause of it, not me.'

Natalie felt furious. Why shouldn't I? she thought. She's supposed to be supporting me, she's the one with the authority here, she's the one who signed my bloody accreditation papers and she'll have to fill in the next lot, too. Natalie felt firmly ticked off, and decided to change her tactics.

Taking a few deep breaths, she said: 'Could you tell me what it is about today that is different? I mean. is this a new supervision style, or what? You're always really helpful. I'm feeling got at. I'm confused enough, anyway, as I said.'

'It's you that's different today', Daphne said, 'You remember? You couldn't work it all out? That's not like you. Your notes are usually very clear.'

Natalie's head began to ache. So it's *my* fault, she thought. Dammit. So what am I not doing? Notes! Of course, I'm not *thinking* about it. My boundaries have got skewed. What I'm doing is *feeling* everything. Well, that's OK, that's obviously what I need to do. That's what all my clients are doing – and they're all feeling terrible.

Aloud, she said: 'Sylvia appears to be suicidally depressed, but actually she's stubborn and proud and ashamed of herself for being dumped in the loony bin. She's shattered that the son has kicked her out. She's lost everything – Valentine, her home, her friends, money, her life, her identity. She's cutting herself off from *lesbians*, hurting herself.

'Vita's frustrated, yes, but she's mostly ashamed of being so hooked on

SM *and* offending her Black friends. She also dislikes SM because *she's* getting hurt, and not getting any love or sex. She's fed up with being the powerful one. She isn't strong, obviously not as physically strong as Vi. Or maybe Vi actually *likes* being hurt.

'Jill's full of pain. She's feeling powerless, upset, angry, betrayed by the Government – she was involved in the access rights campaign too, did I say? – and by the woman who says she's bisexual and is into gay men. She's just betrayed *herself* – thumping the one person she really cares about. I don't know what that is. I must ask her what Lena said or did, what button got pushed, if there was one.'

Daphne said: 'There's some very powerful stuff going on there – rage, grief, loss, betrayal, despair, oppression, power games, violence, sexual violence too. It sounds to me like everybody hates everybody this week. I think you hate me a bit too. I've let you down somehow – no, don't say anything. Think. What is all this about? What is it that *you* are stuck with?'

'Where's your famous intuition got to?'

Natalie smiled at her bleakly. The list sounded very heavy. Trust Daphne to list all the lesbian stereotypes one after the other. Wasn't there anything *positive* she could think of? She said: 'My intuition works for other people, but not this week. It doesn't work for me. That's what you're here for. I'm relying on *your* intuition.'

'Oh?' Daphne was surprised. 'And all along I thought it was my amazing brain – you often tell me how logical and perceptive I am. But not today.'

'Because you haven't got it in writing', Natalie said, pointedly. 'OK', Daphne said. 'We can take extra time to argue this out if you like. But let's try and stay focused. Clients.'

Natalie tried to centre herself. Sylvia. Vita. Jill. Strong feelings, strong actions, strong ... what? Resistance? Sylvia definitely said she wasn't going to commit suicide and she refused to take anti-depressants and be 'shut up', but her pride was making her shut *herself* up. What was that about? What *didn't* she want to say to people – lesbians, anyone, me?

'Sylvia', she said. 'Any ideas? I can't think – maybe it's me that's going crazy.'

'Hah!' said Daphne. 'You've just answered yourself. Have you ever asked Sylvia what it was like in the psychiatric ward? *Why* she discharged herself? I know that hospital – it's not exactly a rest home. Mixed wards, and all that ...'

'*Mixed wards?*' Natalie said, horrified. 'Oh no. I never asked her. You're right. She *hates* men. When she's talking about hating everyone she mentions men – Valentine's son, her ex-husband, the doctor who wants to shut her up – they're all men. It must have been hell for her. No Valentine, and stuck in a ward with a lot of depressed men – or maybe noisy, pestering men. Dreadful for her. Thank you. I know what I can do.'

'Yes?'

'I heard of a new group starting, at a women's centre, it's for women survivors of the mental health system – over 50, all women welcome. I guess Sylvia really wants peace and quiet, so that she can grieve in her own way and cope with being shoved out like a leftover. Maybe I should ask her what it is about men. I don't know if it would be right to suggest the group.'

'Suggest it', said Daphne. 'I wouldn't usually say that, but in this case I think what's happened is that all the men around her who should have been taking care of her have let her down – the son, the doctor – one day she might tell you where that all came from. I expect Valentine was quite strong – she gave up alcohol, remember. But *she* let Sylvia down – she didn't make a will. Now Sylvia's got a psych record. Doesn't help her confidence. But she's angry and stubborn and proud – so she'll be able to fight her way out of it. After all, she found you. First, she needs to get rid of whatever stigma she's feeling.'

'Being a mad lesbian', Natalie said quickly. 'Plain old-fashioned hetero-sexism. Maybe she told them in the hospital who had died. Maybe they laughed or ignored it or something. She *didn't* have a "breakdown". She couldn't tell the doctor it was grief, because she'd have to say she was a lesbian. She can't fight the son, because there's no law protecting lesbian partnerships – though she could get some legal advice on that, I should think. She must have contributed to the household expenses all these years, perhaps she even paid the mortgage. They both had full-time jobs until Sylvia was made redundant.

'She can't discuss being depressed with her lesbian friends if she thinks she's sick, or they do, or they're scared that she is. What she needs is somewhere safe, not another huge overwhelming change – she's had two, no, three already – new friends, some support, to find out that she isn't sick after all. I hope the women in the group aren't anti-lesbian.'

'Why should they be?' Daphne asked.

Natalie decided at that moment that she would have to find a new supervisor, But this wasn't the time to say so. She coughed. 'I'd like to move on. All this is about different ways of being a lesbian, having something or someone to believe in, and losing that, and being shocked about it, and realizing how vulnerable you are, also how *dangerous* it is to be vulnerable, unless you can be both tough *and* vulnerable like Vita.

'Come to think of it, I've got that completely the wrong way round. Vi is in control, not Vita. In fact, Jill too – that's what happened. She's discovered her tough side, so has Vita, and she doesn't like it. Sylvia won't acknowledge hers, so she comes across as stubborn and proud. OK. I feel a bit clearer now.'

'And you?'

'Me? Me, tough?' (Daphne didn't respond.) 'OK. Where do I go for my toughness, my power, my strength? You, for one. My intuition, which never lets me down, usually – except when I'm feeling too much. Oh, no.' She suddenly clasped both her hands around her head.

'What is it?'

'I feel a bit bad now. I never told you . . . that women's group I was going to? It was a self-healing group. I met this fantastic healer at some conference or other, turned out that she lived round the corner. Anyway, it wasn't what I expected. The meditation was good, very relaxing and grounding, and we massaged each other's shoulders – that was lovely . But then it got onto a different level altogether – spiritual healing, channelling, all that. We had to chant and cleanse our chakras.'

Daphne smiled. 'All the usual things. Good, sometimes', she said gazing sympathetically at Natalie, knowing what was coming.

'Yes, but, can you imagine what it felt like, there was this feminist guru – this amazing wise woman, earth mother, whatever, sensitive soul of souls – telling us all that our healing energy came down through the top of our head – crown chakra, I think. And kundalini or something came from the bottom of our *spine*? The base chakra? The source of all energy and power and healing?' Natalie began to cry. Daphne crossed over to her side of the room and knelt beside the wheelchair and placed her hand gently on Natalie's shoulder, giving her tissues from time to time.

She felt like crying herself. She remembered when Natalie had first told her about the 'accident'. It was a family secret that Natalie had only found out from her older sister after their father died. Their father was supposed to be taking care of Natalie while her mother fed the baby. He had been too drunk to notice the two little girls who were waiting in the street for him to take them round to Granny's in the car. He backed the car out and reversed around the corner, showing off the driving skills he'd learned in the Army. He hit both of them.

Natalie's sister recovered fairly quickly, but three vertebrae at the base of Natalie's spine were damaged. She had not been able to walk until she was almost seven, and then only with crutches, and, later, walking sticks.

About three years ago, she had been advised to use a wheelchair, as any further operations might sever her spinal cord and she would lose the use of her legs. So *that's* why she wanted healing – to prevent it from getting worse, or perhaps she was still suffering from shock. She had loved her father and looked up to him. She remembered nothing about the accident and nothing before it. Perhaps all these feelings were coming back for her now. Eventually, Natalie stopped crying. Daphne made some tea.

'Can we go on with supervision, please?' Natalie said. 'I thought of something just now. What it all means for me, and I think it's there for the others too. What Jill's friends should be doing is going to a women's rights centre, or the CAB or something. All they can see is what's *wrong*, they've forgotten that there are some ways of putting things right, not many, but some. The woman that's getting into gay men's issues? Gay men are a very strong community now, but she's not being more of a feminist, as a result. I mean it's her choice, but it's a put down for lesbians.

'It's about authority letting us down, isn't it? Fathers, lovers, politics, ideals, gurus, faith healers, lesbians, supervisors ... ' She grinned.

Daphne smiled at her. 'I'm sorry. I've been really insensitive today. Please think about what relates to you. Your intuition *does* work for you, doesn't it? You don't need a guru in your life. I think you're saying that you and your clients are finding out that what's important isn't control but personal power – autonomy – and making other people responsible for what they do.

'What you feel for your clients ... you're very empathic, and these are *your* feelings too. I'm still wondering, though, why today, in particular, you were convinced that you were stuck. You said your intuition didn't work for you, only for other people?'

'Oh, yes. For one thing, why didn't I ask Sylvia about the hospital? She could get the psychiatric diagnosis taken off her medical records, I should think. Really, though, it was about the group – we were supposed to heal the world. How we got healed ourselves, apparently, was by channelling it to others. I was sitting in my wheelchair while this woman blabbed on, and I must have been feeling really upset, and, well, I can't be me and be truly spiritual. All I could think about was: "*What if I haven't got chakras?*" '

Lesbian women go to therapy because they want to be themselves. This is the real meaning of 'coming out of the closet'. An anti-oppressive practitioner always asks the next question: why are lesbians (and gay men) still in closets, twenty-five years on from Stonewall?

First, they are locked into them by prejudicial social attitudes, psychoanalytic theories, their inherited self-prejudices, and the multiple oppressions which form the heterosexist system. Now, they are also locked in by Government policy which more or less states 'You must intentionally promote heterosexuality'.

Second, they are locked *out* of full participation in society. They are not considered worth counting, even from sociological curiosity.

Lesbians *are* 'promoted', of course. Consider all those lesbian Rambos and murderous bisexual women in recent exploitation films. Women leave their husbands, take to the road, murder rapists, create general havoc, then, after a passionate bonding kiss, they hold hands and soar to their deaths. Or they are serial killers: they track their college sweethearts and, in a frenzy of SM passion, slice the husbands and lovers to death. Lesbian love is a basic instinct or a fatal attraction, a neat Hollywood inversion of the real story. Alternatively, lesbian characters vie for ratings in rival TV soaps, are profiled as the new ravers in youth culture magazines, or iconized as comedy or rock anarchists.

And so, lesbians (and gay men) are unfit to practise psychoanalysis, invisible in modern therapy, have no particular needs as clients, nothing of value to contribute to professional debates, are not welcome at fundraisers for children in need or as foster parents for children possibly in more urgent need . . . These and several other examples of prejudice and aggression are reported regularly in *The Pink Paper*.

These contemporary media images, along with the ghost of Stephen

Gordon, come into therapy again and again. It is reasonable to assume that lesbians do not come to therapy if they are being themselves, feeling good about themselves, and leading contented and fulfilling lives, but the Pride frontliners are only a small proportion of the lesbian population. A more representative body would be the total membership of the local lesbian social groups, which meet once a month or so in a suburban house, or the lifelong partners, perhaps with children, who don't *know* there's a local social group, or the business partners who can't be seen by possible customers going to the local bar or bi-monthly disco – which is probably full of gay men.

Lesbian vigour can also be inhibiting. Like gay men who won't go to Pride and be seen with screaming queens, there are lesbians, many of them older lesbians, who cannot relate to the scene or to politics or to any kind of fashionable categorizing. They do not want to be labelled any more. They want to be their own kind of lesbian, and perhaps they don't want to name themselves as 'lesbian'.

This is what therapy is for, to enable a woman to be herself – a lesbian if that is how she self-identifies – and to expand her world. When therapy becomes another closet, then it is reoppression.

For this reason, all the casework examples focus on the lesbians' *own* 'therapeutic methods': what they are doing themselves to cope with a crisis or external stress, or to escape from their personal traps, or to break into the world that they want, or to try to make a new one. The 'coping skills' are not the answer. The solution is in the problem, and the reason that it is expressed in an alienating or self-harmful way is because oppression has twisted it round like that, and so disorientated it – and, often, problematized it, so increasing the lesbian's isolation.

Lil copes by escaping. That was, probably, her first consciously lesbian decision. Her problems are indirect ways of asking for attention. She has acknowledged the more empowering option, of asking for help to achieve what she wants to do. This is to build her own family unit within a supportive lesbian community, do the work she is good at, live and love her partner and be loved by her. First, she needs to identify what is preventing her from doing any of these quite ordinary things, and to be enabled to find her *own* way (in this case, a legal way) of challenging the oppression she is bringing home each day.

Mara does not think she *has* any 'coping skills', only problems. She believes she is a monster from an alien family. She wants a 'cure' or perhaps a 'fix', something to stop the pain of being abandoned and isolated yet again. She blames herself for this. Her own solution – her best 'pain-killer' – is to keep her relationship going, to express a different, mutually supportive kind of love, to stay *friends* with her 'ex'.

Bella fantasizes about glamour and fame, and creative achievement – a way of saying '*this* is who lesbians are'. She does not want to go back to the lost days of alcoholism – her standard way of coping. She already has what she wants. All she needs is permission to be herself, *from* herself, through her most valuable creative source – her sexuality. Her real creative achievements were her daughters, freeing herself from addictions, a good relationship and a comfortable home. Her glamour is in her lesbian sexuality, and her appeal to a wild and irresponsible younger woman with dash and fire. That is what her book was going to be about – her message to herself.

Katie is struggling with the dilemma of following her natural path and loyalties to people she has long grown away from: family, ex-partner, her closeted, encircling lover-recycling social group who drink and chat and argue their lesbian lives away, always looking for the next new arrival to come in. Katie wants to go out and find whatever the world has to offer her. She wants to be her own 'ideal lesbian' and perhaps, one day, she will be able to truly 'see' herself.

Donna is sick of being a token, and of carrying the responsibility for men's prejudice and insensitivity about the effects of different oppressions on women, while she has committed herself to support work at an AIDS project. Racism, sexism, lesbian-oriented heterosexism – she is 'teaching' them for free, since it isn't her contracted job, getting neither payment nor support, nor interest in her as an individual with important ideas to contribute to the project. She picks up resentment and guilt, and feels increasingly disempowered. Donna's natural response is to talk – give information, challenge and assert herself.

She wants therapy in order to find out how to avoid being scapegoated, being 'more different than she is already', or to find out if she's doing something wrong so that she can change it. She has already realized that the job feels like too much responsibility, and decides to share this responsibility with someone who isn't going to put career above lesbian needs.

Her most empowering solutions are: change the power imbalance by stating her legal position, validate her natural teaching capabilities and highly developed communication skills, and claim her right to a *genuinely* equal opportunity to show what she can do. And if they don't want to know, she'll take her formidable catalogue of skills and insights somewhere they will be appreciated – where *she* will be appreciated as a Black Lesbian Woman.

Devorah is desperately trying to be self-reliant, but is cutting off from herself. She has made a joke of everything that is important to her and her cultural heritage. She has the strong Jewish sense of community survival. She wants to support adventurous young travellers, to help oppressed people everywhere to receive proper education. She *knows* her best 'therapy' is to honour her grandmother's unconditional love and nurturing, to accept her attention and her classic (if stereotypical) 'cure-all' chicken soup (which, incidentally, if free-range, is packed with immunity-building substances), to hear good music, to be accepted as a full member of her own community, and at the same time be independent – to gain a qualification, a chance she missed by being hospitalized solely because she was a lesbian. And she needs to heal the damage caused by her parents, who walked in on her most important sexual relationship.

She is empowering herself, convincing herself that she is, after all 'sane', and, in her idiosyncratic, self-parodying way, controlling the aggression which she has been brought up to fear.

'Jay' (Chapter 3) 'escapes' too – in the way she was conditioned from birth to do – into heterosexual fantasies, the expression of the dilemma which offers no choices that Anna Freud described in her earliest paper: 'altruistic surrender' versus 'identifying with the aggressor' (Freud, A., 1922). Anna Freud was also writing about being a woman and a Jew. 'Jay's' crowded mind is surely evidence of the effects of internalized oppression in the collective psyche of the twentieth-century lesbian, the almost obsessive and lonely attempts to make sense of it all. 'Jay' (who is three very different women) was also in her SM fantasies trying to be in control of the aggression – this was her 'coping skill'. 'Her' eventual solution was to share her fears with other lesbians, to de-stigmatize the issue, to perceive it in its political context, and to stop thinking about 'therapy' and, instead, of consciousness-raising among other lesbians.

And Robyn? (Chapter 5.) She's been fighting her partner, the epitome of internalized heterosexism, for fourteen years. Her solution is to leave, by choice – not to 'escape' into another socially-designated and self-defeating role – and to find the life she has wanted since she was seven or eight years old. What she did (for those who are interested) was to start by fighting spiritual oppression – the cause of her denial of sexuality at the important age – and joining the campaign to ordain women priests in the Anglican Church. She abandoned nursing and became a lesbian sexual health adviser at a drug and alcohol addiction recovery centre. Her partner, stunned at Robyn's assertiveness, booked herself into a therapeutic community in the heart of beautiful countryside.

Sylvia became isolated and lost her lesbian values with the death of her lifelong partner – the people she turned to for help and support de-valued them further, and rendered them meaningless. So she finds a lesbian counsellor – that's her 'therapeutic statement'. Once her grief becomes more manageable, she may decide to learn from other survivors how to re-build her life. Ageism has made her redundant and so devalued her talents and achievements. But she still has rights, and a great deal to offer to lesbian communities, where she will still be valued, and her contribution to society acknowledged.

Vita and Vi? Vita already has her answer. It is to create their own sexual values based on equality, and an acknowledgement of the sexual oppression of all women. In rejecting these values, if Vita and Vi want to stay together they must do what most lesbians are doing – creating a new sexuality, based on equality and mutual respect. When two people are complete, separate individuals and they enjoy each other's differences – *that's* when the sparks fly.

Jill has given up trying to find reasons for everything that she can't change. She knows the reasons. She feels betrayed, and that's why she feels depressed. In facing reality, she can demand justice instead of worsening the situation by logic-battering sessions with her separatist sisters. The answer is to identify their legal rights. That's how feminism was founded, before the industrial revolution. Jill's group could create a lesbian Charter for a community where all lesbians are welcome, and bisexual women too if they want to support anti-heterosexist causes. They could join with established groups and make sure that *all* lesbian rights are recorded and that this Charter is freely distributed. An inventive lesbian needs to learn only how to exploit the system. The advantage of being politically aware is understanding the system better than it understands itself – knowledge, as always, is power.

Many of Natalie's issues are, at their heart the same as her clients'. Lesbian values can be sexual, political, personal, relationship and spiritual. She refuses to be totally immobilized by her increasing physical disability. She is trying to deny this reality. She states this repeatedly. Her supervisor misses this essential point – possibly why Natalie couldn't tell her about the obvious resource for anyone whose body is becoming weak or ill, or unreliable, or dying. She wants to find some meaning for her life – then she might be able to face the reality that she will need to use a wheelchair for the rest of her life. She wants a 'lesbian spirituality' – healing for the internalized prejudices which have come to haunt her along with her increasing disability, and the pain of acknowledging what her father did to her, the symbol of authority's failure to care for its dependants.

Her supervisor likes a certain amount of authority and something tangible to see – the way *she* likes to work – this counter-transference bounces through Natalie and through her clients, to their partners and their friends. Natalie missed some important clues by losing faith in her own intuition. But in dictating her own supervision terms, trusting that her confusion was a statement of needs, she could identify the common experiences of internalized heterosexism, and explain the hostile feelings which bounce back again out of lesbian women, though so many are unaware why.

Natalie is searching for an empowering guide to enable her to keep working with confidence and commitment, something any heterosexual counsellor would take as her due. She has just earned accreditation. She has agreements with her clients, and does not want debility or disability to interfere with her reliability unless it becomes unavoidable. She knows she must plan for this eventuality, but she was disempowered by investing her faith in an external authority. Her own spirituality, however she identifies this – intuition, she says – is her best authority, and this – her autonomy, the only part of her which no one can damage or disable – can guide her through the rest of her working life. Perhaps too, through the re-validation of herself, she will remember that she is a *sexual* woman, and not keep herself alone.

She has said she wants less responsibility. She *needs* and is entitled to support, in order to be able to accept her personal reality, as well as the truth about the New Age 'healing' con. She also wants some fun. She is unusually 'cheeky' to her counsellor. Part of her is intrigued by Vita and Vi's spicing up their sex life, and she knows that deep love is possible towards someone weak and abusive – her own father.

She hasn't got it in her to hate him; and she can relate to Jill's desire for independence and peaceful co-existence and her hatred of incompetent authority. Natalie demonstrates her (and, incidentally, all of her clients') best option, in her supervision – to negotiate. She changes the form of communication, just as she must learn to change the way she relates to and participates in the able-bodied world. She has no choice but to take physical life as it comes, but, like Sylvia, she can begin to plan for her future – as a lesbian woman.

*a*ppendix

Methodology

All the women quoted in the text identify as lesbians, except where indicated. Preliminary research was based on two talks on therapy-related subjects with lesbian groups in London, and feedback from a series of equalities training, heterosexism awareness, and lesbian/gay issues workshops in different UK locations with practitioners in counselling, clinical psychology, mental health service user/advocacy groups, and lesbian and gay health workers.

THE QUESTIONNAIRE

The questionnaire was based on twelve interviews with lesbians training and working in therapy (voluntary and paid) and four with heterosexual women. Both groups included supervisors/trainers.

As this was not intended to be an academic survey, the questions were open, and completion of each segment was voluntary; there were separate groups of questions for client (individual and group), voluntary, training, and practice experience. Apart from clients (some of whom were also volunteers), most contributors completed all sections, including the general comments. Some wrote on the back of the form.

RESEARCH METHODOLOGY: CONTACTING LESBIANS IN THERAPY

(A) Notices were placed in the main general and specialist UK press (including membership bulletins) serving the following readership: (1) lesbians, (2) all women/feminists, (3) lesbians and gay men, (4) counsellors, (5) humanistic psychotherapists, (6) mental health workers/service user advocacy groups, (7) a national newspaper women's page (*The Guardian*).

(B) Notices were delivered or sent direct, with a request to pin on appropriate boards or to circulate as appropriate, to:

(a) lesbian, women's, and lesbian/gay centres which offered counselling services, (b) lesbian network newsletters, (c) general women's centres in principal cities, (d) transcultural counselling and mental health service user projects, (e) therapy/counselling training centres (one with a student newspaper) known to include equalities training or to welcome lesbian/gay trainees (most of the latter were in London).

(C) Direct contact was made with lesbian practitioners who advertised in lesbian and women's publications.

RESPONSE

There were 130 requests for: questionnaires for completion (82), interviews (18) (by telephone), and questionnaires/further information (31). (All questionnaires were sent with an explanatory letter outlining the book proposal.)

In several cases, respondents had seen the notice in more then one place. Most of the trainee/practitioner responses came from the notices in *Counselling* and the bulletin of the Association for Humanistic Psychology in Britain (AHPB).

Most of the client/volunteer responses came from the notices in *Lesbian London* and centres such as London Friend, the London Women's Centre, the newsletters of Pink Therapy and the Association for Lesbian, Gay and Bisexual Psychologies (again, the notice had also been seen elsewhere in most cases) and from direct approaches – most lesbians contacted offered to network and place notices on their centre boards. One response came from *The Guardian*.

There were very few *client-only* responses from outside London, apart from the North East and the Midlands as a result of local workshops at conferences such as the British Association for Counselling and MIND.

Although the *overall* response was national (including Northern Ireland) there was no opportunity to check if notices sent direct to locations outside London had been pinned up/circulated. The general impression gained was that therapy training centres – even those known to be welcoming to lesbian/lesbian and gay trainees and clients – had not pinned up the notices. The highest level of participation was through:

(1) the practice-oriented journals, (2) lesbian and lesbian/gay media, (3) direct contact (including the Pink Therapy/ALGBP bulletins).

An observation here is that confidentiality was a major concern and that either personal contact or a known reference point encouraged participation. This did not apply where respondents were isolated. Where there was more than one questionnaire from, for instance, a medium-sized regional city, the lesbian trainees/practitioners were unaware of each other's existence.

Many of the women who asked for questionnaires were too busy to complete them, felt they could not support the project, or disliked the style/content (some wrote and stated this). Still, the lack of participation by experienced lesbian practitioners (either in senior positions or well-established in private practice), who had been sent information and questionnaires, was felt to require follow-up. Of those who could be reached, most offered the reasons given above. One agreed that her writing on lesbian issues could be quoted, but without referring to her as a 'lesbian' practitioner. Some contributed their own research or new writing for inclusion or background. Seven explained that they were occupied with coursework or writing on lesbian therapy issues for future publication (quoted where available). Four offered in-depth interviews instead. One disliked the 'politically correct' approach, and another criticized the non-academic format of the questionnaire. Eight did not return the messages left on answerphones.

In summary, then, the content of this book cannot be said to be fully representative of a 'lesbian approach' to therapy in the UK at present, only of the views and opinions of the contributors who offered full participation. However, the high level of anti-lesbian prejudice, especially in the analytical schools and psychology, must be taken into account. This includes the internalized heterosexism which led some of the non-participants to comment that a 'lesbian approach' to therapy was unnecessary, or even inappropriate, since practitioners' openness about their personal lives is considered (again, in analytical schools) contrary to therapeutic ethics and detrimental to the therapy process.

Thirty-eight questionnaires were returned, four marked 'not for quoting', and two completed anonymously. Most were signed or initialled as consenting to be quoted (anonymously), and some completed neither box. It was assumed that those who did not mark the 'No' box were prepared to have their information included. However, because of this ambiguity and the possibility of breaching confidentiality, there is no detailed profile of respondents here.

Of the requests for interviews, 15 in-depth telephone interviews were completed (in addition to the initial 12). A core of 14 contributors offered a very high level of participation, right up to the time of editing.

TYPICAL CLIENT PROFILE

Most of the client responses showed experience of more than one type of therapy (described also as counselling) including short-term and long-term individual therapy (NHS and private practice), self-help groups, and facilitated (mixed) groups. The highest number of therapy experiences from any one respondent was five. Very few had only one experience.

'Lesbian age' ranged from one to 30 years. As not all questions were answered, no statistics can be given for the number of lesbians who came out in therapy, or of women who decided during therapy that they were not lesbians.

Most frequently, the lesbians who went to therapy (and who replied to this question) did so because of issues other than sexual identity. These were: general concerns, illness, depression, addiction recovery and partnership issues. Also, problems caused by hostility and prejudice from: birth family, male partners (including fathers of their children), friends, colleagues or co-students, neighbours or landlords, and race or class prejudice (in particular, though not exclusively) within lesbian/lesbian and gay communities. The high degree of stated prejudice and lack of awareness from heterosexual therapy practitioners (and trainers) altered the entire perspective of this book.

TYPICAL TRAINEE/PRACTITIONER PROFILE

Most of the core respondents began to study counselling, a humanistic or body-oriented therapy, or psychotherapy, either (a) as a result of voluntary counselling/helpline/group work experience, for skills development and personal learning and support; or (b) because of a good experience of therapy – usually, a second (in one case, a third) experience – the earlier therapy being negative. Four noted that they had studied because of bad experiences and had hoped that training would both inform and empower them and redress the balance of this negativity.

The respondents who contributed most fully all included in their backgrounds: voluntary befriending/counselling helpline work (especially the latter) in lesbian, lesbian and gay, or women's projects, including rape crisis centres and battered women's refuges.

Of those who had received training on equalities issues as a part of the curriculum, most named the approach studied as Person-Centred, Feminist-based or Humanistic. Training on lesbian or gay issues was non-existent outside six London centres, one of which ran a specialist sexuality awareness training course. Usually, the (sole) lesbian trainee raised these issues herself. The more 'formal' and theoretical the approach taught, the less equalities issues were covered.

The counselling/counselling skills courses situated in Adult Education centres provided basic equalities training and extended their policies to staff – these were, mainly, courses defining their training as 'self-directed'. The most intensive training in (all) equalities issues, sexuality awareness, and specific issues such as living with stigma were, as would be expected, those which were specialist HIV/AIDS and sexual health counselling trainings. Many of the respondents on formal courses attended short trainings on HIV/AIDS and sexual health issues, often because these were the only available courses in their regions which addressed *any* equalities issues. The attention paid to the principal equalities issues of race and gender on most formal psychotherapy trainings was alarmingly low (in several cases, nil). There was no specific anti-oppressive training (that is, awareness of interlinked prejudices) in any school attended by respondents, apart from two with a feminist remit, one of which was not strictly a training centre for therapists but made 'working with women' courses available to other practitioners. Some respondents had studied, in addition to formal counselling or psychotherapy, various arts therapies and body-oriented therapies, and had attended workshops on other approaches (such as Gestalt), or specialist issues – in particular, sexual abuse, addiction recovery, HIV/AIDS, bereavement, and women's health.

INDIVIDUAL PROFILES

The questions of self-identity (race, ethnicity, class, ability/disability, religion, parental status, age, political identity etc.) were not answered by everyone. None of the questionnaire respondents defined herself as disabled (in two cases, new disability as a consequence of illness was given). Of those who identified by race, all but three were white. Most who listed class defined themselves as middle-class (including first-generation middle-class) or working-class. Where separate ethnic identity was named, this was mainly given as Irish, in two cases Scottish, and in three cases white/non-British. Political identity (where given) varied from left-wing, feminist, and lesbian feminist. None gave her age, though some defined as middle-aged. Few gave religions; those who did were Jewish or Christian. One was Roman Catholic, and another atheist. There was a high awareness of women's spirituality issues.

Data analysis

This survey was not intended to produce statistics, but to draw, from the very detailed information, common themes which applied to:

1. Issues lesbians bring to therapy.

2. Evaluations of therapy as a personal resource.

3. Causes of negative experiences of therapy.

4. Evaluations of differences (in addition to gender/sexual orientation) which affected the therapy.

5. General awareness from practitioners of: (a) women's issues, in particular sexuality (including sexual abuse, sexism, sexual harassment, gender-role expectations, connections between sexual and other forms of discrimination); and (b) lesbian-specific issues – personal, sexual, relationship and social, including awareness of anti-lesbian prejudice, internal lesbian/gay community prejudices, and heterosexism.

6. General comments on politics and therapy.

7. Proposals for lesbian-affirmative/anti-oppressive approaches.

There were no questions on coming out (initial self-identification of sexual orientation) as there is other literature available on this subject.

Follow up

As a result of the high degree of heterosexism, anti-lesbian prejudice, and a general lack of awareness in professional therapy reported by the respondents, formal and informal interviews were carried out with representatives of the following organizations or groups:
the Equal Opportunities Commission (training department);
the British Association for Counselling (re: training criteria);
the UK Council for Psychotherapy (re: training criteria and Intercultural Committee survey);

the Lead Body for Advice, Guidance, and Counselling (now also for Psychotherapy), and the consultants devising the NVQ/SVQ standards in counselling and therapy practice;
MIND (National Association for Mental Health);
selected training centres (counselling/humanistic psychotherapy).

Observations

The level of awareness of equalities issues in counselling (as represented by the BAC personnel involved in 'professionalization') and in humanistic psychotherapy (personnel or institutes in the Humanistic and Integrative Section of the UKCP) was abysmally low at the time of the survey (during 1994). Awareness was better by comparison in service or other organizations involved in care, counselling, health or mental health disciplines – including, it hardly needs stating, lesbian and gay projects. This began to change during 1995 (see Introduction).

The most forward-thinking approaches in therapy to equalities issues (especially for women), and to anti-oppressive practice, were expressed by MIND, and (in terms of professional training/competence) the Lead Body and their consultants.

An interview, arranged as this book went to press, for a comment on the new equalities standards in the NVQs/SVQs with a BAC Equalities Officer was cancelled. A request for an interview with his colleague (at his suggestion) was never answered.

Separate contacts were made with counsellors involved in race equality training during the past eight years, who had set up independent multiracial groups, or who had a long tradition of holding race equality workshops with counsellors. So the 'new' professionalism may not be representative of the views of traditional counsellors.

It is intended that elements of the survey not included in this book – extensive information on a range of subjects – will be covered in future publications, in particular the membership bulletins of the lesbian and gay trainee and practitioner associations. The author would be pleased to receive comments from lesbian women in therapy in the UK on any of the issues raised above or in the book. Alternatively, contributions/comments may be submitted to these associations for inclusion in newsletters or future conference workshops. (See Resources for addresses.)

bibliography

Note: Several references to writings by Sigmund Freud are from *The Essentials of Psycho-Analysis*, *The Definitive Collection*, edited by Anna Freud, with introduction and commentaries, in 1981, and published in 1986 (London, Penguin). SE refers to the Standard Edition of Sigmund Freud's collected works, translated by James Strachey (London, Hogarth). Anna Freud's own *Writings* (8 vols; London, Hogarth) are listed as *Writings* with volume number. Whenever possible, paperback editions are given.

Abbott, S. and B. Love, *Sappho Was a Right-On Woman: A Liberated View of Lesbianism*. New York, Stein & Day, 1972.

Agana, P.J., in M. Wilson (ed.), 1994.

AGC&P Journal No. 4. *Networks*. Lead Body for Advice, Guidance, Counselling and Psychotherapy, 1994.

Annesley, P., 'Clinical psychologists' knowledge, skills and attitudes in working with lesbian clients'. Unpublished MSc dissertation, University of Surrey, Department of Psychology, 1995.

Arnot, M. (ed.), *Race and Gender: Equal Opportunities Policies in Education*. London, Open University/Pergamon, 1985.

Barnes, M. and N. Maple, *Women and Mental Health: Challenging the Stereotypes*. London, Venture, 1992.

Bass, E. and L. Davis, *The Courage to Heal: A Guide for Women Survivors of Childhood Sexual Abuse*. London, Mandarin, 1988.

Beck, E.T. (ed.) *Nice Jewish Girls: A Lesbian Anthology*. Trumansburg, NY, The Crossing Press/London, Persephone, 1982.

Becker, C.S., *Unbroken Ties: Lesbian Ex-Lovers*. Boston, Alyson, 1988.

Beckett, E, 'Personal history', in Hall Carpenter Archives/Lesbian History Group, 1989.

Berger, R.M., 'Older gays and lesbians', in R.J. Kus (ed.), 1990.

Bettelheim, B., 'Freedom from ghetto thinking', in *Recollections and Reflections*. London, Penguin, 1990.

Bettelheim, B., *Freud and Man's Soul*. London, Chatto & Windus, 1993.

Bettelheim, B. and A. Rosenfeld, *The Art of the Obvious*. London, Thames & Hudson, 1993.

Bland, L., 'Purity, motherhood, pleasure, or threat? Definitions of female sexuality 1900–1970s', in S. Cartledge and J. Ryan (eds), 1983.

Braun, G. and D. Bell, 'Dealing with ethics and equality in national standards', in *Competence and Assessment*, 25 March 1995.

Browne, A., *When Battered Women Kill*. New York, Free Press, 1989.

Burch, B., 'Psychological merger in lesbian couples: a joint ego psychological and systems approach', *Family Therapy*, no. 10, 1982, pp. 201–8.

Burstow, B., *Radical Feminist Therapy: Working in the Context of Violence*. New York, Sage, 1992.

Caprio, F.S., *Female Homosexuality*, New York, Evergreen, 1962.

Card, C. (ed.), *Hypatia*, vol. 7, no. 4: *Lesbian Philosophy*. Indiana University, 1992.

Carrington, K.L., 'Women loving women: speaking the truth in love', in R.H. Hopcke *et al.* (eds), 1993.

Cartledge, S. and J. Ryan (eds), *Sex and Love: New Thoughts on Old Contradictions*. London, Women's Press, 1983.

Chapman, D. with M. Farnham, 'Personal history', in Hall Carpenter Archives/ Lesbian Oral History Group, 1989.

Chesler, P., *Women and Madness*. New York, Avon, 1973.

Chetwynd, T., A *Dictionary of Symbols*. London, Granada, 1982.

Chodorow, N., *Feminism, Masculinities, Sexualities: Freud and Beyond*. London, Free Association, 1994.

Christmas, M., 'Jewish gays and lesbians', in R.J. Kus (ed.), 1990.

Christopher, E., *Psycho-Sexual Problems*. London, British Association for Counselling, 1993.

Clarkson, P. and M. Pokorny (eds), *The Handbook of Psychotherapy*. London, Routledge, 1994.

Comely, L., C. Kitzinger, R. Perkins and S. Wilkinson, 'Anti-lesbianism in the British Psychological Society', *Self and Society*, vol. 21, no. 1, 1993, pp. 7–9.

Dana, M. and M. Lawrence, *Women's Secret Disorder*. London, Grafton (pb), 1988.

Davies, D. and C. Neal (eds), *Pink Therapy: A Guide for Counsellors and Therapists Working with Lesbian, Gay and Bisexual Clients*. Milton Keynes, Open University Press, 1996.

Denman, F., 'Prejudice and homosexuality', *British Journal of Psychotherapy*, vol. 8, no. 3, 1993, pp. 346–57.

Doress, P. B. and D. L. Siegal, in co-operation with The Boston Women's Health Book Collective, *Ourselves Growing Older*. New York, Simon and Schuster/ Touchstone, 1987. UK edn: J. Shapiro (ed.), London, Fontana, 1989.

Dublin Lesbian and Gay Men's Collectives, *Out for Ourselves: The Lives of Irish Lesbians and Gay Men*, Dublin; Lesbian and Gay Men's Collective and Women's Community Press, 1986.

Duffy, M., *The Microcosm*. London, Panther, 1967.

Eichenbaum, L. and S. Orbach, *Outside In, Inside Out – Women's Psychology: A Feminist Psychoanalytic Approach*. London, Penguin, 1982.

Elliott, M. (ed.), *Female Sexual Abuse of Children: The Ultimate Taboo*. London, Longman, 1993.

Ellis, M.L., *Lesbians, Gay Men and Psychoanalytical Training*. London, Free Association, 1994.

Ernst, S., 'Can a daughter be a woman? Women's identity and psychological separation', in S. Ernst and M. Maguire (eds), *Living With the Sphinx: Papers From The Women's Therapy Centre*. London, Women's Press, 1987.

Ernst, S. and L. Goodison, *In Our Own Hands: A Book of Self-Help Therapy*. London, Women's Press, 1981.

Fein, S.B. and E.M. Muehring, 'Intrapsychic effects of stigma: a process of breakdown and reconstruction of social reality', *Journal of Homosexuality*, vol. 7, no. 1, 1981 (USA).

Freud, A. (1922) *Beating Fantasies and Daydreams, Introduction to Psychoanalysis. Writings*, vol. 1. London, Hogarth.

Freud, A. (1936) *Writings*, vol. 2, *The Ego and the Mechanisms of Defence*. London, Hogarth.

Freud, A. (1981) Introduction and commentaries to S. Freud, *The Essential of Psycho-Analysis – The Definitive Collection of Sigmund Freud's Writing*. London, Penguin, 1986.

Freud, M., *Glory Reflected*. London, Thames & Hudson, 1957.

Freud, S., *The Complete Letters to Wilhelm Fleiss (1887–1904)*, ed. J.M. Masson., Cambridge, MA, Harvard University, 1985.

Freud, S. *Leonardo* (1910), trans. A.A. Brill as *Leonardo da Vinci: A Study in Psychosexuality*. New York, Modern Library Edition, 1917.

Freud, S., 'The psychogenesis of a case of homosexuality in a woman' (1920), in *Collected Papers* II, trans. Joan Riviere, 1924. Quoted in D. Klaich, *Woman + Woman: Attitudes Towards Lesbianism*. New York, Morrow, 1974.

Freud, S., Footnote (1925) to *Three Essays on the Theory of Sexuality*. (1905) 6th edn, trans. J. Strachey. SE, vol. 7, London, Hogarth, 1953.

Freud, S., *The Future of an Illusion* (1927). SE, vol. 21. London, Hogarth.

Freud, S. and J. Breuer, *Studies in Hysteria* (1895). SE, vol. 2. London, Hogarth, 1925.

Friday, N., *My Secret Garden: Women's Sexual Fantasies*. London, Virago, 1975.

Fromm, E., *Sigmund Freud's Mission*. New York, Harper, 1959.

Gil, E., *Treatment of Adult Survivors of Childhood Abuse*. California, Launch, 1988.

Gilroy, B., 'Black old age ... the diaspora of the senses?' in M. Wilson (ed.), 1984.

Gorman, J., *Out of the Shadows*. London, MIND, 1992.

Greene, B. and G.M. Herek (eds), *Psychological Perspectives on Lesbian and Gay Issues*, vol.

1: *Lesbian and Gay Psychology: Theory Research and Clinical Applications*. Thousand Oaks, CA, Sage, 1994.

Greer, G., 'The politics of female sexuality', in *Female Energy*. Sydney, Oz Magazine, 1970.

Greer, P. and J. Breckenridge, ' "They throw the rule book away": sexual assault in Aboriginal communities', in J. Breckenridge and M. Carmody (eds), *Crimes of Violence*. Sydney, Allen & Unwin, 1992.

Guntrip, H., *Schizoid Phenomena, Object-Relations, and The Self*. London, Hogarth, 1983.

Hall, M. and A. Gregory, 'Love and work in lesbian relationships', in B. Sang *et al.* (eds), 1991.

Hall, R., *The Well of Loneliness*. London, Jonathan Cape, 1928. (Banned until 1948 in the UK, and republished by Falcon.)

Hall, R., L. Tice, T. Beresford and A. Hall, 'Sexual abuse in patients with anorexia and bulimia', *Psychosomatics*, vol. 30, no. 1, 1989, pp. 73–9.

Hall Carpenter Archives/Lesbian History Group, *Inventing Ourselves: Lesbian Life Stories*. London, Routledge, 1989.

Hansen, M. and M. Harway (eds), *Battering and Family Therapy: A Feminist Perspective*. CA, Sage, 1993.

Hay, L., *Heal Your Body*. London, Eden Grove, 1988.

Heenan, C., 'Out on a limb? Lesbian psychotherapists', *Changes*, vol. 12, no. 4, 1994, pp. 284–9.

Hemmings, S., *Older Lesbians* (information leaflet). London, Lesbian Line, 1989.

Hendessi, M., *Four in Ten: Report on Young Women Who Become Homeless as a Result of Sexual Abuse*. London, CHAR, 1992.

Hepburn, G. and B. Gutierrez, *Alive and Well: A Lesbian Health Guide*. CA, Crossing Press, 1988.

Hitchings. P., 'Psychotherapy and sexual orientation', in P. Clarkson and M. Pokorny (eds), 1994.

Hite, S., *The Hite Report: A Nationwide Study of Female Sexuality*. New York, Dell, 1976.

Hopcke, R.H., K.L. Carrington and S. Wirth (eds), *Same Sex Love and the Path to Wholeness*. Boston, Shambala, 1993.

Hossack, A., 'Difficulties working with the intellectual schizoid – a care study', *Counselling*, vol. 5, no. 4, 1993, pp. 277–80.

Jacobs, M. (ed.) *The Care Guide: A Handbook for the Caring Professions and Other Agencies*. London, Cassell, 1995.

Janes, J., 'Equal opportunities and the Equal Opportunities Directory', *Competence and Assessment*, no. 27. London, Department of Employment, 1994.

Jeffreys, S., *The Lesbian Heresy: A Feminist Perspective on the Lesbian Sexual Revolution*. London, Women's Press, 1994.

Jordan, S. 'Glad to be gay?' *Self and Society*, vol. 22, no. 2. London Association for Humanistic Psychotherapy, 1994.

Kasl, C.D., *Women, Sex and Addiction*. London, Mandarin, 1990.

Kaye-Kantrowitz, N. and I. Klepfisz (eds), *The Tribe of Dina: A Jewish Women's Anthology*. Rockland, ME, Sinister Wisdom, 1986.

Kirkland, G. with G. Lawrence, *Dancing on My Grave*. New York, Doubleday, 1986/London, Penguin.

Kitzinger, C. and A. Coyle, 'Lesbian and gay couples: speaking of difference', *The Psychologist*, February 1995, pp. 64–9.

Kitzinger, C. and R. Perkins, *Changing Our Minds: Lesbian Feminism and Psychology*. London, OnlyWomen, 1993.

Klaich, D., *Woman Plus Woman: Attitudes Towards Lesbianism*. New York, Simon & Schuster, 1974/Morrow (paperback), 1975.

Klein, C., *Counselling Our Own: The Lesbian/Gay Subculture Meets the Mental Health Service* (2nd edn). Seattle, Consultant Services North West, 1991.

Kramer, M., *Jewish Grandmothers*. New York, Beacon, 1976.

Kurdek, L.A., 'The nature and correlates of relationship quality in gay, lesbian, and heterosexual co-habiting couples: a test of the individual difference, interdependence and discrepancy models', in B. Greene and G.N. Herek (eds), 1994.

Kus, R.J. (ed.), *Keys to Caring: Assisting Your Gay and Lesbian Clients*. Boston, Alyson, 1990.

Loulan, J., ' "Now when I was your age": one perspective on how lesbian culture has influenced our sexuality', in B. Sang *et al.* (eds), 1991.

Luke, H., *Kaleidoscope: The Way of Woman*. New York, Parabola, 1993.

Macdonald, B. and C. Rich, *Look Me in the Eye: Old Women, Age and Ageism*. San Francisco, Spinsters Ink, 1985.

McKenzie, S., 'Merger in lesbian relationships', *Women and Therapy*, vol. 12, no. 1/2, 1992, pp. 151–60.

McLelland, L. Mynors-Wallis and J. Treasure, 'Sexual abuse, disordered personality and eating disorders', *British Journal of Psychiatry*, vol. 158, no. 10, 1991, pp. 63–8.

McLeod, E., *Women's Experience of Feminist Therapy and Counselling*. London, Open University, 1994.

Macourt, M., *How Can We Help You? Information, Advice, and Counselling for Gay Men and Lesbians*. London, Bedford Square, 1989.

Marie, Personal history, in S. Neild and R. Pearson (eds), 1992.

Mason-John, V. (ed.), *Talking Black: Lesbians of African and Asian Descent Speak Out*. London, Cassell, 1995.

Mason-John, V. and A. Khambatta (eds), *Lesbians Talk: Making Black Waves*. London, Scarlet, 1993.

Mercier, L.R. and R.M. Berger, 'Social service needs of lesbian and gay adolescents: telling it their way', *Journal of Social Work and Human Sexuality*, vol. 8, no. 1, 1989, pp. 75–94.

Miller, A., *The Drama of Being a Child* (1979), trans. R. Ward. London, Virago, 1987.

Miller, A., *Thou Shalt Not Be Aware: Society's Betrayal of the Child*. London, Pluto, 1984.

Millett, K., *Sexual Politics*. New York, Knopf, 1971/London, Virago, 1979.

MIND, *Stress on Women Campaign Pack*. London, MIND Publications, 1993.

Montsho, Q. 'Behind locked doors', in V. Mason-John (ed.), 1995.

Moon, L., 'Working with lesbian and gay clients', *Counselling*, vol. 5, no. 1, 1994, p. 26.

Neal, C., 'Queer in the head?', *Self and Society*, vol. 21, no. 1, 1993, pp. 4–5.

Neild, S. and R. Pearson (eds), *Women Like Us*. London, Women's Press, 1992.

Neisen, J. H., 'Healing from cultural victimization: recovery from shame due to heterosexism', *Journal of Gay and Lesbian Psychotherapy*, vol. 2, no. 1, 1993.

O'Connor, N. and J. Ryan, *Wild Desires and Mistaken Identities: Lesbianism and Psychoanalysis*. London, Virago, 1993.

Off Pink Collective, *Bisexual Lives*. London, Off Pink, 1988.

Orzek, A.M., 'The lesbian victim of sexual assault: special considerations for the mental health professional', in E.D. Rothblum and E. Cole (eds), 1989.

Parmar, P., 'Black lesbians' in 'Loving women: lesbian life and relationships', in A. Phillips and J. Rakusen (eds), 1989.

Pearlman, S.F. 'Distancing and connectedness: impact on couple formation in lesbian relationships', in E.D. Rothblum and E. Cole (eds), 1989.

Peters, U.H., *Anna Freud: A Life Dedicated to Children* (1979). trans. Schockenbooks/London, Weidenfeld and Nicolson, 1985.

Phillips, A. and J. Rakusen (eds), *The New Our Bodies Ourselves* (2nd edn). Boston Women's Health Book Collective/London, Penguin, 1989.

Phillips, M., *War of the Words*. London, Virago, 1994.

Pink Therapy, *Journal of Pink Therapy* (the UK Lesbian and Gay trainees, counsellors' and psychotherapists' group), 1994.

Proctor, G. 'Lesbian clients' experiences of clinical psychology: a listeners' guide', *Changes*, vol. 12, no. 4, 1994.

Radical Therapist/Rough Times Collective, *The Radical Therapist Anthology*. Somerset, MA, Collective, 1971.

Rakusen, J., 'Loving women: lesbian life and relationships', in A. Phillips and J. Rakusen (eds), 1989.

Reich, W., *The Mass Psychology of Fascism* (1933), ed. M. Higgins, trans. C.M. Raphael, 1969; V.R. Carfagno (3rd edn). London, Souvenir, 1970.

Rendel, M., 'The winning of the Sex Discrimination Act', in M. Arnot (ed.), 1985.

Renzetti, C.M., 'Violence in lesbian relationships', in M. Hansen and M. Harway (eds), 1993.

Rothblum, E.D. and Cole, E. (eds), *Loving Boldly: Issues Facing Lesbians*. New York, Harrington Park, 1989.

Rowan, J., 'Rowan's trivia: going halfway', *AHPB Newsletter*, September 1994. London: Association for Humanistic Psychology in Britain.

Rowan, J., 'What is counselling about?', *Counselling*, vol. 6, no. 1, 1995, p. 12.

Ryan, J., 'Psychoanalysis and women loving women', in S. Cartledge and J. Ryan (eds), 1983.

Samuels, A., *The Political Psyche*. London, Routledge, 1993.

Sang, B., 'Midlife and older lesbians', in S.H. Dworkin and F.J. Gutierrez (eds), *Counselling Gay Men and Lesbians: Journey to the End of the Rainbow*. Virginia, American Counselling Association, 1992.

Sang, B., J. Warshow and A.J. Smith, *Lesbians at Midlife: The Creative Transition*. California, Spinsters Book Company, 1991.

Sayer, J., *Mothering Psychoanalysis*. London, Penguin, 1991.

Shapiro, J., 'The menopause: entering our third age', in P.B. Doress and D.L. Siegal (eds), 1989.

Shelley, M., 'Lesbianism', in Radical Therapist/Rough Times Collective, 1974.

Shidlo, A., 'Internalized homophobia – conceptual and empirical issues in measurement', in B. Greene and G.M. Herek (eds), 1994.

Smith, A.J., 'First of all, I'm Jewish – the rest is commentary', in B. Sang *et al.* (eds), 1991.

Solomon, M., Oral history (interview by Margaret Farnham), in Hall Carpenter Archives/Lesbian History Group, 1989.

Sophie, J., 'Internalized homophobia and lesbian identity', *Journal of Homosexuality* (USA), vol. 14, nos 1–2, 1987. (USA).

Southgate, J. and R. Randall, *The Barefoot Psychoanalyst*. London, The Association of Karen Horney Psychoanalytic Counsellors, 1978.

Stevens, C.T., 'Individuation and eros: finding my way', in R.H. Hopcke *et al.* (eds), 1993.

Taylor, J. and T. Chandler, *Lesbians Talk Violent Relationships*. London, Scarlet, 1995.

Thomas, P., 'A therapeutic journey through the Garden of Eden', *Counselling*, vol. 2, no. 4, 1991, pp. 143–5.

Thorn, L., 'Getting it all back', Counselling, vol. 1, no. 2, 1990.

Trigangles, R.G. *Anthology of Writing by Jewish Lesbians*. Trumansburg, NY, Crossing Press, 1986.

Tweedie, J., Introduction to N. Friday, 1975.

Tweedie, J., *In the Name of Love*. London, Jonathan Cape, 1979.

Wilkinson, S. and C. Kitzinger (eds), *Heterosexuality: A Feminism and Psychology Reader*. London, Sage, 1993.

Wilson, M. (ed.), *Healthy and Wise: The Essential Health Handbook for Black Women*. London, Virago, 1994.

Wittman, C. and M. Francis, *The Gay Liberation Manifesto*. Chicago, Seed Magazine, 1970.

Wolff, C., *Love Between Women*. London, Duckworth, 1971.

Wood, D., *The Power of Words: Uses and Abuses of Talking Treatments*. London, MIND Publications, 1994.

Young, V., 'Menopause', in M. Jacobs (ed.), 1995.

Young, V., 'Working with older lesbians', in D. Davies and C. Neal (eds), 1996.

resources

UK

For other national/local resources, refer to lesbian, women's, and gay media listings, trade unions or campus lesbian and gay groups, or send s.a.e. to appropriate organization. Groups are often unfunded or poorly funded. Some of the larger London centres are national resources or can provide details of local groups. Most funded helplines have Minicoms, and some also list lesbian therapy services.

Association of Greater London Older Women (AGLOW)
Older Lesbians Group
9 Manor Gardens
London N7 6LA

Association for Lesbian, Gay and Bisexual Psychologies UK (ALGBP)
c/o C. Neal
North End Practice
8a Burghley Road
London NW5 1UE

Bisexual Women's Group
BM LBWG
London WC1N 3XX

Black Lesbian and Gay Centre (BLGC)
BM Box 4390
London WC1N 3XX
(For a national list of Black/minority ethnic lesbian groups, see Mason-John and Khambatta, 1993).

Body Positive Women's Group
51b Philbeach Gardens
London SW5 9EB

GEMMA (Lesbians/bisexual women with/without disabilities)
BM Box 5700
London WC1N 3XX

Irish Lesbian Network
c/o London Irish Women's Centre
59 Stoke Newington Church Street
London N16

Jewish Lesbian and Gay Helpline
0171 706 3123

Leicester Lesbian, Gay, and Bisexual Community Resource Centre
(Lesbian sexual health information)
0116 254 7412

Lesbian and Gay Bereavement Project
via Switchboard 0171 837 7324
or (recorded message) 0181 455 8894 for duty counsellor

Lesbian and Gay Coalition Against Racism (LAGCAR)
PO Box 306
London N5

Lesbian and Gay Employment Rights (LAGER)
Unit 1G, Leroy House
436 Essex Road
London N1 3QP
Lesbian line: 0171 704 8066
Gay line: 0171 704 6066

Lesbian Custody Project
ROW
52–54 Featherstone Street
London EC1Y 8RT

Lesbian History Group (LHG)
and
Lesbian Archive and Information Centre (LAIC)
c/o London Women's Centre
Wesley House, 4 Wild Court
London WC2B 4AU

Lesbian Information Services (LIS)
and
Lesbian Youth Information/Support Service (LYSIS)
PO Box 8
Todmorden
Lancashire OL14 5TZ
Helpline: 01706 817235

Lesbian Line
BM Box 1514
London WC1N 3XX
0171 251 6911 Minicom: 0171 253 0924

London Friend
Lesbian Helpline: 0171 837 2782
Lesbian and Gay Helpline: 0171 837 3337
(Minicoms on both lines)

MIND
Granta House
15–19 Broadway
London E15 4BQ
0181 519 2122
Information line: 0181 522 1728

National Friend
(network of 38 befriending/helpline resources)
BM National Friend
London WC1N 3XX

National Union of Civil and Public Servants
Lesbian and Gay Group (NUCPS LGG)
BM 1645
London WC1N 3XX
0171 960 2038

Older Lesbian Network (OLN)
BM OLN
London WC1N 3XX

PACE (Project for Advice, Counselling and Education)
34 Hartman Road
London N7 9JL
0171 700 1323

Pink Therapy
c/o ACAS
34 Electric Lane
London SW9 8JT

Positively Women
5 Sebastian Street
London EC1V 0HE
0171 490 5155/0171 490 5501

QUEST
(Lesbian and gay Catholics)
BM Box 2585
London WC1X 3XX
0171 792 0234

Regard
(disabled lesbian/gay befriending/campaign group; quarterly journal *Regard Rights/Writes*)
BM Regard
London WC1N 3XX

Society of Telecom Engineers
Lesbian and Gay Group (STE L&G Group)
PPG8, Meridian House
34–35 Farringdon Street
London EC4A 4ED

Switchboard
(London Lesbian and Gay Switchboard)
LIGS, BM Switchboard
London WC1N 3XX
0171 837 7324

UNISON
(formerly NALGO)
Lesbian and Gay Group
1 Mabledon Place
London WC1H 9AJ
0171 388 2366

Wages Due Lesbians
(Black and white lesbian campaign against anti-lesbian discrimination)
0171 837 7509 (Minicom)

Women's Health
52–54 Featherstone Street
London EC1Y 8RT
0171 251 6580

Women's Therapy Centre
6 Manor Gardens
London N7 6LA

Publications

Cassell's Pink Directory:
Lesbian and Gay Organizations, Businesses and Services in the UK and Eire
L. Gibbs and T. Purcell (eds)

The Pink Paper
13 Hercules Street
London N7 6AT
Tel: 0171 272 2155

Perversions: International Journal of Lesbian and Gay Studies
BM Perversions
London WC1N 3XX

National AIDS Manual (NAM Publications)
and *UK Directory of Helpines Offering HIV/AIDS and Sexual Health Advice*
52 Eurolink Centre
49 Effra Road
London SW2 1BZ
Tel: 0171 737 1846

IRELAND/NORTHERN IRELAND

Belfast AIDS Helpline
01232 326117

Cara (Friend)
Belfast: 01232 22023

Cork AIDS Alliance
(00353) 21 275837

Cork Lesbian Collective
24 Sullivan's Quay
Cork

Cork Lesbian Line
(00353) 21 967026

Dublin AIDS Alliance
(00353) 1 8733799

Gay Switchboard (Dublin)
(00353) 1 721055

Irish Gay Rights Movements
(IGRM)
4 McCurtain Street
Cork

Lesbians and Gays at Work
(Trade union group covering 32 counties)
PO Box 97
Cork

National Gay Federation (NGF)
(for other group contacts/collectives)
Hirschfield Centre
10 Fownes Street
Dublin 2

Northern Ireland Gay Rights Association (NIGRA)
PO Box 44
Belfast BT1

Tel-A-Friend (TAF)
(Dublin)
Lesbian Line/Parents' Enquiry: (00353) 1710608

SCOTLAND

Edinburgh Lesbian Line
0131 557 0751

Edinburgh Gay Switchboard
0131 556 4049

Glasgow Lesbian Line
0141 353 3117

Strathclyde Gay and Lesbian Switchboard and Counselling Service
0141 221 8372

WALES

Cardiff Friend
01222 340101

Cardiff Lesbian Line
01222 374051

NETHERLANDS

ALGP Europe
(European Association for Lesbian and Gay Psychologies)
c/- Schorerstichting
PC Hoofstraat 3
1071 BL Amsterdam

HomoDok
Lesbian and Gay Studies Bibliographical Resources Centre
University of Amsterdam
Oudezijds Achterburgwal 185
1012 DK Amsterdam

SAD
(Lesbian and Gay Counselling Service)
PC Hoostraat 5
1071 BL Amsterdam

AUSTRALIA

Feminist Bookshop
Orange Grove Plaza
315 Balmain Road
Lilyfield
NSW 2040
(02) 810 2666

Gay and Lesbian Counselling Service of NSW
197 Albion Street
Surry Hills
NSW 2010
(02) 360 3063

Gay and Lesbian Counselling Service of SA
PO Box 2011
Kent Town
South Australia 5071
(08) 362 3223

Gay and Lesbian Counselling Service of WA
79 Stirling Street
Perth
Western Australia 6000
(09) 328 9044

Lesbian Counselling and Information Service
PO Box 1078
Fortitude Valley
Queensland 4006
(07) 839 3288

Lesbian Network
PO Box 215
Rozelle
NSW 2039

Louisa Lawson Centre for Counselling and Therapy for Women
112 West Botany Street
Arncliffe
NSW 2205

CANADA

London Battered Women's Advocacy Centre
Committee Confronting Lesbian Battering
69 Wellington Street
London
Ontario N6B 2G4

USA

Complete listings can be found in the *Directory of Homosexual Organizations* under the 'Counseling' and 'Mental Health' classifications, or directories published by the National Lesbian and Gay Health Foundation including the *National Gay Health Directory* and the *Sourcebook on Lesbian/Gay Health Care*.

Association of Lesbian and Gay Psychologists
210 5th Avenue
New York, NY 10010

Battered/Abused Gays/Lesbians
PO Box 8141
Omaha, NE 68108

Gay and Lesbian and Bisexual Caucus
American Association of Sex Educators, Counselors, and Therapists
418 Elk Street
Albany, NY 12206

Gay and Lesbian Counseling Service
600 Washington #219
Boston, MA 02136

Homosexual Community Counseling Center
30 E 60th Street
New York, NY 10022

National Association of Lesbian and Gay Alcoholism Professionals
204 West 20th Street
New York, NY 10011

National Coalition Against Domestic Violence
Lesbian Task Force
1500 Massachusetts Avenue
NW Suite 35
Washington, DC 20005

Seattle Counseling Service for Sexual Minorities
1505 Broadway
Seattle, WA 98122

Society for the Psychological Study of Lesbian and Gay Issues
Division 44, American Psychological Association
1200 17th Street NW
Washington DC 20036

index